INTERNATIONAL FINANCIAL INTEGRATION

International Financial Integration

The Limits of Sovereignty

David T. Llewellyn

Professor of Money and Banking
University of Loughborough
England

A HALSTED PRESS BOOK

JOHN WILEY & SONS
NEW YORK

© David T. Llewellyn 1980

First published in Great Britain 1980 by
The Macmillan Press Ltd

Published in the U.S.A. by
Halsted Press, a Division of
John Wiley & Sons, Inc.
New York

Printed in Hong Kong

Library of Congress Cataloging in Publication Data

Llewellyn, David T
International financial integration.

(Problems of economic integration)
"A Halsted Press book."
Includes bibliographical references and index.
1. International finance. 2. Capital movements.
3. Monetary policy. I. Title.
HG3881.L556   332.4'5   80–11699
ISBN 0–470–26960–X

Dedicated affectionately to
WENDY

Contents

Preface

This book is about the nature and extent of international financial integration and its policy implications. The orientation of the study is the extent to which such integration limits national sovereignty in the execution of economic policy in general and monetary policy in particular.

The substantial volume of international capital flows is a major feature of the international monetary system, and has an important impact on the domestic economy. And yet many basic textbooks tend either not to consider this aspect of the macro-economy, or confine the analysis to an appendage of the main argument. It is hoped that this book will help to redress the balance somewhat by placing international financial linkages and capital flows at the forefront of the analysis of the macro-economy.

Only weeks after the typescript was sent to the publishers the British Government abolished all remaining exchange-control regulations which had previously inhibited capital outflows from the United Kingdom. This move could prove to be one of the most important changes in the monetary environment of the United Kingdom since 1945, and it certainly increases the extent to which the country is financially integrated with the international money markets. Although the orientation of the book is not specifically the United Kingdom, the text has been amended to take note of the fact that exchange control in the United Kingdom was abolished in October 1979.

My interest in this topic was developed during a three-year period at the International Monetary Fund in Washington, and my intellectual debt to former colleagues at the Fund is gratefully acknowledged. But the book itself arose out of a course of lectures given at the Universities of Loughborough and Nottingham, and a week's course given regularly for the Bank of America in London and Paris. Indeed, the book is an attempt at integrating the basic, sometimes rather abstract, analytical framework of the economist, and the expertise and orientation of the practical banker. The analysis of international financial integration is conducted in terms of the actual operation of institutions and financial markets. It is hoped that both economist and banker can learn from each other, and that an attempt at something of a synthesis of their respective traditions will prove useful. The book is therefore addressed to economists, bankers and students and has been written with each in mind. Thus, while economists can learn from the operators who make the markets they analyse, similarly bankers can benefit from the broader analytical framework of the economist.

At various points in the book, therefore, examination is made of the operation and procedures of relevant financial markets (such as the forward exchange market) and of banking operations. This is based on a belief that an appreciation of banking techniques, and the mechanics of money markets, must be a necessary ingredient of a full understanding of the operation and conduct of monetary policy and the implications of international financial integration.

The book will hopefully prove useful for bankers, fellow economists and students. It should be relevant for many third-year undergraduate courses in macro and monetary economics, banking, international finance and international economics at universities and polytechnics. The emphasis of the discussion is upon issues of policy and relevant empirical evidence is surveyed. Institutional mechanisms are discussed while purely theoretical constructs have been kept to a minimum. No attempt at all has been made to offer a comprehensive review of the enormous theoretical literature on the monetary aspects of the open economy. Indeed, the framework of the study is set in Chapter 2 in terms of the extended IS/LM paradigm.

I owe a considerable intellectual debt to many colleagues and, of course, to the many economists whose research and writing has extended the subject enormously over the past decade. I owe a particular debt to Professor Brian Tew of the University of Nottingham, whose perception and ready willingness to discuss issues is very much appreciated by many. I have also benefited from many discussions with Mr G. E. J. Dennis of the University of Loughborough, with whom I collaborate in writing 'Trends in International Banking and Capital Markets' for the *Financial Times*. I also wish to offer my sincere thanks to the many bankers and officials in various countries who have patiently dealt with my many questions, and who have given so freely of their time. I also gratefully acknowledge the generous financial assistance given to my department by the Midland Bank. The editor of *The Banker* has also kindly allowed me to reproduce substantial parts of my article in the January 1979 issue.

There have been several delays in the writing of this book. I would like to record my sincere thanks to George McKenzie of the University of Southampton, and to Macmillan for their encouragement and patience during the delays. My secretary, Mrs Brenda Moore, has been of very great assistance. She has patiently endured several drafts of various chapters, and her speed and efficiency in typing the manuscript when other demands have been substantial, are very much appreciated.

Above all, I wish to thank my family for their constant help and encouragement, and I dedicate the book to my wife, Wendy.

University of Loughborough   DAVID T. LLEWELLYN
25 September 1979

ACKNOWLEDGEMENTS

The author and publishers wish to thank the following who have kindly given permission for the use of copyright material:
The Bank of England for an extract from *Quarterly Bulletin*, December 1976;
The Board of Governors of the Federal Reserve System, Washington D.C. for a chart from Document H.13, *Selected Interest Rates and Exchange Rates*;
North-Holland Publishing Company for equations from *National Monetary Policies and International Financial Markets* by R. J. Herring and R. C. Marston;
Organisation for Economic Co-operation and Development, Paris, for extracts from the Report *Capital Movements in the OECD Area - An Econometric Analysis* by W. H. Branson and R. D. Hill (1971).

1
Introduction

A major development in the international monetary system over the 1970s was the substantial rise in the volume of international capital flows. The high degree of capital mobility, and the volume of funds involved, is a major feature of the international monetary system and the world economy. The degree of financial integration between countries that has now been reached, in large part associated with international capital flows and the expansion of euro-currency markets, has important implications for the conduct of monetary policy. This has become particularly important in the United Kingdom since the abolition of exchange control in October 1979. The extent of financial integration has a major bearing upon both the effectiveness of monetary policy in any one country and the extent to which individual countries are able to pursue a monetary policy strategy independently of that of other countries. Increasingly, monetary policy has had to be framed within the constraints imposed by a high degree of financial integration in the world economy.

Various aspects and the policy implications of international financial integration are explored in the following chapters. In particular, the ultimate focus of attention is the extent and nature of the constraint imposed upon monetary policy by international financial integration. While the major emphasis is given to integration through international capital flows, the more general two-way causal link between the balance of payments and domestic monetary conditions is also considered. Although the emphasis is on policy issues, these must necessarily be set in the context of the operation of financial markets. For this reason, several chapters are devoted to fairly detailed analysis of the foreign-exchange market and the techniques of international arbitrage and, where possible, empirical evidence is reviewed.

MEASURES OF FINANCIAL INTEGRATION

International financial integration may be measured in several alternative, though related, ways and at various points in the analysis emphasis is given to one rather than the others. Broadly, integration may be viewed in terms of: (1) the interest-rate sensitivity of international capital movements and the volume of funds available for international arbitrage; (2) the extent to which arbitrage capital flows induce equilibrating movements in the spot exchange rate, the forward rate and interest rates to eliminate profitable arbitrage opportunities; (3) the extent to which movements in high-powered money (the monetary base) or the money supply in different countries are causally related; and (4) the extent to which interest rates in different financial centres move in parallel.

With respect to the first, two components need to be identified: (i) the degree to which wealth holders *desire* to optimise a portfolio structure on the basis of a mix of financial assets in different countries and/or currencies and (ii) the extent to which they are technically able to do so. The first relates essentially to the substitutability of financial assets in different countries and currencies and the extent to which, in terms of risk-return calculations, wealth holders seek to optimise their position through internationally and multi-currency diversified portfolios. The second component incorporates questions related to information costs, transactions costs and, in particular, exchange control and other officially imposed constraints on the development of internationally diversified portfolios. Thus the first component may be high, and yet the actual volume of arbitrage funds may be comparatively small because of official and market constraints. In this case, interest rates and other variables may diverge from equilibrium levels, and apparently profitable arbitrage opportunities may be sustained.

The second aspect of integration to be discussed (particularly in Chapters 4 and 7) focuses upon the extent of deviations from the interest-parity condition, i.e. the extent to which the forward exchange-rate premium or discount does not equal interest-rate differentials between currencies and countries. Considerable attention is given to the forward exchange market because movements in the forward exchange rate tend to limit the volume of capital flows (and hence the degree of financial interdependence), but also because official (central bank) intervention in the forward market can be a powerful policy technique.

Third, the power, and international transmission, of monetary policy may also be analysed in terms of the causal links between movements in monetary aggregates in different countries. Thus, with a fixed exchange rate, a policy-induced rise in high-powered money in country A may, through international financial flows, induce a rise in the monetary base in country B. This mechanism tends to limit the effectiveness of monetary policy in country A, but also to reduce the monetary independence of country B whose domestic money supply is not entirely under its own control.

At several points, a distinction has been made between currencies and countries. In some cases, of course, the two may be synonomous in that a movement of funds between countries also involves changes in the currency structure of a portfolio. This is not necessarily the case, however, because of the role of euro-currency markets (markets in bank deposits denominated in currencies other than those of the country in which the banks are located). Indeed, the euro-currency markets have served to increase the extent of international financial integration. Thus a wealth holder has a twofold decision to make: the currency structure of his portfolio and the location of the assets, and in particular whether to hold bank deposits in the domestic or euro segment of a currency market. This distinction is highlighted in Chapters 7 and 9. Arbitrage flows may, therefore, be between national money markets, between different currency segments of the euro-currency market and between euro and domestic money markets.

POLICY CONSTRAINTS

Much of the analysis in the chapters that follow concentrates upon the constraints on policy (particularly monetary policy) imposed by international financial integration. This is based upon what might be termed two *incompatible trinities*. The international trinity relates capital flows, exchange rates and the domestic money supply. The evidence of the Bretton Woods regime, and of the experience of 'managed floating' rates since the mid 1970s, strongly indicates that fixed exchange rates, freedom of international capital flows and precise control over the domestic money supply are basically incompatible. Thus, policy-induced changes in the money supply create profitable arbitrage opportunities and, if exchange rates are fixed, the resultant capital flows induce changes in domestic money supplies due to the domestic financial counterpart to central bank intervention in the foreign exchange market.

Towards the end of the 1960s an attempt was made to resolve this fundamental conflict by imposing controls on capital movements (see Chapter 8). As these were circumvented, and introduced their own unintended distortions, the conflict was later resolved by adopting floating exchange rates. Floating exchange rates mean that although in principle the money supply is domestically determined, the monetary authorities lose control over the exchange rate. This dilemma has, at times, been particularly acute for Germany and Switzerland. In 1973 when, as a result of the domestic monetary counterpart of substantial foreign exchange market intervention by the Swiss central bank to stop the Swiss franc appreciating, the rate of inflation was unacceptably high, the Swiss franc, together with many other currencies, was allowed to float. Monetary stability was exchanged for exchange-rate stability. In October 1978 (after a year when the effective Swiss franc exchange rate had appreciated by 30 per cent), the Swiss authorities announced a maximum limit for subsequent appreciations against the Deutsche Mark. Foreign-exchange-market intervention was to be used to secure this limit. As a result of the domestic monetary consequences of this intervention, early in 1979 the Swiss authorities ceased to conduct monetary policy on the basis of publicly announced targets for the growth of the domestic money supply. Thus, with substantial international capital mobility, a fundamental conflict may emerge between official monetary and exchange-rate targets both within a country and between countries.

The related domestic *incompatible trinity* links the growth in the money supply, the level of interest rates and the size of the Government's own financial deficit. Policy-makers cannot arbitrarily choose simultaneous targets for all three variables. With a given financial deficit (public sector borrowing requirement in the United Kingdom) either the money supply or the level of interest rates is market- (demand-) determined. As noted in the final chapter, either trinity taken alone imposes constraints on the conduct of monetary policy. The constraints when both trinities are relevant can become particularly acute.

EXCHANGE-RATE SYSTEM

One of the key factors determining the constraint imposed upon monetary policy by international financial integration is, therefore, the exchange-rate system. Most of the analysis is conducted in terms of fixed v. floating exchange rates. In practice, the 'managed floating' regime conforms to neither polar case. As already noted, the rigid Bretton Woods fixed-exchange-rate system was eventually abandoned after close on thirty years in part because of the problems created for monetary control by international capital flows. The adoption of floating exchange rates was associated in no small part with a desire on the part of governments in Europe and elsewhere to determine their own monetary policy. In particular, and for reasons discussed in detail in Chapter 12, the nature of the Bretton Woods system (or at least the way it was operated) meant that monetary conditions in Europe were dominated by the stance of monetary policy adopted in the United States.

The asymmetrical nature of the reserve currency system meant that, in practice, a balance-of-payments deficit in the United States had no effect upon the U.S. money supply but, as a result of foreign exchange market interventions by central banks in surplus countries, the money supply in surplus countries was raised. Towards the end of the 1960s and in the early 1970s U.S. monetary policy became more expansionary than in Europe. The attempt at resolving the resultant conflict was eventually made in terms of abandoning the rigid fixed-exchange-rate system of the 1950s and 1960s. Floating rates were viewed not only as conferring monetary autonomy, but as a means of reducing the monetary dominance of the United States in particular.

The efficacy of floating rates has, however, come to be questioned in three main areas. It is not clear that, in practice, domestic objectives are more easily attained by floating exchange rates, nor that governments are able to frame monetary policy exclusively on the basis of domestic policy objectives. Second, the power of exchange-rate movements to secure real-wage and balance-of-payments adjustment is questionable in the long run. Third, the volatility of exchange rates, and their overshooting of long-run equilibrium values, has been greater than early theoretical models predicted and certainly greater than desired by policy markers.

THE EVIDENCE SUMMARISED

International financial integration, and the resultant policy constraints, is a question of degree. It is clear that monetary policy is in practice substantially constrained through offsetting capital flows when exchange rates are fixed. But the evidence also indicates that some monetary independence is retained. This is because: (i) there are limits to the responsiveness of capital to interest-rate differentials (Chapters 4 and 12); (ii) certain market mechanisms both limit capital flows and insulate domestic monetary conditions from those flows that do take place; and (iii) the monetary authorities are able, at least in the short term, to offset or *sterilise* the domestic monetary consequences of capital flows and the balance of payments in general (Chapter 12). In particular, equilibrating movements in the forward exchange rate afford a substantial degree of insulation and limit the extent to which capital flows in response to interest-rate changes. However, by definition, equilibrating forward-exchange-rate adjustments apply only to those capital flows that are covered in the forward market and not to uncovered (essentially speculative) capital flows. A degree of insulation is also achieved in some cases by extensive exchange control to limit capital flows. However, this degree of insulation was removed for the United Kingdom in October 1979 when all remaining exchange controls were removed.

The evidence also indicates that, at least in the short run, externally induced changes in the money supply can be *sterilised*. However, problems emerge if several countries simultaneously attempt sterilisation beyond a certain degree (Chapter 12) as this indicates a major conflict in monetary policy between countries. The longer-run viability of sterilisation policy is also questionable.

Overall, neither of the two polar cases identified in Chapter 2 is confirmed by the empirical evidence. Thus, while monetary policy clearly is constrained by international financial integration, there is no evidence that monetary conditions in any country are totally dominated by external influences. The 'small-country' model, where the domestic interest rate is constrained at the world level, is clearly not consistent with the experience of either fixed or floating rates except, perhaps, in some analytical 'long run' of little interest to policy-makers.

Over the 1970s the environment in which monetary policy was conducted underwent substantial changes. The decade started with the strains imposed by a collapsing fixed exchange rate system buttressed in many European countries by a battery of controls and other measures designed to limit capital inflows (see Chapter 8). Since 1973 the international monetary system has been based upon varying degrees of 'managed-floating'. The euro-currency markets also grew at a substantial rate, as did the volume of international capital flows. Rates of inflation reached unprecedented levels in the early 1970s in many countries and the decade witnessed marked divergencies in the rates of inflation between countries. The strategies of monetary policy also changed markedly, with increasing emphasis being given to the control of monetary aggregates as the target of policy rather than interest-rate levels. There were also significant changes in the intellectual climate, with monetarist analysis increasingly emphasising the limited role for discretionary monetary policy and the role of monetary policy in contributing to policy objectives with respect to real magnitudes such as the level of output and employment. Increasing doubts were also raised with respect to the power of exchange-rate changes to adjust relative real wages and the balance of payments in the long run. The link between the balance of payments and the money supply were also increasingly emphasised.

An important background to these policy and intellectual trends was the clear constraint imposed by international financial integration. It is to the details of this that we now turn.

SELECTED BIBLIOGRAPHY

Cooper, R. N. (1968) *Economics of Interdependence* (New York: McGraw-Hill).

Holtrop, M. W. (1963) *Monetary Policy in an Open Economy: Objectives, Instruments, Limitations and Dilemmas*, Essays in International Finance, No. 43, Princeton University.

Llewellyn, D. T. (1979) 'International Financial Intermediation', in *A Framework of International Banking*, ed. S. Frowen (Guildford: Philip Thorn Associates).

2
Stabilisation Policy in an Open Economy

A convenient means of focusing upon the impact international capital movements have on the domestic economy is through the analysis of stabilisation policy. An extensive literature establishes that the response of income and employment to fiscal and monetary policies[1] depends both upon the exchange-rate system and the interest-rate sensitivity of international capital movements. The analysis of stabilisation policy is reviewed in this chapter within a generalised, essentially Keynesian, framework which incorporates the monetary aspects of the balance of payments.

The major analytical and empirical issues involved and featured throughout the book are: (i) the extent to which international capital movements are sensitive to interest-rate changes; (ii) their impact upon the domestic money supply and exchange rate; (iii) the impact capital movements have on the power of stabilisation policy to alter domestic income and employment; (iv) the extent to which the monetary effects of the balance of payments can be sterilised; (v) the relative power of monetary and fiscal policy with fixed and floating exchange rates with varying degrees of international capital mobility; and (vi) the degree of insulation of the domestic economy from foreign disturbances that is afforded by a floating exchange rate. Together, these largely determine the degree of monetary independence of non-reserve currency countries.

Through the 1960s it became increasingly apparent that a major aspect of the fixed-exchange-rate system was that, in a world of substantial capital mobility, monetary policy in countries outside the United States was frequently undermined by the domestic monetary implications of the balance of payments. The domestic monetary counterpart of official intervention in the foreign-exchange market might conflict with domestic monetary policy. The domestic money supply was found not to be entirely exogenous in a fixed-exchange-rate system, as a substantial proportion of any domestically induced change in the money supply could be offset by monetary flows resulting from the balance of payments. For instance, contractionary domestic monetary policy could be offset by capital inflows either at the initiative of foreign investors attracted by high interest rates, or by attempts by domestic bank and non-bank residents to restore the supply of money balances by borrowing in international money markets. In both cases the impact on the domestic money supply resulting from official exchange market intervention to prevent the exchange rate rising would tend to offset the original contractionary domestic monetary policy.

Immediately after the German central bank ceased supporting the Deutsche Mark in the exchange market in 1971, the Bundesbank claimed in its regular *Bulletin*: 'The Bank is now released from the compulsion of having to create central bank money by the purchase of foreign exchange. . . . The Bundesbank thus no longer has to fear that its restrictive course in credit policy is more or less automatically undercut by monetary inflows from foreign countries.' (Bundesbank Monthly Report, Mar 1971.) The case for floating exchange rates was seen in the early 1970s largely in terms of the supposed greater independence and power afforded to monetary policy.

THE BASIC MODEL

A simplified, essentially Keynesian, model of an open economy may be employed to illustrate the analysis of monetary and fiscal policy. This model is adopted, not because it is necessarily the most appropriate analytical framework for considering stabilisation policy in an open economy, but because it offers a simple and consistent analytical structure in which to survey the major issues involved in international interdependence. In particular, the importance of international capital movements for the domestic economy can be readily appreciated using the standard *IS/LM* paradigm. This standard paradigm can be easily adapted to highlight the issues under review. The model is used simply to illustrate the major issues, and no attempt is made to survey the vast literature on stabilisation policy in an open economy, most of which has progressed beyond the simple *IS/LM* paradigm. For an alternative structural model, which incorporates the rational expectations hypothesis and offers a synthesis of Keynesian and monetarist models, see Beenstock (1978).

Equation (2.1) gives the traditional *IS* curve, and equation (2.2) the *LM* curve which also indicates that the supply of money has a domestic and foreign component.[2] The latter is measured by the central bank's holdings

$$Y = C(Y) + I(i) + G + X(r) - M_p(Y, r) \tag{2.1}$$

$$M = H + R = La(Y) + L_d(i) \tag{2.2}$$

$$B = \Delta R = T + K_1(i) + K_2(r - r_e) \tag{2.3}$$

of reserves of gold and foreign exchange. Throughout the analysis it is assumed that a rise in the domestic interest rate does not induce any change in interest rates in other countries, and that capital movements take place on an uncovered basis. This means that complications with respect to offsetting changes in the forward exchange rate can be ignored. This assumption is dropped in Chapter 4. The model relates to a small country and is presented in the normal Keynesian flow formulation. This implies that wealth effects (specifically those deriving from an unbalanced budget and current account) are not incorporated and hence equilibrium is not constrained to the requirement that the budget and current account deficits sum to zero. The model solves for Y, i and r with a floating exchange rate, and Y, i and B when the exchange rate is fixed. It also follows that the money supply is domestically determined with a floating exchange rate (as R is fixed), but is endogenous with a fixed exchange rate.

The basic model is summarised in Figure 2.1 where combinations of Y and i for internal, money market and balance-of-payments equilibrium are given by the IS, LM and F schedules. Balance-of-payments equilibrium is defined as zero excess demand for foreign currency in the foreign-exchange market. The F schedule is upward-sloping as a rise in income induces a deterioration in the current account due to a rise in imports, while a rise in the domestic interest rate induces a capital inflow. The position of the schedule is determined by the exchange rate[3] (which determines the level of exports at each level of income), and the volume of speculative capital flows; unless otherwise stated, the analysis assumes the latter to be constant. The elasticity of the balance-of-payments schedule is determined by the relative magnitudes of the marginal propensity to import and the interest-rate sensitivity of international capital movements. For a given marginal propensity to import the greater is the interest sensitivity of capital movements the more elastic is the F schedule while, other things being equal, the larger is the marginal propensity to import the more inelastic is the schedule. The analysis to follow demonstrates the importance attached to two particular aspects of the elasticity of the F schedule: (1) whether it is greater (F_3 in Figure 2.1) or less (F_2) than that of the LM curve (which is determined by the interest rate and income elasticity of the

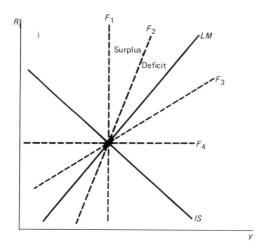

FIGURE 2.1   The basic model

demand for money); and (2) whether it is infinitely elastic (F_4) implying that the equilibrium level of the domestic interest rate is determined uniquely at the world level. When the F schedule is infinitely elastic, capital flows are so responsive to interest-rate movements that the emergence of a small differential in favour of the domestic economy induces such a large capital inflow that the interest rate can be sustained only at the original (world) level. In the latter case domestic policy can have no long-run effect on the domestic interest rate unless the country is large enough to be able to influence the world interest-rate level.

MONEY SUPPLY AND THE BALANCE OF PAYMENTS

In general, as implied in equation (2.2), a balance-of-payments deficit (surplus) with a fixed exchange rate induces a contraction (rise) in the volume of high-powered money (and hence, through the bank credit multiplier, a potential multiple fall (rise) in the domestic money supply). External influences on the domestic money supply are, however, absent with a floating exchange rate. With a fixed exchange rate high-powered money is destroyed or created through the domestic monetary counterpart to central bank intervention in the foreign-exchange market. Central bank purchases of foreign currency (balance-of-payments surplus) have the same effect upon the volume of high-powered money as do open-market purchases of bonds from the private sector. In Figure 2.2 the balance of payments is viewed in terms of stable supply and demand curves for foreign exchange related to the exchange rate. The overvalued exchange rate E_0, implied by the balance-of-payments deficit AB, can be sustained only by the central bank buying domestic currency and selling

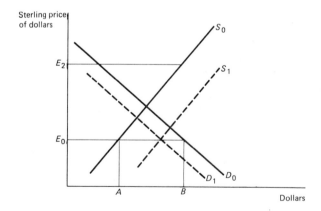

FIGURE 2.2   The foreign exchange market

reserves (AB). In the process the domestic counterpart is a reduction in the volume of high-powered money. Maintained for long enough, the effect of the reduced money supply with the exchange rate fixed would be an automatic balance-of-payments adjustment (and shifts from D_0 to D_1 and S_0 to S_1) through the monetary effect on expenditure and interest rates. Conversely, the domestic money supply is increased with a balance-of-payments surplus at an exchange rate E_2.

With a floating exchange rate the rate adjusts automatically to any *ex ante* excess supply/demand for foreign exchange. The absence of official foreign-exchange-market intervention (and its domestic monetary counterpart) implies an entirely domestically determined supply of money.[4]

In the fixed-exchange-rate case, the impact the balance of payments has on the domestic money supply may, at least in the short term, be *sterilised* by appropriate domestic operations of the central bank. Thus the effect on high-powered money of a balance-of-payments surplus may be offset by central bank sales of bonds to the non-bank private sector. The precise mechanisms and experience of European countries in this respect are discussed in detail in Chapter 12. The evidence indicates that a degree of *sterilisation* does seem to be feasible, though the process becomes increasingly complex when several countries simultaneously attempt to offset the monetary effects of inconsistent balance-of-payments and monetary policies. At this stage it suffices to note that effective *sterilisation* may occur in one of four ways: (1) through deliberate policy measures adopted by the monetary authorities (e.g. open-market operations in government debt, changes in reserve requirements of the domestic banking system, swap facilities between the central bank and commercial banks, official forward exchange transactions with domestic banks, etc.); (2) automatically through the portfolio choice of non-residents when, for instance, the balance-of-payments surplus derives from a capital inflow and non-resident investors purchase newly created public sector debt; (3) through the automatic operation of particular institutional mechanism such as the Exchange Equalisation Account in the United Kingdom; and (4) through portfolio adjustments of banks when, for instance, they repay loans from the central bank when bank reserves rise due to a balance-of-payments surplus. Thus a balance-of-payments surplus does not invariably induce a rise in the volume of high-powered money, and any rise that does take place can, in principle, be offset by appropriate domestic measures.

Through whatever mechanism *sterilisation* occurs, the implication is that external payments surpluses and deficits last longer (as the monetary adjustment mechanism fails to operate) and reserve changes are larger. In practice an effective limit to the magnitude of *sterilisation* is given by: (i) the technical ability of the central bank to control the domestic money base through its policy instruments; (ii) the constraint, when in deficit, of limited external reserves or borrowing capability; (iii) the domestic consequences of continuing to supply excess money balances; and (iv) the limit of surplus countries' willingness to supply real resources in exchange for money balances. There is also the constraint that the *sterilisation* strategies of different countries may be in fundamental conflict which, as noted in Chapter 12, may produce an unstable international monetary system.

The automatic *sterilisation* mechanism is particularly significant for countries which are *reserve currency centres*; i.e. those whose currency is used as a means of holding external reserves (e.g. U.S. dollar and sterling). To the extent that surplus countries choose to hold U.S. dollars in their reserves (rather than demand primary reserve assets from the United States), an *ex ante* balance-of-payments deficit in the United States implies no loss of reserves by the United States. The implication is that, with fixed exchange rates, the United States is less subject to balance-of-payments constraints than are countries in Europe, and a deficit in a reserve currency country's balance of payments may increase the world money supply as the rise in the money supply in the surplus country is not matched by a corresponding fall in the deficit country. There is, therefore, an asymmetrical external monetary effect between countries which are, and those which are not, reserve currency centres. For this reason, monetary policy in the reserve currency centre is an important determinant of the world interest-rate level, and monetary conditions outside the reserve currency centre may be dominated by the monetary policy being pursued by the reserve currency country.

In the analysis to follow, a distinction is therefore made between *equilibrium*, with the three sectors (real economy, balance of payments and money market) each in equilibrium, and *quasi-equilibrium*[5] where the monetary effects of a balance-of-payments surplus or deficit are *sterilised*. The traditional definition of equilibrium in the Keynesian model (intersection of *IS* and *LM*) is therefore defined here as *quasi-equilibrium* if, at that level of income and the rate of interest, the balance of payments is unbalanced.

Basic propositions

In the standard *IS/LM* paradigm the major analytical conclusions with respect to stabilisation policy in an open economy are conveniently described in Cooper.[6] In formal terms:

$$\frac{(dY)}{(dM)_{\text{flexible}}} > \frac{(dY)}{(dM)_{\text{fixed}}} \qquad (2.4)$$

$$\frac{(dY)}{(dG)_{\text{flexible}}} \gtreqless \frac{(dY)}{(dG)_{\text{fixed}}} \qquad (2.5)$$

Equation (2.4) indicates that when capital movements are responsive to interest-rate differentials monetary policy has a comparative advantage in terms of its impact on domestic income with a floating exchange rate. The direct effect on income of a rise in the money supply is reinforced, with a floating rate, by the exchange-rate depreciation due to the inevitable *ex ante* balance-of-payments deficit. The relative power of fiscal policy (change in government expenditure) as between a fixed and floating exchange rate is indeterminate and depends upon the relative elasticities of the LM and F schedules. While an expansionary monetary policy always worsens the balance of payments with a fixed exchange rate (as the level of income is raised and the rate of interest falls) an expansionary fiscal policy has an indeterminate effect on the balance of payments with a fixed exchange rate as the capital inflow induced by the higher interest rate may be greater than the income-induced rise in imports. With a floating exchange rate, therefore, the domestic impact of fiscal policy may either be reinforced or partly offset by exchange-rate movements. The analysis of fiscal and monetary policy in terms of the extended IS/LM paradigm is reviewed in the remainder of this chapter.

FISCAL POLICY: FIXED EXCHANGE RATE

A pure expansionary fiscal policy implies a budget deficit financed by the sale of bonds to the non-bank private sector so that the budget deficit leaves the domestic money supply unchanged.[7] This assumption is made throughout the analysis. It is further assumed that the financing mechanism has no wealth effect which enables the model to develop an equilibrium position with an unbalanced budget, or with a budget deficit which is not equal to the current account deficit.

The effect of a rise in government expenditure is illustrated in Figure 2.3 below. The impact on the balance of payments depends upon the relative elasticities of the LM and F schedules. As a rise in income induces, through the effect of an increased demand for money balances, a rise in the domestic interest rates, the capital account may improve by more than the current account deteriorates through the income-induced rise in imports. If the combined effect induces a balance-of-payments surplus, *quasi-equilibrium* income rises from y_0 to y_1 in Figure 2.3A, while the secondary monetary effects of the balance-of-payments surplus induces a further rise in income to y_E. On the other hand, if the elasticity of LM is greater than F, the balance of payments moves into deficit and, in the absence of *sterilisation*, the power of fiscal policy is reduced by the negative effect on the domestic money supply induced by the balance-of-payments deficit. In Figure 2.3B equilibrium income (y_E) is below *quasi-equilibrium* income (y_1). The relative elasticities of the LM and F schedules therefore determine: (i) the power of fiscal policy and (ii) the type and extent of *sterilisation* operations required of the central bank (sales of bonds in the first and purchase of bonds in the second case).

Fiscal policy becomes most powerful in the fixed-exchange-rate case when the F schedule is infinitely elastic (the rate of interest determined at the world

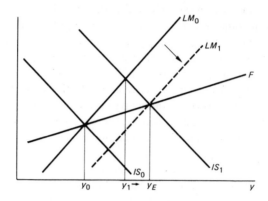

FIGURE 2.3A   Fiscal policy with fixed exchange rate: *ex ante* surplus

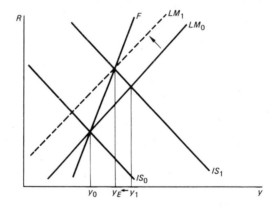

FIGURE 2.3B   Fiscal policy with fixed exchange rate: *ex ante* deficit

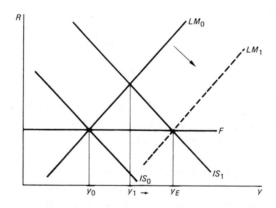

FIGURE 2.3C   Fiscal policy with fixed exchange rate: perfect capital mobility

level), as the externally induced rise in the money supply will continue until the initial interest-rate level is attained. The change in equilibrium income in this case is determined by the simple Keynesian national income multiplier (Figure 2.3c).

The conclusion is that, with a fixed exchange rate and in the absence of *sterilisation*, the interest-rate sensitivity of international capital has an effect on the power of fiscal policy through the monetary effects of the balance of payments. The power of fiscal policy is enhanced when the elasticity of the *LM* is less than that of the *F* schedule; i.e. when: (1) the interest elasticity of demand for money is low; (2) the income elasticity of the demand for money is high; (3) the marginal propensity to import is low and/or; (4) the interest-rate sensitivity of capital movements is high.

FISCAL POLICY: FLOATING EXCHANGE RATE

With a floating exchange rate (zero central bank intervention in the foreign-exchange market) the balance of payments has no direct effect upon the domestic money supply. However, the movement in the exchange rate resulting from an *ex ante* balance-of-payments surplus or deficit has a secondary effect on income via its expenditure-switching effect on the volume of exports and imports. The analysis for fiscal policy is summarised in Figure 2.4 below. Throughout the analysis of floating rates the effect of the change in the exchange rate on the real value of nominal money balances is not incorporated.

When, with a fixed exchange rate, the balance of payments moves to a surplus following an expansionary fiscal policy, the exchange-rate appreciation with a floating rate detracts from the power of fiscal policy. Thus in Figure 2.4A the rise in income following a rise in government expenditure from IS_0 to IS_1 (i.e. $y_0 y_E$) is less than when the exchange rate is fixed and the monetary effect of the balance of payments are not sterilised ($y_0 y_1$). The effect of the exchange rate appreciation (which shifts the curves from IS_1 to IS_2 and F_0 to F_1) is to moderate the rise in income by an amount $y_E y_1$.

Conversely if, with a fixed exchange rate, an expansionary fiscal policy creates a balance-of-payments deficit, the exchange-rate depreciation in Figure 2.4B (F_0 to F_1 and IS_1 to IS_2) stimulates income further with the ultimate rise in income ($y_0 y_E$) greater than would have been the case with a fixed exchange rate ($y_0 y_1$). The rise in income will also be greater than that with a fixed exchange rate coupled with *sterilisation* ($y_0 y_p$).

In the extreme case (*F* schedule infinitely elastic) fiscal policy has no effect on domestic income and employment. The rise in the exchange rate continues until the effect on income (via its adverse effect on exports) reduces the demand for money balances to the original level. At this point the interest rate has attained its previous (world) level. Equilibrium is determined uniquely at y_0 with IS_0, LM_0 and F_0 in Figure 2.4c.

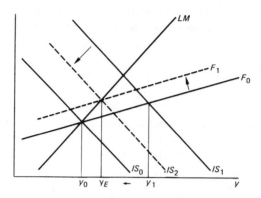

FIGURE 2.4A   Fiscal policy with floating exchange rate: *ex ante* surplus

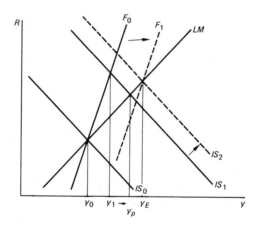

FIGURE 2.4B   Fiscal policy with floating exchange rate: *ex ante* deficit

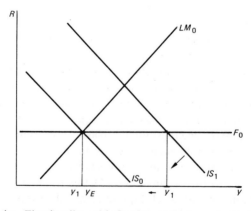

FIGURE 2.4C   Fiscal policy with floating exchange rate: perfect capital
mobility

MONETARY POLICY: FIXED EXCHANGE RATE

Unlike an expansionary fiscal policy, a rise in the domestic money supply (induced by, for instance, central bank purchases of bonds) will always tend to produce a balance-of-payments deficit with a fixed exchange rate as both the current and capital accounts move into deficit. The rise in imports worsens the current account position while a lower domestic interest rate[8] induces a capital outflow. In the absence of *sterilisation*, the money supply therefore reverts to its initial level (LM shifts back to LM_0 in Figure 2.5). Monetary policy is therefore totally ineffective as a means of increasing income and employment, irrespective of the marginal propensity to import and the interest-rate sensitivity of international capital. In effect, central bank purchases of bonds to create high-powered money are offset by central bank purchases of high-powered money with foreign currency. The net effect is a change in the composition of the central banks' assets; from foreign currency to bonds. Similarly, an initial increase in the domestic component of high-powered money is, through the resultant balance-of-payments deficit, offset by a reduction in the external component.

However, the elasticity of the balance-of-payments schedule does affect the power of monetary policy to the extent that it determines the feasibility of *sterilisation* measures. The more elastic is the F schedule (greater the induced balance-of-payments deficit) the more difficult it will be for the central bank to offset the external monetary effects. Maintenance of *quasi-equilibrium* at y_1 in Figure 2.5 implies permanent *sterilisation*.

Thus the sensitivity of international capital movements to interest-rate

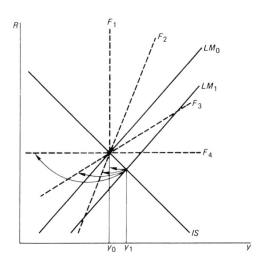

FIGURE 2.5 Monetary policy: quasi-equilibrium

changes does not affect the long-run power of monetary policy when the exchange rate is fixed. However, in the short term it influences the feasibility and magnitude of *sterilisation* (and hence the ability to sustain a *quasi-equilibrium* rise in income) and determines the speed at which full equilibrium is approached in the absence of *sterilisation*.

MONETARY POLICY: FLOATING EXCHANGE RATE

As a rise in the domestic money supply invariably worsens the balance of payments when the exchange rate is fixed, it induces a depreciation of a floating rate. Thus while with a fixed-exchange-rate monetary policy is totally ineffective, it becomes a powerful means of changing income when the exchange rate adjusts automatically in the foreign-exchange market to eliminate excess supply/demand positions. The power of monetary policy is enhanced even compared with the *quasi-equilibrium* position as, in Figure 2.6A (when the effect of the exchange-rate depreciation from IS_0 to IS_1 and F_0 to F_1 is included) the equilibrium level of income must be greater than y_1, which is the *quasi-equilibrium* level with a fixed exchange rate.

It can be demonstrated that, unlike the fixed-exchange-rate case, the interest-rate sensitivity of capital movements does affect the power of monetary policy with a floating exchange rate as, the more sensitive are such flows, the greater is the *ex ante* balance-of-payments deficit and hence the exchange-rate depreciation and secondary effect on income. Indeed in the limiting case where the F schedule is infinitely elastic, and where there can be no net reduction in the domestic interest rate (Figure 2.6B), the power of monetary policy is given by the quantity theory (proportional change in income to that of the change in the domestic money supply). A rise in the money supply which induces an initial fall in the rate of interest induces a capital outflow which depreciates the exchange rate until the resultant rise in income is sufficient to induce the public to hold the increased stock of money at the initial interest rate, i.e. when the rise in income is sufficient to cause the whole of the increased money stock to be held in transactions balances (y_E in Figure 2.6B).

POWER OF STABILISATION POLICY: SUMMARY

The main conclusions of the simple model with respect to the effect of stabilisation policy may be summarised:

(1) With a fixed exchange rate the power of fiscal policy is enhanced when it induces a balance-of-payments surplus (when the elasticity of the *LM* schedule is less than that of the F schedule) and is reduced when it induces an external deficit. This is because of the domestic monetary counterpart to the balance-of-payments effects.

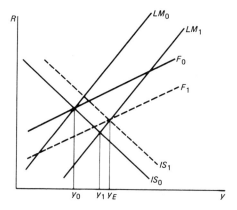

FIGURE 2.6A

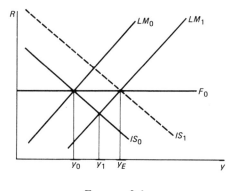

FIGURE 2.6B

FIGURE 2.6   Monetary policy: floating exchange rate

(2) Conversely, with a floating exchange rate exchange-rate movements (the mirror image of externally induced changes in the money supply with a fixed exchange rate) reduce the power of fiscal policy in the former and enhance it in the latter case.

(3) When international capital movements are so responsive to interest rates that the domestic interest rate is determined uniquely at the world level, fiscal policy becomes most powerful with a fixed exchange rate (the full national income multiplier case), but totally powerless with a floating rate.

(4) Monetary policy has no long-run effect on income with a fixed exchange rate (i.e. when the monetary effects of the balance of payments are not *sterilised*) irrespective of the sensitivity of international capital movements

to interest-rate changes. On the other hand, the power of monetary policy is unambiguously increased with a floating exchange rate (even compared with *quasi-equilibrium* under fixed exchange rates), as both the current and capital accounts move into *ex ante* deficit with an expansionary monetary policy. But this power derives from induced exchange-rate adjustments.

(5) The more sensitive is international capital to interest-rate movements the greater is the power of monetary policy with a floating exchange rate. In the extreme case (F schedule infinitely elastic) the rise in income is proportional to the rise in the money supply.

Thus, in the model described, a floating exchange rate unambiguously enhances the power of monetary policy while its effect on fiscal policy is indeterminate. The comparative effect on income of expansionary fiscal and monetary policies, is summarised in Figure 2.7. Given the model as described it also follows that:

$$\left[\frac{(dY)}{(dG)} \middle/ \frac{(dY)}{(dM)} \right]_{\text{flexible}} < \left[\frac{(dY)}{(dG)} \middle/ \frac{(dY)}{(dM)} \right]_{\text{fixed}}$$

i.e. the effect on income of a given increase in the money supply, relative to that of a given expansion in government expenditure, is greater with a floating than with a fixed exchange rate. If comparison is made of increases in the money supply and government expenditure which, with a fixed exchange rate, induce the same rise in income, with a floating exchange rate the rate will be more depreciated (and hence income will be higher) in the case of monetary policy. This is because at each level of income the rate of interest is lower, and hence the capital outflow is greater.

The focus of the analysis has not been specifically on the problem of simultaneously achieving internal and external balance, nor therefore on the assignment of policy instruments to specific policy targets. If a target level of income is established, policy has to be framed allowing for the monetary effects of the balance of payments. With a fixed exchange rate monetary policy is powerless to change equilibrium income with the implication that a target level of income can be attained only through fiscal policy or exchange-rate adjustments. On the other hand, with a floating exchange rate monetary policy becomes a powerful means of attaining a target level of income, though monetary measures must be devised allowing for their exchange-rate consequences. Similarly, with a fixed exchange rate, the framing of fiscal policy to achieve a target level of income must also allow for monetary and exchange-rate effects deriving from the balance of payments.

It also follows that the traditional view of the targets–instrument approach (that there must be an equal number of instruments as targets), is valid in the internal/external balance case only when: (i) sterilisation is being practised in a situation where the external balance target is defined other than zero excess

	MONETARY POLICY	FISCAL POLICY F > LM	FISCAL POLICY F < LM
Fixed exchange rate: no sterilisation	Zero	AD	PQ
Fixed exchange rate: Sterilisation	AB	AC	PR
Floating exchange rate	AC	AB	PS

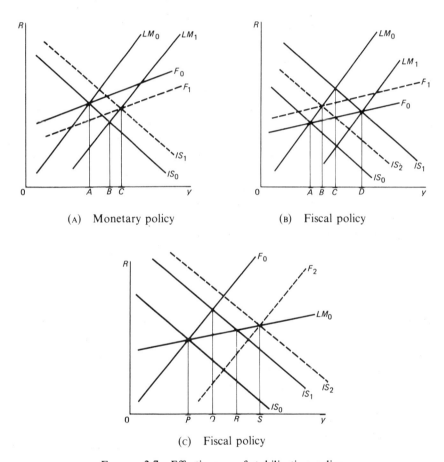

(A)   Monetary policy   (B)   Fiscal policy

(c)   Fiscal policy

FIGURE 2.7   Effectiveness of stabilisation policy

demand for foreign currency; and (ii) the external policy target relates to the structure of the balance of payments as well as the overall total. The rule is redundant when automatic equilibrating monetary and exchange-rate effects of the balance of payments are allowed to operate.

INSULATION WITH FLOATING RATES

The exchange-rate regime has a bearing also upon the impact on the domestic economy of disturbances originating in other countries. The degree of insulation afforded by a floating exchange rate depends, however, upon the nature of the disturbance. Although a floating rate insulates the domestic money supply from balance-of-payments effects, total insulation is not secured. In some cases complete insulation is afforded as, for instance, when the disturbance is an outward shift in the Phillips Curve overseas.

The resultant rise in import prices (which, with a fixed exchange rate, induces a rise in domestic prices) is offset by an appreciation of a floating exchange rate.[9] On the other hand, the effect on domestic output of an exogenous rise in export demand is partly, though not totally, offset by an appreciation of the exchange rate.

Exogenous (speculative) capital inflows may also have effects on income dependent upon the exchange-rate system and the relative elasticities of the LM and F schedules. An exogenous capital inflow alters the equilibrium conditions for external equilibrium from F_0 to F_1 in Figure 2.8. With a fixed exchange rate (Figure 2.8A) the effect on income is either zero (if *sterilisation* is complete), or positive when the balance-of-payments surplus induces a rise in the money supply. With a floating exchange rate a speculative inflow induces a fall in income through its effect on the exchange rate. Income is reduced by $y_0 y_1$ in the case where the elasticity of the F schedule is greater than that of the LM curve (Figure 2.8B), and by $y_0 y_2$ in Figure 2.8C.[10]

Thus a floating exchange rate affords only partial insulation from disturbances to the domestic economy originating in other countries.

LMITATIONS OF THE ANALYSIS

Inevitably there are many limitations to any simplified economic model. The model as described is subject to the general limitations inherent in the comparative static IS/LM framework: assumption of constant prices, a narrow monetary transmission mechanism, the absence of wealth effects from either monetary or fiscal policy, an assumed independence of the demand for money function and the supply of money, and the assumption of zero growth, etc. In addition, the analysis is conducted on the basis of comparative statics which enables the analysis to proceed without incorporating the complications of differential time-lags in the attainment of equilibrium in the three sectors of the model. An important feature of the model with respect to monetary policy is that a rise in the supply of money induces a fall in the domestic interest rate, which implicitly assumes that the demand for money function is specified independently of the supply of money. This may not be appropriate when increases in the money supply are associated with expectations of faster inflation, as speculators are likely to revise their expectations about future

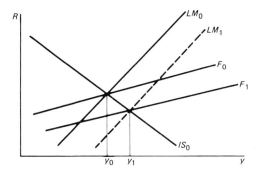

FIGURE 2.8A

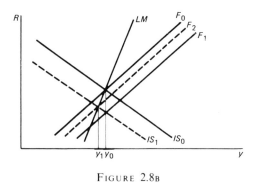

FIGURE 2.8B

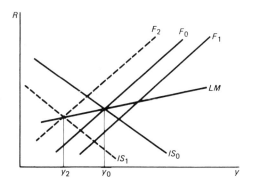

FIGURE 2.8C

FIGURE 2.8 Speculative capital inflow

interest rates, and hence the demand for money at each level of interest rate changes. In such cases a rise in the money supply may induce a rise in interest rates and vice versa as appeared to be the case in the United Kingdom in the period 1972–7. This may also arise if the rise in the money supply is in excess of publicly announced targets for the growth of monetary aggregates when investors believe that the central bank will be forced to sell more public sector debt (at higher interest rates) to regain control over the money supply.

Apart from the general limitations of the *IS/LM* framework there are also more specific qualifications to be made in the context of analysis which explicitly incorporates the balance of payments. First, the theory of capital movement implies that capital flows at a constant rate through time while a particular interest-rate differential persists; this is implicit in a stable *F* schedule. A more appropriate framework (both theoretically and empirically) stresses stock-adjustments with finite capital movements associated with *changes* in interest-rate differentials (see Chapter 4). In these models there is no unique combination of income and the rate of interest for a given balance-of-payments position except to the extent that capital flows are associated with steady increments to total wealth. Stock-adjustment models predict that a change in interest-rate differentials induces a rearrangement of portfolios and these take place over a finite period. A continuous *flow* of capital (to match a flow of imports related to a maintained level of income) requires, therefore, a constantly changing interest rate at each level of income. Second, the analysis has assumed either that capital movements are made on an uncovered basis (and hence are partly speculative), or that the forward exchange rate is uniquely determined at its current level. Either assumption implies that the effect on capital movements of changes in interest rates is not offset by equilibrating movements in the forward exchange rate.

Third, the analysis assumes a high degree of stability implied by an external equilibrium schedule related to levels of the exchange rate. To the extent that, in the short term, expectations about the future exchange rate are determined by current movements in the rate a high degree of instability is introduced into the balance-of-payments schedule. Fourth, it has been implicitly assumed that movement in the exchange rate effectively equilibrates the balance of payments, which implies that: (i) exchange-rate movements have an effect upon real wages, and (ii) trade responds to net exchange-rate movements. Both assumptions can be challenged (see Chapter 14).

PORTFOLIO BALANCE CONSTRAINTS

In the basic model adopted in this chapter, wealth effects of neither the budget deficit nor the balance of payments are incorporated. Wealth effects on expenditure include the consequences of changes in *net* wealth, and changes in the composition of wealth. Changes in *net* wealth derive from surpluses or deficits in either the budget or the current account of the balance of payments.

Both induce changes in *net* financial assets of the community which may in turn induce changes in expenditure and income, etc. Alternatively, changes can occur in the composition of net wealth between, for instance, bonds and money, and between domestic and external assets. Thus an open-market purchase of bonds by the central bank increases the volume of money balances but, as only an exchange of assets is involved, there is no change in *net* wealth. Similarly, with a balanced current account position, a capital inflow with a fixed exchange rate forces the central bank to create more domestic money balances. There is, however, no change in the community's *net* wealth as the rise in money balances is matched by a rise in liabilities to foreigners. Using the terminology of Gurley and Shaw, budget deficits and current account positions induce changes in *outside* money (changes in *net* wealth), while capital flows and open-market operations represent *inside* methods of changing the domestic money supply. Wealth effects deriving from the budget position occur irrespective of whether the budget deficit is financed through the issue of bonds or money.

Changes in *net* wealth may affect the level of expenditure and income in two ways: (i) a rise in *net* financial assets may induce a direct balance-sheet effect as the stock of physical commodities in wealth-holders' portfolios is low relative to the stock of financial assets, and this induces a balance-sheet adjustment in a way that increases expenditure on real goods; and (ii) the traditional real-balance effect induces individuals to raise current levels of consumption to make wealth holdings commensurate with their level of income. In these cases full equilibrium in the economy requires portfolio equilibrium and no endogenous changes in *net* wealth. A weakness of the traditional *IS/LM* paradigm is that such portfolio constraints are not incorporated.

In a simple closed economy model, where the only changes in *net* wealth derive from the Government's budget, equilibrium requires a balanced budget. In this case the fiscal policy multiplier is: $\left(\dfrac{1}{w}\right)$ where w is the income-tax rate (%) as a proportion of income. An initial rise in government expenditure induces a rise in income (through the wealth effect upon expenditure) until income rises sufficiently to generate a rise in tax receipts equal to the original rise in government expenditure. Conversely, changes in the money supply via open-market operations have no lasting effect upon income as the initial rise in income due to the rise in the money supply induces a rise in tax receipts and hence a budget surplus. The reduction in *net* welath that this implies induces an offsetting reduction in expenditure and income.[11] The equilibrium level of income is constrained by the requirement that the budget is balanced.

In an open economy the portfolio constraint becomes more complex.[12] There is no net change in the volume of financial assets when the budget deficit equals the current account deficit, as the former increases *net* wealth while the latter drains financial assets from domestic residents. This becomes the equilibrium condition and, with a fixed exchange rate, the government expenditure multiplier becomes $\left(\dfrac{1}{m+w}\right)$, where m is the marginal propensity to import. This must necessarily be smaller than the closed-economy multiplier. Any rise in government expenditure induces a rise in income, imports and tax receipts. If m is 0.3 and w is 0.2 the multiplier is 2 and a 100 increase in government expenditure induces a rise in income of 200. The resultant rise of 40 in tax receipts and 60 in imports absorbs the initial creation of 100 of *net* financial assets through the budget deficit. However, as before and for similar reasons, monetary policy can have no long-run effect upon the level of income with a fixed exchange rate.

With a floating exchange rate a rise in government expenditure induces an initial rise in *net* financial assets in the form of either money or bonds, and two opposing forces on the exchange rate: (i) the income-induced rise in imports causes the exchange rate to depreciate which is positive on income while (ii) the rise in the domestic interest rate induces an offsetting capital inflow. If the two are equal, the multiplier remains at $\left(\dfrac{1}{m+w}\right)$. At one extreme, where capital is totally unresponsive to changes in interest rates, the budget must ultimately be balanced as the current account must also be in balance in full equilibrium. Income rises under the impact of the expansionary fiscal policy and the depreciating exchange rate, and this continues until the rise in income is sufficient to generate increased tax receipts equal to the initial rise in government expenditure. The multiplier is $\left(\dfrac{1}{w}\right)$, which is the closed-economy multiplier. At the alternative extreme, where the F schedule is infinitely elastic, the domestic interest is fixed at the world level. The increased supply of bonds (the financing of the budget deficit) is purchased by foreigners who, by assumption, stand ready to buy any excess supply of bonds at the given (world) level of interest rates. As income rises there develops an excess demand for money, but, as the rate of interest is constrained at the world level, there is no mechanism by which the system can equilibrate the excess demand for money other than by a fall in income brought about by the appreciation of the exchange rate. Equilibrium income cannot change and the multiplier becomes zero.

With a floating exchange rate, therefore, the fiscal multiplier ranges between zero and $\left(\dfrac{1}{w}\right)$. While the conclusions of the analysis are not fundamentally different from the *IS/LM* model without wealth effects, the portfolio balance constraint alters the precise magnitude of income changes associated with monetary and fiscal policy.

CONCLUSIONS

Notwithstanding the limitations of the simplified model adopted, the significance of international capital movements is clear. In particular, the power of monetary and fiscal policy is determined in part by the sensitivity of capital flows to changes in interest rates, and autonomous (speculative) capital movements have effects on the domestic economy through their monetary or exchange-rate effects.

SELECTED BIBLIOGRAPHY

Beenstock, M. (1978) *The Foreign Exchanges* (London: Macmillan).

Branson, W. H. (1972) *Macroeconomic Theory* (New York: Harper & Row) chap. 15.

Cooper, R. N. (1976) 'Monetary Theory and Policy in an Open Economy', *Scandinavian Journal of Economics*, May 1976.

Fleming, J. M. (1962) 'Domestic Financial Policies under Fixed and Floating Exchange Rates', *IMF Staff Papers*, Nov 1962.

Galbis, V. (1975) 'Monetary and Exchange Rate Policies in a Small Open Economy', *IMF Staff Papers*, July 1975.

Helliwell, J. F. (1969) 'Monetary and Fiscal Policies for an Open Economy', *Oxford Economic Papers*, 1969.

Herring, R., and Marston, R. (1977) *National Monetary Policies and International Financial Markets* (Amsterdam: North-Holland) chap. 2.

Llewellyn, D. T. (1974) 'Stabilisation with Fixed and Floating Exchange Rates: A Generalised Approach', mimeo, University of Loughborough.

Mundell, R. A. (1968) *International Economics* (New York: Macmillan Co.) chaps 11, 14, 15, 16, 17 and 18.

Oates, W. E. (1966) 'Budget Balance and Equilibrium Income', *Journal of Finance*, Sep 1966.

Ott, D. J., and Ott, A. F. (1965) 'Budget Balance and Equilibrium Income', *Journal of Finance*, Mar 1965.

Ott, D. J., Ott, A. F., and Yoo, J. H. (1975) *Macroeconomic Theory* (Tokyo: McGraw-Hill Kogakusha) chap. 11.

Swoboda, A. K. (1972) 'Equilibrium, Quasi-Equilibrium and Macro-economic Policy', *Quarterly Journal of Economics*, pp. 162–71.

3

The Monetary Approach

In the previous chapter the domestic monetary effects of the balance of payments were incorporated in the standard IS/LM paradigm, and the two-way direction of causation between changes in the domestic money supply and the balance of payments was highlighted. In this extended model full macro-economic equilibrium requires zero excess demand/supply of foreign exchange so that, with a fixed exchange rate, there are no continuing externally induced changes in the money supply, and the exchange rate is in equilibrium in the floating-rate case. It also establishes that, with a fixed exchange rate and in the absence of sterilisation, monetary policy has no long-run effect upon the level of real income irrespective of the interest-rate sensitivity of capital movements. In the identity $M \equiv H + R$, policy-induced changes in the domestic component of high-powered money are offset by equal and opposite changes in the external reserves and external component of the monetary base. On the other hand, monetary policy becomes potentially powerful combined with a floating exchange rate though this power derives from induced exchange-rate movements.

The so-called *monetary approach* to the balance of payments reaches similar conclusions in the fixed-rate case (though the theoretical mechanisms are different), but challenges the role of monetary policy in the floating-rate case. The IS/LM paradigm is generally not appropriate for analysis of monetarist theoretical mechanisms. The central feature of the monetary approach is the proposition that the balance of payments is essentially a monetary pheno-menon. The focus of attention is on the relationship between the supply and demand for real-money balances, with a balance-of-payments deficit (or depreciating exchange rate) a reflection of an excess supply of money. The external deficit or depreciating exchange rate represents the equilibrating mechanism through which actual and desired real-money balances are reconciled. Thus with a fixed rate an excess supply of money induces a balance-of-payments deficit which continues until, under the influence of declining external reserves and external component of the monetary base, the *nominal* money supply has been reduced to a level consistent with the demand for *real* money balances. Similarly, a depreciating floating rate equilibrates the supply and demand for domestic money balances through the effects of the resultant rise in the domestic price level which reduces the *real* value of a given level of *nominal* money balances. Indeed with a floating exchange rate the impact of an excess supply of money is likely to be reflected in faster inflation in a shorter period than with fixed rates through the induced effect on the domestic price level of the depreciating exchange rate.

In both cases the external adjustment represents a phase of stock-adjustment which eliminates an *ex ante* discrepancy between the supply and demand for real money balances. A balance-of-payments deficit or depreciating exchange rate is the mechanism through which portfolio equilibrium of wealth-holders is restored. The corollary is that balance-of-payments analysis is conducted in terms of stocks rather than flows which are emphasised in the *IS/LM* paradigm. It also implies that a balance-of-payments deficit is inherently temporary and, unless the monetary effects are sterilised, reflects a once-for-all portfolio-adjustment.

There is, therefore, an automatic balance-of-payments adjustment mechanism through the effect upon the money supply. In practice, however, while in the long run a balance-of-payments deficit may be adjusted *via* the money supply, it is likely that the country will face an external reserves constraint before full adjustment has occurred. For this reason the loss of reserves will likely force more speedy balance-of-payments adjustment policies. Permanent deficits in the monetarist analysis reflect attempts by the central bank to prevent the domestic money supply adjusting to external disequilibria. In this case a continuous excess supply of money is being created.

Similarly the monetarist theory of the determination of the exchange rate emphasises asset rather than goods markets, with the equilibrium exchange rate between two currencies ensuring that the two stocks of domestic money balances are willingly held. The exchange rate is viewed as the price of domestic money in terms of foreign currency, and the price moves to eliminate any excess supply or demand of one against the other. In the short run the exchange rate is determined by stock-equilibrium conditions and in the long run by flow-equilibrium conditions.[1]

The monetary and asset-market approaches emphasise the supply and demand for real money balances; this is the centrepiece of the analysis. This does not, however, imply that excessive domestic money or credit creation is invariably the *proximate* cause of a balance-of-payments disequilibrium which may reflect a failure to adjust the domestic money supply to changes in the demand for money. If, for instance, the growth rate decelerates without a corresponding deceleration in the rate of domestic credit creation, the concomitant excess supply of money balances induces a balance-of-payments deficit. Similarly, according to monetarist analysis, countries such as Germany and Switzerland moved into current-account surplus after the 1973 oil price rise because the rise in domestic prices induced an increased demand for nominal money balances while the monetary authorities failed to fully accommodate this demand through their domestic monetary policy.

The extreme form of the monetarist approach to the balance of payments (termed *global monetarism*)[2] is based upon the assumption of perfect arbitrage in traded goods and financial asset markets, and upon the assumptions made in other standard monetarist analysis. In terms of the familiar formulation $M = kPY$ an excess supply of money cannot be equilibrated by a rise in real income which, in the long run, is determined at the full-employment (or natural unemployment) level and independently of the money supply. Similarly, the domestic price level, with fixed exchange rates, is determined at the world level by perfect arbitrage in traded goods (law of one price). As, in the long run, the demand for money function is viewed as stable and independent of changes in the supply of money, there can be no equilibrating movements in K (via interest rate movements) in response to an excess supply of domestic money balances. It follows that, with these constraints and the multitude of implicit assumptions in monetarist models, any excess domestic money creation can be offset only by an externally induced reduction in nominal money balances (fixed-exchange-rate case), or a reduction in the real value of a given nominal money supply (floating-rate case). An excess supply of money balances induces portfolio diversification into foreign goods and financial assets.

The analysis in these terms highlights the long-run orientation of the monetary approach to the balance of payments which is implicit in the law of one price, the stable demand for money function and the invariability of real income to changes in the money supply. In many cases monetarist models proceed from the *assumption* of perfect arbitrage in asset markets and the markets in internationally traded goods. And yet, as noted in Chapters 6, 7 and 12, these assumptions are not generally supported by empirical evidence. The relevance of the monetarist approach therefore lies in the analytical long run which may well be beyond the policy-makers' horizon.

POLICY IMPLICATIONS

The ultimate policy implication of the monetary approach is that balance-of-payments adjustment occurs through the money supply and that instruments to adjust the balance of payments operate *via* their impact upon the demand or supply of real money balances. Thus, an exchange-rate adjustment is an effective means of inducing a once-for-all rise in external reserves by reducing the real value of a given volume of nominal money balances. In effect, a single devaluation is equivalent to a once-for-all reduction in the domestic money supply with the concomitant excess demand for money inducing an external surplus. However, the effect of the devaluation is temporary and associated with the once-for-all reduction in the real value of money balances. If the original deficit is due to an excessive expansionary monetary policy, and this is not restrained, the effect of the devaluation is transitory. The approach emphasises that, in the final analysis, permanent balance-of-payments adjustment requires that changes in the domestic component of the money supply are consistent with the demand for money. At the same time monetary policy has no long-run or permanent effect upon the real magnitudes in the economy. It also implies that, to secure an improvement in the balance of payments *via* monetary policy, the domestic component of the monetary base must be contracted, or expanded at a slower rate than the projected rise in the demand for money given the assumed course of real income, prices and interest rates over the policy period. The implied excess demand for money is equilibrated through reserve inflows.

It also follows that floating exchange rates do not offer an escape from the contraints on domestic monetary policy and, contrary to the previous analysis, do not enhance its power. In particular, floating rates do not enable an independent monetary policy to secure a level of real income and employment above the *natural* level. Indeed, to the extent that balance-of-payments adjustments of any kind (tariffs, exchange-rate adjustments, etc.) operate *via* their impact on the excess supply/demand for money, they are not permanent alternatives to an appropriate domestic monetary policy. It is in this sense that the monetarist approach questions the role of floating exchange rates as a means of enabling countries to pursue an independent monetary policy. The *monetarist* approach attributes much of the volatility of floating rates experienced since 1973 to monetary factors and postulates that stable exchange rates require a stable and predictable monetary policy. In particular, speculators are not viewed as irrational and unpredictable, but as wealth-holders who use all available information in determining their expectations about the future level of the exchange rate. Monetary policy is seen as an important ingredient in the formation of expectations. Thus a stable path of *actual* exchange rates requires a stable path of *expected* rates which in turn necessitates a stable and predictable monetary policy. The observed instability of exchange rates is due, therefore, not to erratic speculators but to erratic monetary policy which increases uncertainty.

Ultimately, in the monetary approach, a balance-of-payments deficit is a reflection of a degree of excess money balances above that in other countries. If excess money balances are being created in all countries, the world price level rises but no balance-of-payments problems necessarily emerge. One possibility, therefore, for a stable international monetary system is internationally co-ordinated monetary policy strategies between countries. This, as noted in Chapters 12 and 14, is a particularly significant issue in fixed-exchange-rate systems (e.g. the European Monetary System) but, given the limited effective power of exchange-rate adjustments in the monetarist models, is equally valid with floating exchange rates.

SOME CRITICISMS

In line with most monetarist analysis it is the long run that is emphasised. The assumptions made, and mechanisms implied, pertain to the analytical long run which, if related to years, is almost invariably longer than the policy-makers' horizon. This makes for difficulties in empirically testing the propositions of the monetary approach. Thus it is only in the long run that monetarist models have the level of real income determined independently of monetary policy, and the evidence is very much against the law of one price in either commodity or asset markets in the short run. The evidence also indicates (see Chapter 12) that monetary authorities are able, at least in the short run, to effectively sterilise the monetary effects of the balance of payments, and this power has been used. Exchange-rate adjustments may also affect real magnitudes in the short run. The evidence has been carefully and comprehensively reviewed by Kreinin and Officer (1978), who report mixed results. With respect to the *Global Monetarist* approach they conclude: 'By any strand of argument, there is almost no evidence to support the hypothesis of the law of one price in the commodity, bond or equity markets. Global monetarism must be rejected in the present state of the globe.' But this does not deny the usefulness of the insights offered by the monetary approach. Indeed, the predictions are relevant even without the assumption of perfect arbitrage though, as noted in Beenstock (1978), (who integrates short- and long-run analysis in a structural model of the economy and the balance of payments) this lengthens the long run. In the final analysis, the monetarist approach questions the ultimate value of so-called independent monetary policy that is afforded by floating exchange rates. But in the short run the alternative elasticities and absorption approaches to balance-of-payments analysis remain valid.

CONCLUSIONS

In the two broad alternative approaches discussed in this and the previous chapter (the *monetarist* analysis and the Mundell–Fleming extension of the neo-Keynesian model to an open economy) monetary factors were seen to be important in balance-of-payments analysis. Both question the ability of governments to pursue independent monetary policies with fixed exchange rates. The two approaches also stress the powerful monetary linkages between countries, and particularly the effect that money creation in one country has on the domestic money supply in other countries when exchange rates are fixed.

The analysis has been conducted in terms of the polar cases of fixed and floating exchange rates. In practice, since 1973 *managed floating* has been the predominant policy, with central banks attempting to moderate exchange-rate movements. Nevertheless, the analysis is equally relevant to this hybrid system. In many cases governments have attempted to secure simultaneous and inconsistent exchange-rate, monetary and interest-rate targets. In this system, while balance-of-payments pressure has an effect on exchange rates, official intervention in the foreign-exchange market has also had the normal monetary and interest-rate effects discussed earlier. Attempts have also been

made to sterilise the monetary effects of foreign-exchange-market intervention. The logic of the analysis, when applied to the managed-floating-
rates case, implies similar conclusions to the fixed-rate case though more
complexities arise. This may be illustrated by considering the effects of a
speculative capital outflow. In the fixed-rate case, the domestic money supply
contracts unless full sterilisation is attempted, while with floating rates the
exchange rate depreciates. In the hybrid system the exchange rate declines and
pressure is exerted on the domestic money supply. If, in this model, central
banks always seek to *limit* the depreciation (but not prevent it completely)
sterilisation of the monetary effect may tend, in the long run, to induce a
greater exchange-rate depreciation than in the pure floating-rate case. This is
because of the exchange-rate effect of a higher *ex ante* money supply which
adds to the exchange-rate pressure originally induced by speculation. This
may be particularly powerful if speculators base their expectations in part
upon the course of monetary policy. The net result is likely to be both a greater
exchange-rate depreciation, and a larger loss of reserves. In effect, the central
bank's domestic monetary policy is inconsistent with its exchange market
intervention policy: the central bank buys domestic currency to limit the
exchange-rate depreciation, but simultaneously sells domestic currency in the
domestic money market to sterilise the monetary effect of its exchange market
intervention. Disequilibrium in the money market is therefore larger, and
maintained for a longer period, with the implication that the ultimate
exchange-rate adjustment is larger. The *monetarist* analysis suggests that it is
largely this monetary policy that has induced the large exchange-rate
adjustments experienced since 1973. Monetary authorities cannot, in the long
run, secure arbitrarily chosen target levels for the exchange rate and the
domestic money supply.

SELECTED BIBLIOGRAPHY

Beenstock, M. (1978) *The Foreign Exchanges* (London: Macmillan)
    chaps 2–5.
Bilson, J. F. O. (1978) 'Monetary Approach to the Exchange Rate: Some
    Evidence', *IMF Staff Papers*, Mar 1978.
Black, S. (1973) *International Money Markets and Flexible Exchange Rates*,
    Studies in International Finance No. 32, Princeton University Press.
Blackwell, C. (1978) 'Monetary Approach to Balance of Payments', *IMF
    Survey*, 20 Feb, 6 Mar.
Currie, D. A. (1976) 'Some Criticisms of the Monetary Analysis of Balance of
    Payments Correction, *Economic Journal*, Sep 1976.
Dornbusch, R. (1973) 'Devaluation, Money and Non-Traded Goods',
    American Economic Review, Dec 1973.

Dornbusch, R. (1975) 'A Portfolio Balance Model of the Open Economy', *Journal of Monetary Economics*, Jan 1975.

Frenkel, J. A., and Johnson, H. G. (1976) *Monetary Approach to the Balance of Payments* (Toronto: University of Toronto Press).

Frenkel, J. A., and Rodriquez, C. A. (1975) 'Portfolio Equilibrium and the Balance of Payments: A Monetary Approach', *American Economic Review*, Sep 1975.

Humphrey, T. M. (1977) 'A Monetarist Model of Exchange Rate Determination', *Federal Reserve Bank of Richmond Economic Review*, Jan 1977.

Johnson, H. G. (1973) 'The Monetary Approach to Balance of Payments Theory', in Connolly, M., and Swoboda, A. (eds) *International Trade and Money* (London: Allen & Unwin).

Johnson, H. G. (1975) 'The Monetary Approach to Balance of Payments Theory', *Manchester School*, Sep 1975.

Johnson, H. G. (1976) 'Money and the Balance of Payments', *Banca Nazionale del Lavoro Quarterly Review*, Mar 1976.

Johnson, H. G. (1977) 'Monetary Approach to Balance of Payments Theory and Policy', *Economica*, Aug 1977.

Kemp, D. S. (1975) 'A Monetary View of the Balance of Payments', *Federal Reserve Bank of St. Louis Review*, Apr 1975.

Kouri, P. (1976) 'The Exchange Rate and the Balance of Payments in the Short and Long Run: A Monetary Approach', *Scandinavian Journal of Economics*, May 1976.

Kreinin, M. K., and Officer, L. H. (1978) *The Monetary Approach to the Balance of Payments*, Princeton Studies in International Finance, No. 43, Princeton University Press.

Rhomberg, R., and Heller, H. R. (eds) (1977) *Monetary Approach to the Balance of Payments* (Washington: IMF).

Various (1976) *Scandinavian Journal of Economics*, May 1976.

Whitman, M. V. (1975) 'Global Monetarism and the Monetary Approach to the Balance of Payments', in *Brookings Papers on Economic Activity*, No. 3 (Washington, D.C.: Brookings Institute) pp. 491–536.

4

The Forward Exchange Rate

The analysis of international capital flows, and their impact on exchange rates and the domestic economy, becomes more complex though more realistic when forward as well as spot exchange transactions are incorporated. The role of the forward market is important in three ways: (i) movements in the forward exchange rate affect arbitrage calculations which determine international capital flows: (ii) forward exchange transactions and changes in the forward rate are important elements in interest-rate and monetary linkages between countries; and (iii) official (central bank) intervention in the forward exchange market is a potentially powerful means of influencing the volume and pattern of capital flows. More specifically, autonomous forward exchange transactions (such as speculative forward sales of a currency) may influence the relative rates of return between investments in different currencies, and hence cause wealth-holders to rearrange their portfolio of wealth between countries. Also, counterpart forward transactions to spot capital flows induce movements in forward rates which in turn alter the arbitrage calculation resulting from interest-rate changes. In this sense, movements in the forward rate have an equilibrating effect and tend to moderate the magnitude of capital flows in response to changes in interest-rate differentials. In this way the forward exchange market can be an important insulating mechanism which limits the extent of international financial interdependence through capital account transactions.

In the forward exchange market, transactions are made for delivery of currency at some specified date in the future (e.g. three months hence) but at a price agreed between the transactors today; the forward exchange market is a futures market which enables interest arbitrageurs, traders and investors to eliminate the risk of movements in spot exchange rates. Thus, an American investor purchasing three-month U.K. treasury bills may incur a capital loss measured in dollars if, at the time of maturity, sterling has depreciated in the exchange markets. This risk is eliminated if, at the time sterling is purchased spot to invest in the U.K. money market, sterling is also sold forward against dollars at a predetermined rate. Similarly, a British importer of German goods may borrow from his German supplier and the risk that the sterling value of his debt might be increased through an appreciation of the Deutsche Mark or depreciation of sterling can be eliminated by buying Deutsche Marks forward for the maturity of his debt.

Forward transactions may be made with banks for a variety of maturities though the bulk are made in the one- to six-month range. The forward rate is said to be at a *premium* if it is appreciated against the current spot rate (e.g. if spot sterling were £1 = $1.75 while the three-month forward rate were £1 = $1.80), and at a *discount* if it is depreciated against the spot rate.

The aim of this chapter is to identify the role of forward exchange transactions in international capital movements rather than to present an exhaustive presentation of forward exchange theory *per se*, or to integrate the forward rate into a full macro model.[1] Nevertheless, to appreciate the role of forward transactions a review of the basic theory of forward exchange rate determination is necessary. In this and the following chapter two alternative analytical frameworks are considered and these may be termed: (i) the *structural* model, and (ii) the *Cambist* approach. The former views the forward premium as determined by the interaction of speculative and interest arbitrage supply and demand for forward currency by banks and non-banks. This is compared with the *Cambist* approach which considers the forward premium to be determined simply by the difference between relevant interest rates in different currencies. This chapter concentrates on the more general theoretical view, while Chapter 5 reviews the *Cambist* approach. In the final analysis, while the debate between the two has been long and heated, there is little analytical difference between them; the distinction is more apparent than real.

FORWARD EXCHANGE TRANSACTIONS

Traditionally, the theory of forward exchange distinguishes four types of transaction: *interest arbitrage, speculation, commercial covering* and *hedging* of non-self-liquidating assets. For most purposes, however, these may be reduced to two, as the third and fourth may be subsumed within the first two without loss of significant analysis. Interest arbitrage is directly related to international capital flows and occurs when, for instance, an investor purchases foreign currency so as to invest temporarily in a foreign asset and covers the potential exchange-rate loss (which would result from a depreciation of the foreign currency) by simultaneously selling/buying the foreign/domestic currency forward. The *arbitraguer* is therefore a risk-averter.

A speculator, on the other hand, deliberately incurs risk in anticipation of profit to be derived from a movement in the spot exchange rate before the forward contract matures. Indeed, because the speculator need not have funds at the time of opening a speculative forward position,[2] the forward exchange market is particularly attractive to speculators. Profit (or loss if the assumption proves to be false) derives from the difference between: (i) the price (exchange rate) at which the speculator commits himself to deliver, or accept delivery of, foreign exchange at the maturity of the forward contract, and (ii) the prevailing spot rate at the time of maturity. Speculators sell foreign currency forward (i.e. purchase domestic currency forward) when their expectation is that in three months' time the spot exchange rate of the domestic currency will have appreciated by an amount which is greater than the current forward premium (per cent) against the current spot rate; in other words, when the *expected* future spot rate is appreciated against the current forward rate. This is because in three months' time, and in order to meet his forward commitment to supply foreign currency, the speculator is able to buy the foreign currency with less domestic currency than he receives as the counterpart to his forward sale of foreign currency. Conversely, if the expected future spot rate is depreciated against the current forward rate the speculator sells domestic currency forward (buys foreign currency). No speculative purchases or sales are made when the expected future spot rate and the current forward rate are the same. The volume of forward sales and purchases by speculators is likely to be determined by the confidence with which expectations are held, the size of the expected profit (i.e. difference between current forward rate and expected future spot rate) and the extent of previously incurred forward commitments.

INTEREST ARBITRAGE

Covered interest arbitrage transactions are profitable providing the interest gain through investing in the foreign money market rather than domestically is greater than the capital loss made on the forward transaction when the forward rate is at a discount to the current spot rate. Put more formally, *covered* interest arbitrage is profitable providing the uncovered interest rate differential between the two countries is greater than the forward discount/premium.

If X_t is the forward exchange rate, X_0 the spot rate (both measured in terms of domestic currency per unit of foreign currency)[3] R_d is the sterling interest rate and R_f the interest rate in the United States, capital will flow from London to New York when:

$$\frac{X_t(1 + R_f)}{X_0} > (1 + R_d),$$

i.e. when the forward discount (per cent) on sterling is greater than the uncovered interest-rate differential in favour of investment in the United Kingdom. Conversely, capital flows to London when the equation is reversed. There is no incentive for capital to flow between the two countries when the two sides of the equation are equal, which is when sterling's forward discount is exactly equal to the interest-rate differential in favour of London. At this point the forward exchange rate is said to be at *interest parity*.

INTEREST-PARITY THEORY

The interest-parity theory of the forward exchange rate, upon which the *Cambist* formulation is based, postulates that equilibrium in the forward exchange market is achieved when the forward exchange rate is at its interest-parity level, i.e. when the forward discount/premium equals the interest-rate differential between relevant currency assets. At this rate there is no incentive for arbitrage capital flows. In a situation where the spot and forward exchange rates are not held constant by the monetary authorities, and both the domestic and foreign interest rates adjust under the impact of international capital flows, all four prices adjust to any exogenous disturbance to an initial equilibrium. Through such adjustments parity is re-established. Thus, if a covered interest differential were to open in favour of domestic assets, arbitrage inflows would in principle induce: (i) an appreciation of the spot exchange rate; (ii) a depreciation of the forward rate (increased demand for spot sterling and increased sales of forward sterling by interest arbitrageurs); (iii) a rise in the foreign interest rate; and (iv) a fall in the domestic interest rate. In principle, each moves in the direction of reducing the covered interest differential and, if capital flows are not restricted, adjustments continue until parity is restored. However, the crucial condition is that the supply of arbitrage funds is not restricted before parity is achieved.

To the extent that any of the four prices are fixed, or determined at a unique level, a greater proportion of the adjustment is necessarily borne by the others. Thus, even though the forward exchange rate itself may not adjust (perhaps because it is being held at a particular level by official intervention, or is determined uniquely by speculators), the interest-parity condition may still be attained providing there is a sufficient volume of arbitrage funds. If, for instance, speculators have complete confidence that the spot rate will be depreciated by 2 per cent in three months' time, the forward rate will move to a 2 per cent discount as, in principle, there is no limit to the volume of sales of forward sterling by speculators. Speculators will keep the forward rate at a 2 per cent discount while they have total confidence in a depreciation of the spot rate. There will therefore be no adjustment to the forward rate resulting from the capital flows in response to the initial covered interest-rate differential. *Providing there is a perfectly elastic supply of arbitrage funds,* capital will flow from the United Kingdom until there is no further incentive for arbitrage between, say, U.K. and U.S. Treasury bills. As the spot rate is presumed fixed (though changeable by the authorities) and the forward rate is determined uniquely by speculators, equilibrium is restored through adjustments in U.K. and U.S. interest rates. There is therefore nothing implicit in the interest-parity theory of the forward exchange rate that requires the equilibrating adjustment to be made by the forward exchange rate itself; it is one of the four variables determined simultaneously. Neither, therefore, does the existence of speculation in the forward market necessarily impede the attainment of interest parity.

However, if speculation or official intervention prevents the forward rate from adjusting to interest-rate differentials, a greater volume of capital flows is needed to restore the equilibrium parity condition as the adjustment has to be made entirely by interest rates. This is because a given volume of capital flows tends normally to have a greater impact on the forward exchange rate than on interest rates, as it is likely to represent a higher proportion of total forward exchange transactions than money market transactions. It is for this reason that the theory requires an infinite supply of arbitrage funds. But it also implies that if, for any reason, the supply of arbitrage funds is limited, the existence of a substantial forward premium or discount may produce an equilibrium at which a positive or negative covered differential remains.

In the final analysis the theory is a restatement of the general proposition that the same commodity cannot sell simultaneously for two prices unless different segments of the market can be separated. In this sense the theory is applicable only to assets which are homogeneous and alike in all respects (e.g. default risk, maturity, etc.) other than the currency of denomination as this difference is effectively eliminated in the forward exchange market. This requirement will be found to be significant when the parity condition is applied to euro-currency v. national money markets.

A FORMAL MODEL

A formal model of the forward exchange rate may be constructed on the basis of supply and demand schedules for forward exchange by speculators and interest arbitrageurs. The equilibrium forward rate is determined when the net supply of forward exchange by one group of transactors is matched by the net demand from the other. In effect one group provides the other with forward exchange. The important issue for covered capital movements is the volume of forward currency made available to arbitrageurs by either speculators or central banks if the latter are intervening in forward markets. The basic theoretical model is outlined in Figure 4.1. The forward exchange *rate* is measured on the vertical axis in terms of the number of units of domestic currency per unit of foreign currency. Whether any particular forward rate is at a premium or discount depends upon the current spot rate, which may also be indicated on the vertical axis. The volume of forward exchange supplied and demanded by speculators and arbitrageurs is indicated along the horizontal axis. To the left is measured arbitrageurs sales of forward exchange/purchases of forward sterling (associated with a spot capital outflow) and speculators' sales of forward sterling. In the analysis to follow it is initially assumed that both the spot rate and foreign and domestic interest rates are determined exogenously, and remain constant.

(i) *Arbitrageurs*

The supply and demand curves of interest arbitrageurs is given in Figure 4.1 as

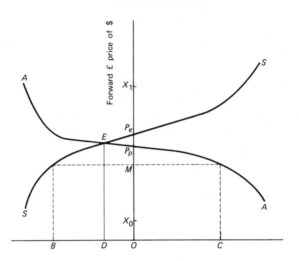

Arbitrageurs' purchases/speculators'
sales of forward sterling

SPOT CAPITAL OUTFLOW

Arbitrageurs' sales/speculators'
purchases of forward sterling

SPOT CAPITAL INFLOW

FIGURE 4.1   Determination of the forward exchange rate

AA. When the spot rate and domestic and foreign interest rates are known, the
parity level of the forward rate is determined at P_p; at this rate no arbitrage
capital flows take place, as the covered interest differential is zero. The
arbitrageurs' schedule therefore cuts the vertical axis at the parity level of the
forward exchange rate and at this rate there is zero net demand or supply of
forward exchange by arbitrageurs. At other points along AA the arbitrageurs'
net supply or demand of forward exchange is measured along the horizontal
axis. To the left the forward rate is depreciated against its parity level which,
with a given spot rate, implies a covered interest-rate differential against
domestic assets. This implies a spot capital outflow and hence arbitrageurs' net
sales/purchases of forward exchange/sterling. Conversely, to the right of P_p
the capital inflow implies net forward sales of sterling by arbitrageurs. Thus,
the arbitrageurs' schedule is a demand curve for forward sterling to the left of
zero but a supply curve of forward sterling to the right. If the spot rate is X_0 the
implication is that the domestic interest rate is higher than the foreign rate as
the parity level of the forward rate (P_p) is at a discount to the spot exchange
rate. Thus, at a forward rate below P_p (e.g. M) in Figure 4.1 we have:

$$\frac{X_t(1+R_f)}{X_0} < (1+R_d)$$

which induces a capital inflow OC with arbitrageurs selling an amount OC of
forward sterling. The AA schedule indicates not only arbitrageurs' forward

transactions but the corresponding volume of spot capital flows which are the counterpart to their forward transactions.

The slope of the schedule indicates the elasticity of supply of arbitrage funds, i.e. the interest-rate sensitivity of international capital flows. Clearly, the more interest elastic are such capital movements the greater is the elasticity of demand/supply of forward exchange. We shall see that the slope of this schedule is important in determining both the forward exchange rate and the volume of capital flows. The shape of the schedule in Figure 4.1 indicates the possibility that, as the volume of capital flows increases, an increasingly wide covered interest-rate differential is needed to induce further capital flows.

The slope of the AA schedule is determined, therefore, by those factors (such as degree of exchange control, investors' estimates of non-exchange risks to foreign investment, availability of funds, etc.) which determine the interest-rate sensitivity of international capital flows. The *position* of the schedule is determined by: (i) the spot exchange rate, and (ii) the uncovered interest-rate differential between domestic and foreign assets. Thus, a rise in the domestic interest rate is represented by an upward shift in the AA schedule as the uncovered differential moves in favour of domestic assets, and hence the parity level of the forward exchange rate depreciates.

(ii) *Speculators*

The speculators' supply and demand schedule is represented by SS in Figure 4.1. No speculative sales or purchases of forward exchange are made when the forward rate is equal to the expected future spot rate. Thus the SS schedule cuts the vertical axis at the level of the expected future spot rate (P_e). The schedule indicates the volume of speculative forward sales/purchases of foreign/domestic currency at each forward exchange rate. At a forward rate OM the expected future spot rate (P_e) is depreciated against the current forward rate and hence speculative forward sales of (OB) sterling are made. Conversely, at forward rates appreciated against the expected future spot rate, forward purchases (sales) are made of sterling (foreign currency). The slope of the SS schedule is determined by: (i) the degree of certainty with which expectations about the future spot rate are held, and (ii) the degree of risk-aversion of speculators. Clearly, the greater the certainty with which a particular expectation is held the more elastic will be the speculators' schedule. When expectations are held with substantial confidence the SS schedule is highly elastic as a small divergence between the present forward rate and the expected future spot rate induces speculators to sell or buy substantial amounts of forward currency as they believe risks to be low. Conversely, if expectations are held with little confidence, and speculators exhibit significant risk-aversion, the SS schedule will be inelastic as a substantial divergence between the forward rate and the expected spot rate is necessary to induce speculators to incur the risks of even relatively small forward commitments.[4]

EQUILIBRIUM FORWARD RATE

The equilibrium forward rate and volume of capital flows are determined at E and OA in Figure 4.1. At this rate the net demand for forward sterling by interest arbitrageurs (OD) associated with the capital outflow is met by the net supply of forward sterling by speculators. This is because at E the forward rate is appreciated against the expected future spot rate (P_e). If equilibrium were in the right-hand segment of Figure 4.1 (i.e. if the expected future spot rate P_e was appreciated against the interest-parity level of the forward rate), equilibrium in the forward market would imply a capital inflow with consequent sales of forward sterling by arbitrageurs, matched by demand for forward sterling by speculators. Clearly, any position such as M could not be an equilibrium rate as, in that particular case, both speculators and arbitrageurs are selling forward sterling by amounts OB and OC respectively. The forward rate would depreciate under the impact of excess supply of forward sterling until supply and demand were in balance.

In Figure 4.1 the equilibrium forward rate (E) is different from the interest-rate-parity level (P_p) and hence, in principle, arbitrageurs are forgoing apparently profitable investment opportunities. Clearly this is a consequence of a less than perfectly elastic arbitrage schedule. It follows from this representation of the forward exchange rate that the sufficient conditions for the parity theory to be upheld are: (i) the AA schedule is infinitely elastic, which implies an infinite supply of potential arbitrage funds, or (ii) the expected future spot rate is equal to the parity level at which point there is zero capital flows as the two schedules intersect on the vertical axis. The closer is the expected future spot rate to the parity level of the forward rate the greater the probability that the forward rate will be close to parity irrespective of the elasticities of the two schedules. But the more important analytical condition is that there is an infinite supply of arbitrage funds available to take advantage of any covered interest-rate differential between two currencies. An important corollary, however, is that while the forward rate is determined at its parity level when the supply of funds is infinitely elastic, the *volume of capital flows is determined uniquely by the slope and position of the speculators' schedule*. Thus in Figure 4.2 an infinitely elastic supply of arbitrage funds, with the forward rate determined at its parity level, is consistent with either a capital outflow OC (if the expected future spot rate is depreciated against the parity level of the forward rate), or capital inflow OB in the converse case. Thus while primacy may be afforded to arbitrageurs in determining the forward rate, the volume of capital flows is determined in this case uniquely by speculators who determine the volume of forward sterling or foreign currency to be absorbed by interest arbitrageurs. The importance of speculators (and the slope of the speculators' schedule) derives from their being the counterpart suppliers (demanders) of the forward currency demanded (supplied) by arbitrageurs.

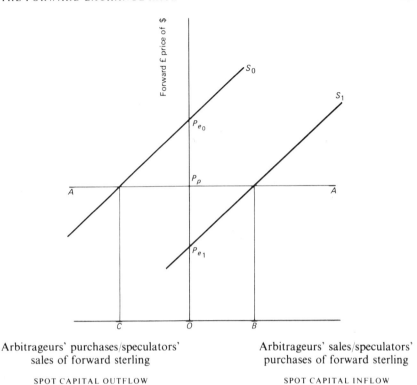

FIGURE 4.2   Determination of capital movements

DETERMINATION OF CAPITAL FLOWS

Not only the forward exchange rate but also the volume and direction of international capital movements are determined by the multitude of factors which determine the position and slope of the speculators' and arbitrageurs' supply and demand schedules for forward exchange. In particular, it has been established that the volume of capital flows may be determined exclusively by speculators' activities in the forward exchange market. In terms of static analysis, for instance, for a given SS schedule the more elastic is the arbitrage schedule (more elastic the supply of potential arbitrage funds) the greater will be the volume of capital flows (in either direction), and the closer will the forward exchange rate be to its parity level. Similarly, for a given arbitrage schedule the more elastic is the speculators' schedule (greater certainty speculators maintain their expectations with respect to the future spot rate) the greater will be the volume of capital flows and the closer will be the forward rate to the speculators' expected future spot rate. Thus, the determination of the volume of capital flows is more complex than represented in the model in Chapter 2 and depends, *inter alia*, upon: (i) uncovered interest-rate differentials, (ii) the interest sensitivity of capital flows, (iii) expectations about the future spot rate and their impact on speculative positions in the forward market, and (iv) the degree of confidence with which these views are held by speculators. The analysis becomes more complex still when policy variables, such as changes in interest rates, may affect these other variables.

Speculative activity in the forward market affects spot capital flows indirectly through its effect upon the covered interest-rate differential. A speculative forward sale of sterling will tend, other things being equal, to cause the forward rate to depreciate and the covered interest-rate differential to move against sterling. Arbitrageurs react by reducing the proportion of their portfolios held in sterling and increasing the proportion in foreign currency assets. In this way speculation conducted entirely in the forward market affects both the magnitude and direction of international capital flows. It can also be verified from the basic Figure 4.1 (p. 40) that the effect upon spot capital movements of *shifts* in the speculators' schedule is in part determined by the *elasticity* of the schedule; the more elastic is the schedule the greater the impact on spot capital flows of changes in speculators' views about the future spot rate.

INTEREST RATES

The basic model may be applied to the analysis of the impact on international capital flows of changes in either domestic or foreign interest rates. Analytically, a rise in the domestic interest rate is represented by an upward shift in the arbitrageurs' schedule from A_0 to A_1 in Figure 4.3. A rise in the domestic interest-rate changes the parity level of the forward exchange rate with the parity forward discount/premium (per cent) increased/decreased by an amount equal to the rise in the interest rate. Thus, with a constant spot exchange rate, the rise in the domestic rate is equivalent to $P_{p_0} P_{p_1}$ in Figure 4.3. The normal effect of a rise in the domestic interest rate would be: (i) a smaller capital outflow or larger capital inflow, (ii) a depreciation of the forward exchange rate as arbitrageurs increase their sales of forward sterling as the counterpart to the spot capital flows, and (iii) a change in the covered interest-rate differential of an amount something less than the initial change in interest rates. Thus, an induced movement in the forward exchange rate will, if the speculators' schedule is less than perfectly elastic, moderate the effect on international capital flows of changes in either domestic or foreign interest rates. In Figure 4.3, for instance, an initial capital outflow of OM (assuming a speculative schedule of S_0) is transformed to a capital inflow ON and the forward exchange rate depreciates from A_0 to B_0. The change in the *covered* interest-rate differential is clearly less than the initial change in interest rates because of the equilibrating movement in the forward exchange rate. Only when the speculators' schedule for forward exchange is infinitely elastic will the change in the covered interest-rate differential be equal to the initial change in interest rates. It is only in this case that, as the forward rate is determined

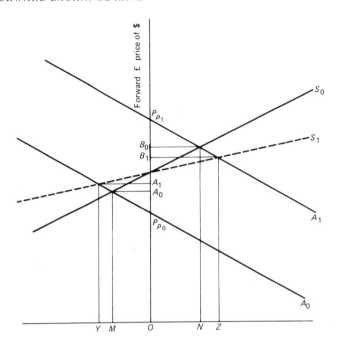

Arbitrageurs' purchases/speculators'   Arbitrageurs' sales/speculators'
    sales of forward sterling   purchases of forward sterling

      SPOT CAPITAL OUTFLOW   SPOT CAPITAL INFLOW

FIGURE 4.3   Rise in domestic interest rate

unambiguously by speculators, there is no change in the forward rate due to
changes in the direction or magnitude of capital flows. Thus, as indicated in
Figure 4.3, the more elastic is the speculators' schedule: (i) the greater will be
the impact of interest-rate changes on international capital flows, and
(ii) the smaller will be the extent of the equilibrating movement of the forward
exchange rate. With the more elastic S_1 schedule in Figure 4.3 the effect on
capital flows is increased by $MY + NZ$.

EMPIRICAL EVIDENCE

The elasticities of the arbitrageurs' and speculators' schedules are key
determinants of the response of capital flows to interest-rate changes, and
hence of the degree of international financial integration. Other things being
equal, the degree of national insulation varies inversely with the elasticities of
the two schedules.

The empirical evidence[5] indicates that, when comparison is made between
national rather than *euro*-currency assets, the arbitrage schedule is less than
infinitely elastic and that the speculators' schedule is inelastic. Beenstock

(1978) estimates the slope of AA to be \$1929 million for the United Kingdom and the speculators' schedule to be very inelastic (\$103 million). Thus, while a rise in domestic interest rates of 1 per cent might induce a \$1929 million inflow with a constant forward rate, the very inelastic SS schedule causes a substantial equilibrating movement in the forward rate which reduces the net inflow to \$102 million. However, this implies that if the Bank of England were to intervene to support the rate by selling forward dollars of \$1827, a 1 per cent rise in interest rates would induce the full \$1929 capital inflow. These estimates relate to the period prior to the abolition of exchange control in 1979. Thus, a covered foreign currency asset is not viewed as a perfect-substitute for a domestic asset as, although the exchange risk has been removed, other risks remain (e.g. default risk, risk of exchange control being imposed by the foreign government, etc.). The arbitrage schedule may also be less than perfectly elastic because exchange control limits the supply of arbitrage funds. There may be other portfolio-balance reasons why investors would not be prepared to supply an infinite volume of funds to a particular foreign market. The speculators' schedule appears to be inelastic, which implies that the effect upon the capital account of changes in interest rates is substantially muted by equilibrating movements in forward exchange rates. This also implies that official intervention in the forward market is a potentially powerful means of inducing capital flows, as such intervention may prevent the forward rate from moving to choke off the capital flow response to interest-rate changes.

The impact of changes in interest rates (whether caused by changes in monetary or fiscal policy) is therefore dependent, *inter alia*, upon the interest-rate sensitivity of international capital flows, but also upon the elasticity of the speculators' schedule for forward exchange. Other things being equal, the more certain are speculators about their view of the future spot rate the greater the influence monetary policy is likely to have on international capital flows.

Three important conclusions emerge with respect to the power of monetary policy: (i) unless speculators have total confidence in their view of the expected future spot rate the effect of a change in interest rates on the relevant covered interest-rate differential is partly offset by a movement in the forward exchange rate; (ii) the power of monetary policy to affect international capital flows depends critically upon the elasticity of the speculators' schedule for forward exchange and upon whether changes in interest rates cause speculators to adjust their view of the future spot rate; and (iii) the more elastic is the speculators' schedule the greater is the likely impact of changes in monetary policy on capital flows and the resultant depreciation of a floating spot exchange rate. The degree of monetary interdependence is therefore in part determined by conditions in the forward exchange market and, in particular, by the slope of the speculators' schedule.

QUALIFICATIONS

Several important qualifications must be made to the analysis. Two particular reservations are made with respect to the theory of international capital flows and the monetary effects of the balance of payments. As with the presentation in Chapter 2, the arbitrage schedule implicitly assumes a flow theory of international capital rather than the theoretically more superior stock-adjustment model. It assumes therefore that capital continues to flow at a constant rate while a particular covered interest-rate differential persists. In this respect the model is more appropriately related to the short run during which a stock-adjustment is being made. Second, as presented the analysis implicitly assumes that monetary consequences of capital flows are effectively neutralised and that the uncovered interest-rate differential is not itself affected by capital flows.

A third reservation to the analysis is that, by definition, it applies only to those international capital movements that are made on a covered basis, i.e. where the investor eliminates the exchange-rate risk of international arbitrage by covering in the forward exchange market. To the extent that investors do not cover (i.e. themselves implicitly become speculators) international capital movements are determined by *uncovered* interest-rate differentials.

In addition, the limitations introduced by the *ceteris paribus* assumption are substantial. In particular it is implicitly assumed that speculators' and arbitrageurs' decisions are made independently of each other. The latter assumption implies that either schedule may change without affecting the other. This effectively eliminates the very real possibility that, for instance, changes in interest rates may affect expectations about the future spot exchange rate.

SUMMARY

The analysis with respect to the determination of the forward exchange rate and the implications for international capital flows are summarised in Table 4.1. In all cases changes in the forward exchange rate and magnitude and direction of capital flows are determined by factors which induce changes in either the position or slope of speculators' and interest arbitrageurs' de-mand/supply for forward exchange. The analysis in the table assumes a constant spot exchange rate, except in case (6). The forward discount is measured as a percentage of the prevailing spot rate and, in all but case (6), a widening of the discount implies a depreciation of the forward exchange rate (and vice versa).

If an exogenous change in the spot exchange rate (case 6) does not induce a corresponding change in speculators' views about the future spot rate the net effect of an appreciation of the spot rate will be a smaller capital inflow, or larger outflow, and a widening of the forward discount. The forward *discount*

TABLE 4.1 Determination of the forward exchange rate

Ceteris paribus		Effect upon	
Exogenous change	*Analytical effect*	*Capital flows*	*Forward discount* (%)
(1) R_d rises or R_f falls	AA shifts up	Inflow greater or Outflow smaller	Widens[1]
(2) Elasticity of supply of arbitrage flows decreases when:			
(i) initial inflow	AA becomes steeper	Inflow smaller	Narrows[2]
(ii) initial outflow		Outflow smaller	Widens[2]
(3) Depreciation of expected future spot rate	SS shifts up	Inflow smaller or Outflow greater	Widens
(4) Rise in perceived risk or risk-aversion by speculators:			
(i) initial inflow		Inflow smaller	Widens[2]
(ii) initial outflow	SS becomes steeper	Outflow smaller	Narrows[2]
(5) Lower reserve requirements on banks' external liabilities	AA shifts up[3]	Inflow greater or Outflow smaller	Widens
(6) Spot exchange rate appreciates	AA shifts down	Inflow smaller or Outflow greater	Widens[4]

[1] Unless perfectly elastic speculators' schedule.

[2] Effect depends upon whether the initial equilibrium position involves a capital inflow (P_e appreciated against P_p) or capital outflow (P_e depreciated against P_p).

[3] Lower reserve requirements against external liabilities imposed by the central bank means that the banks may offer external depositors a higher interest rate as the banks may effectively use a higher proportion of their deposits from non-residents for profitable investment as a smaller proportion has to be maintained in the form of zero or low interest reserves.

[4] Forward rate appreciates but by less than spot rate providing SS is less than perfectly elastic and does not shift.

widens even though the forward exchange rate tends to appreciate in line with the spot rate. The immediate impact effect of a spot rate appreciation is a widening of the forward discount which, other things being equal, would normally induce a capital outflow. Thus, with given domestic and foreign interest rates, the parity level of the forward exchange rate must appreciate by the same extent as the spot rate so as to maintain a constant discount/premium in percentage terms. This is represented in the analysis by a downward shift in the arbitrage schedule. The ultimate effect, however, is a net widening of the forward *discount* as the appreciation of the forward rate would normally be less than the shift in *AA* except where the speculators' schedule is infinitely elastic.

APPENDIX
The Forward Exchange Rate and Stabilisation Policy with a Floating Spot Rate

Having outlined the theory of the forward exchange rate the analysis of stabilisation policy in Chapter 2 may be modified to the case where capital movements are a function of *covered* interest-rate differentials. For simplicity it is assumed that the forward rate is determined uniquely by speculators' expectations about the future spot exchange rate, and that these may be determined by current movements in the spot rate. The conclusion is that, under a floating spot exchange-rate system, the power of monetary and fiscal policy is radically different from that outlined in Chapter 2 when the forward rate is incorporated into the analysis, and depends critically upon how current movements in the spot rate affect expectations about the future spot rate.

Four simple models of speculation are identified where expectations about the future spot rate are said to be: (1) *neutral*, (2) *independent*, (3) *inelastic*, and (4) *elastic* with respect to current changes in the spot rate.[1] When expectations are *neutral* (implicitly assumed in Chapter 2) the expected future spot rate (and hence the current forward exchange rate) is always equal to the prevailing spot rate; the forward premium (per cent) is therefore zero and unaffected by movements in the spot rate. In the *independent* case expectations are formed without reference to current movements in the spot rate with speculators believing the spot rate will eventually move to the current forward rate. It follows that the forward discount/premium (per cent) narrows/widens proportionately to a depreciation of the spot rate. When expectations are *inelastic* expectations about the future spot-rate change in the same direction as current movements in the spot rate, but by proportionately less. If the spot rate declines the forward rate also depreciates but by a proportionately smaller magnitude; the forward discount/premium narrows/widens, but by less than in the *independent* case. When expectations are *elastic*, speculators believe the future spot rate will move further in the same direction as current changes. Thus a depreciation of the spot rate induces expectations of a further depreciation, and hence a widening of the forward discount.

The conclusion of Chapter 2 was that, when capital flows are infinitely elastic with respect to interest-rate differentials and the equilibrium value of the domestic interest rate is determined uniquely at the world level, fiscal policy is powerless but monetary policy is very powerful (Quantity Theory case) when the spot rate is freely floating. With fiscal policy the capital inflow induced by the (temporary) rise in the domestic rate of interest induces an appreciation of the spot rate until the initial level of income is restored when the demand for money regains its previous value at the original (world level) interest rate. With an expansionary monetary policy the exchange rate depreciates due to the capital outflow until the rise in income is sufficient to increase the demand for money balances equal to the rise in the money supply. These conclusions are indicated in the *neutral* case in Table 4.A.1.

TABLE 4.A.1.

	MONETARY POLICY		FISCAL POLICY	
Expectations	*Forward discount*	*Power of policy*	*Forward discount*	*Power of policy*
Neutral	Constant	2 (quantity theory)	Constant	3 (zero)
Independent	Narrows	4 (positive)	Widens	1 (positive)
Inelastic	Narrows	3 (positive)	Widens	2 (positive)
Elastic	Widens	1 (positive)	Narrows	4 (negative)

1   most powerful,   4   least powerful.

When the forward rate is incorporated in the analysis, the *F* schedule relates to the *covered* interest rate. In this case the domestic interest rate may diverge from the world level even when capital flows are perfectly elastic with respect to covered interest-rate differentials. The domestic interest rate may therefore be above/below the world level by the amount of the forward discount/premium. This also means that if the forward rate does not move proportionately to the spot rate the equilibrium domestic interest rate can change with the forward premium even though the *F* schedule is perfectly elastic.

In the analysis to follow, the forward and spot exchange rates are assumed to be initially the same.

Monetary Policy

When expectations are *neutral* the standard conclusions apply as changes in interest rates are not offset by any movement in the forward premium which remains at zero. If expectations are *independent* the power of expansionary monetary policy is limited even though the spot rate depreciates. The capital outflow is moderated as the *covered* interest-rate differential changes by less than the change in interest rates. This is because the forward rate stands at a premium as the spot rate depreciates while the forward rate remains unchanged. In Figure 4.A.1 below the *LM* curve shifts to LM_1 and the spot rate depreciates and the forward rate stands at a premium. With a forward premium the equilibrium domestic interest rate is lower (F_1 in Figure 4.A.1) than its initial level and equilibrium income rises from y_0 to y_1 rather than y_2 as in the *neutral case.*

When expectations are *inelastic* the power of monetary policy is less than in the *neutral* case but greater than when expectations are *independent.* Thus

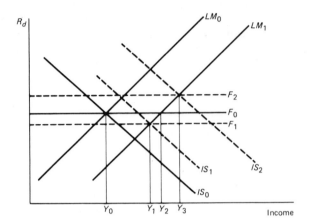

FIGURE 4.A.1   Monetary policy

while the effect of the fall in the domestic interest rate is partly offset by the forward rate moving to a premium (forward rate depreciates by less than the spot rate) the offset is, by definition, less than in the *independent* case where the forward rate remains constant. In Figure 4.A.1 the F schedule lies between F_0 and F_1 and the new level of income is between y_1 and y_2. The *net* depreciation of the spot rate is therefore greater in the *inelastic* case than in the *independent* case.

On the other hand the power of monetary policy is enhanced, even above the *neutral* case, when expectations are *elastic* as the effect on capital outflows of the fall in the domestic interest rate is accentuated by the forward rate moving to a discount. This results from the depreciation of the forward rate being greater than the spot rate. The spot exchange-rate depreciation is therefore greater and, given the interest-parity condition, the outflow induces a net rise in the domestic interest rate. The forward discount means that the equilibrium level of the domestic interest rate rises and, in Figure 4.A.1, the F and IS schedules are F_2 and IS_2 and the level of income rises to y_3.[2] The conclusions are summarised in Table 4.A.1.

Fiscal Policy

The ordering of fiscal policy is the opposite of that of monetary policy (see Table 4.A.1). The power of fiscal policy is increased over the *neutral* case when expectations with respect to the future spot rate are *independent* of current movements in the spot rate. This follows as the capital inflow (due to the rise in the domestic interest rate) induces a rise in the spot rate, but, with a constant forward rate, a forward discount emerges and hence the inflow is moderated.

Fiscal policy regains power with a floating exchange rate. The emergence of a forward discount enables the domestic interest rate to be sustained at a higher level than initially; in Figure 4.A.2, the F schedule shifts to F_1 following an expansionary fiscal policy to IS_1. The net rise in income is $y_0 y_1$ as, unlike the *neutral* case, the exchange-rate appreciation is less than that necessary to entirely eliminate the expansionary effect of the fiscal policy, i.e. IS_1 shifts back to IS_2 and not IS_0 due to the appreciation of the spot rate. This is because, compared to the *neutral* case, there is a smaller capital inflow because of the forward discount.

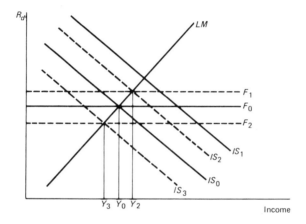

FIGURE 4.A.2   Fiscal policy

When expectations are *inelastic* the same qualitative conclusion emerges but the net effect on income is less than in the independent case as the resulting forward discount is smaller. The equilibrium level of the domestic interest rate is therefore between F_0 and F_1 in Figure 4.A.2. This is because in the *inelastic* case the rise in the spot rate induces a (smaller) rise in the forward rate and hence the forward discount that emerges is smaller. When expectations are *elastic* an expansionary fiscal policy becomes counterproductive and induces a fall in income. Thus the rise in the spot rate induces a forward premium (as the forward rate appreciates by more than the spot rate) which accentuates the capital inflow which, in turn, has a further negative effect on income through the induced greater appreciation of the spot exchange rate. In effect the F schedule shifts below F_0 (to F_2) in Figure 4.A.2 as the forward premium implies a lower equilibrium interest rate. Income falls to Y_3.

Conclusions

Incorporation of the forward exchange rate into the basic model with a floating spot rate radically changes the conclusions derived in Chapter 2. Monetary policy becomes more powerful when expectations are *elastic* (the rise in income is greater than that given by the Quantity Theory when expectations are *neutral*), but less powerful when expectations are *inelastic*. Opposite conclusions emerge with fiscal policy which becomes perverse when expectations are *elastic* (as against powerless in the *neutral* case) though fiscal policy regains some of its power when expectations are *inelastic*.

SELECTED BIBLIOGRAPHY

Argy, V., and Porter, M. (1972) 'The Forward Exchange Market and the Effects of Domestic and External Disturbances under Alternative Exchange Rate Systems', *IMF Staff Papers*, Nov 1972.
Beenstock, M. (1978) *The Foreign Exchanges* (London: Macmillan) chaps 2 and 6.
Grubel, H. (1966) *Forward Exchange, Speculation and the International Flow of Capital* (Stanford: Stanford University Press).
Herring, R., and Marston, R. (1977) *National Monetary Policies and International Financial Markets* (Amsterdam: North-Holland) chap. 3.
Kesselman, J. (1971) 'Role of Speculation and Forward Rate Determination: Canadian Flexible Dollar, 1953–60', *Canadian Journal of Economics and Political Science*, Aug 1971.
Tsiang, S. C. (1959) 'The Theory of Forward Exchange and Effects of Government Intervention', *IMF Staff Papers*, Apr 1959.

5

Forward Exchange Rate:
A Banker's View

The standard theoretical approach to the analysis of the forward exchange rate and capital flows is challenged by foreign exchange dealers on the grounds that it ignores the mechanisms through which banks (which make the market) provide forward exchange facilities. The traditional analysis implicitly assumes either that speculators and arbitrageurs deal direct with each other or, more realistically, that banks act solely as brokers. The alternative analysis of the forward exchange market offered by bankers is frequently termed the *Cambist* approach.

One of the major conclusions of the *Cambist* formulation is that it is not necessary for speculators to supply/demand the forward exchange demanded/supplied by arbitrageurs and that, given the normal banking mechanisms in the market, covered arbitrage by non-banks does not cause a *net* capital movement into a currency. The only significant spot capital flows (in the sense of involving a net movement into a currency and having a potential impact on the country's monetary base) are either those conducted on an uncovered basis, or those resulting from banks automatic spot exchange transactions in response to non-bank forward market speculation. Covered arbitrage transactions by non-banks have no net effect upon the spot exchange rate, reserves or domestic money supply as they are offset by equal and opposite spot transactions by banks.

While the *Cambist* analysis differs in important detail from the formal analysis outlined in the previous chapter, the fundamental conclusions of the analysis remain intact though the mechanisms involved are different.

The *Cambists'* approach challenges a basic element of the standard approach, in that in their view the observation of a non-parity level of the forward exchange rate (i.e. a positive covered interest-rate differential) arises only because inappropriate interest rates are compared. If comparison is made between euro-currency interest rates (the relevant markets for arbitrage transactions by banks), uncovered interest-rate differentials invariably equal forward discounts/premia. Thus the forward exchange rate is always at its parity level against euro-currency interest rates, which implies a perfectly elastic bank arbitrage schedule within these markets. Second, the *Cambists'* challenge the relevance of a non-bank arbitrage schedule as any non-bank arbitrage capital flow is automatically offset by spot transactions by the banks which implies that the AA schedule does not represent *net* spot capital movements. Third, the *Cambist* formulation denies that the effect speculation in the forward market has on capital movements and the spot exchange rate is due to non-bank arbitrage transactions.

The *Cambist* view holds that banks provide the counterpart supply and demand of forward exchange to match the transactions of their customers. The equilibrating mechanism (which ensures that the forward rate does not deviate from its parity level) derives from the banks' *automatic* response in the spot market to their non-bank customers sales/purchases in the forward market. There is, therefore, no meaningful unique non-bank arbitrage function based on the supposed response of non-banks to intrinsic premia/discounts. For this reason the interest-rate-parity theory should be at the centre of the analysis. Automatic adjustments induced by bank transactions always ensure that the forward rate is at its parity level with respect to euro-currency interest rates. The observation of non-parity relationships is due to the wide variety of possible domestic interest-rate comparisons, and the effect of exchange-control regulations which can prevent arbitrage taking place between the domestic and euro segment of a money market.

BANKING MECHANISMS

The central feature of forward exchange operations stressed in the *Cambist* approach is that banks respond to customer's demand (supply) of forward exchange by either: (i) matching it with an equal and opposite customer supply or, more likely, (ii) sell spot whatever the customer is selling forward. Put another way, as the bank always accommodates its customers' requests the bank will sell spot what it is effectively buying forward from its customer. It does this in order to avoid creating an undesired open speculative forward position in its own books. This is not to imply that banks do not speculate in the forward market, but simply that when they do it is on the basis of their own explicit view of future spot-rate movements. A bank will not be forced passively into a speculative position by virtue of its customers' transactions. In the absence of matching forward transactions, two alternative, though very similar, methods of offering forward facilities to customers without forcing banks into open speculative positions are available: (i) the *swap* method, and (ii) the euro-currency market mechanism. In the final analysis they must necessarily yield the same result as otherwise two forward premia could be quoted for the same currency.

(1) *Swap Method*

A currency swap involves an inter-bank transaction where a bank sells a currency spot to another bank and simultaneously buys the currency back forward. If a non-bank customer sells dollars forward the bank has at that point incurred an open forward position as it is committed to deliver, say, Deutsche Marks in three months. In order to avoid this exposure, the bank will immediately sell dollars spot for Deutsche Marks utilising its own dollar bank deposits. At this point the bank has covered against the exchange-rate risk, but its spot dollar position has been reduced below the level it judges to be appropriate. There is no rationality in the bank having a reduced spot dollar position simply because of forward transactions by customers as these transactions will not alter the factors that determine the banks' desired spot position within exchange-control limits. It will therefore seek to restore its spot dollar position. This it will do by a *swap*: (i) it buys spot dollars with Deutsche Marks and, (ii) sells dollars forward by the same amount. The second part is likely as, in three months' time, it will receive spot dollars from the forward transaction with its non-bank customer, and this would otherwise take the banks spot dollar holdings above either the exchange-control limit (relevant to U.K. banks prior to October 1979) or its desired dollar holdings. It would then be forced to sell spot dollars at a possibly disadvantageous rate.

(2) *The Euro-Currency Mechanism*

Under the alternative procedure, the bank: (i) borrows in the euro market the currency being sold forward by its customers; (ii) sells the currency spot for the currency being bought by the customer; and (iii) invests the proceeds of the spot sale in the appropriate euro-currency market.

Thus if a customer sells Deutsche Marks forward to the bank the bank immediately has an open speculative forward position as it is committed to provide, say, dollars in three months' time at a price agreed today. This risk involved is that in three months' time, the Deutsche Mark price of these dollars may be greater than the receipt of Deutsche Marks from the forward contract. The four transactions which give a balanced position for the bank are: (1) a forward purchase of Deutsche Marks from the customer at the latter's initiative; (2) bank borrowing in the euro-DM market at an interest rate of, say 6 per cent, (3) the sale of Deutsche Marks spot for dollars; and (4) the investment of the proceeds in the euro-dollar market at, say 8 per cent. The 'gain' on the transactions (the difference between the two interest rates) determines the forward premium of the Deutsche Mark in a competitive foreign-exchange market. The bank has a totally balanced, and hence riskless, position as it has: a forward asset in Deutsche Marks from (1); a forward liability in Deutsche Marks from (2); a forward liability in dollars from (1); and dollars to meet that liability from (4). Providing the maturity of the forward and euro-currency contracts are precisely matched, the bank incurs no exchange risk as it repays the Deutsche Mark borrowing from the proceeds of the maturing forward contract and it already has the dollars to meet its forward liability to the customer.

The *Cambist* formulation asserts that the mechanism through which the banks provide forward facilities in a perfectly competitive foreign-exchange market ensures that the forward rate can never deviate from its parity level.

Indeed, dealers quote forward exchange rates on the basis of observed euro-currency interest-rate differentials. While this may be true of individual dealers (who are assumed to be only a small part of a competitive market), there is a *fallacy of composition* as combined bank transactions also affect the relevant euro-currency interest rates. While euro-currency interest rates are exogenously determined to any one bank they are mutually determined with forward exchange rates by the market as a whole. Thus the view that forward rates are calculated on the basis of euro-currency interest rates yields an indeterminate system.[1]

CAPITAL MOVEMENTS

The implication is that a *net* spot capital movement into a currency (i.e. combining both bank and non-bank transactions) is possible only if speculative forward positions are being taken by non-banks, and then only through the effect of the banks' automatic response to their customers' forward transactions. Thus a covered capital inflow into German treasury bills from, say U.S. Treasury bills, implies a spot purchase and forward sale of Deutsche Marks by non-bank arbitrageurs. The banks' covering operations imply spot sales of Deutsche Marks which exactly offset the non-bank spot purchases. The net effect of the series of transactions is: (i) no *net* spot demand for Deutsche Marks (no net capital inflow) and hence no impact on Germany's external reserves, monetary base or spot exchange rate; (ii) increased foreign holding of German treasury bills and lower external holdings of U.S. Treasury bills, and (iii) a smaller volume of euro-DM and larger volume of euro-dollar deposits.[2] The effect on money markets is therefore to induce a switch between Treasury bills (domestic money market investment) and the euro segment of the money markets. There are no direct effects on domestic liquidity resulting solely from non-bank covered capital flows.

The position is different if speculative positions are also simultaneously being taken in the forward market, e.g. speculative purchases of forward Deutsche Marks equal to the non-bank arbitrage sales. In this case there are net purchases of spot Deutsche Mark due to the counterpart spot covering of the banks forward sales of Deutsche Marks to non-bank speculators. The series of bank and non-bank spot and forward transactions is summarised in Table 5.1 for the case where non-bank arbitrage inflows into Germany are matched by an equal volume of speculative purchases of forward Deutsche Marks. As already noted, in itself the non-bank arbitrage inflow has little significance and does not imply net spot purchases of Deutsche Marks. However, the banks will also cover in the spot market their forward sales of Deutsche Mark to non-bank speculators. Thus, in response to the forward sales of Deutsche Marks by non-bank arbitrageurs, the banks borrow euro-Deutsche Marks, sell spot for dollars and invest in the euro-dollar market. As

TABLE 5.1   The Banking Mechanism

		Non-banks		Banks
ARBITRAGE	1	Sell spot $	2A	Buy forward DM
	1A	Buy spot DM	3	Borrow DM
	2	Sell forward DM	4	⌠ Sell spot DM
			4A	⌡ Buy spot $
SPECULATION	5	Sell forward $	5B	Sell forward DM
	5A	Buy forward DM	5C	Buy forward $
			6	Borrow $
			7	Sell spot $
			7A	Buy spot DM

transactions (1) and (4A) in Table 5.1 cancel, there are no *net* spot transactions due to arbitrage. However, in response to non-bank speculative forward sales of dollars banks borrow dollars, sell spot for Deutsche Marks and invest in the euro-Deutsche Mark market. The overall effect of the combined transactions is a net purchase of spot Deutsche Marks at (7A).

A rise in the domestic interest rate therefore induces a *net* spot capital inflow (with a potential impact on the domestic money and spot exchange rate) through: (i) any effect interest-rate changes have on uncovered capital movements, and (ii) the banks' spot covering of their forward contracts with speculator customers. The former implies a net spot capital movement into the domestic currency as the inflow induces an uncovered spot purchase of the domestic currency which, being uncovered, involves no offsetting spot sales by the banks as a counterpart to forward contracts with their customers. The second effect derives from the impact of covered flows on the forward exchange rate and the resultant change in speculators' forward transactions. In terms of the previous, partial equilibrium forward exchange model, a rise in the domestic interest rate shifts the arbitrageurs' schedule from A_0 to A_1 which, as depicted in Figure 5.1, changes a covered outflow OB to an inflow OC. In the *Cambist* model the induced rise in the spot exchange rate or external reserves derives not from the spot capital flow *per se* (as there is a counterpart offsetting spot transaction as the banks cover their forward position with customers), but from the change in speculators' forward transactions. With a speculators' schedule S_0, the effect on the forward exchange rate (E_0 to E_1) transforms the position from speculative forward sales OB to purchases OC. According to the *Cambist* view the potential rise in the spot rate or reserves following a rise in domestic interest rates results from the banks' spot purchases of domestic currency as a counterpart to their forward sales to speculators. This implies *net* spot purchases of domestic currency (banks and non-banks) as, by definition, there are no spot transactions by speculators. The magnitude of this impact depends, therefore,

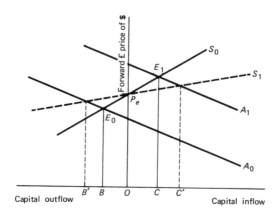

FIGURE 5.1   A rise in the domestic interest rate

upon the elasticity of the speculators' schedule being, for instance, greater with S_1 than S_0 in Figure 5.1.

Thus speculation in the forward market has an impact on spot capital flows. In the theory outlined in Chapter 4 the spot effect resulted from non-bank arbitrage transactions, but under the *Cambist* formulation it results from the automatic spot covering of open forward positions by the banks. Nevertheless, in both analyses speculation in the forward market has an effect on capital movements, and hence upon either spot exchange rates or external reserves. The mechanism differs but the result is basically the same in the two approaches. While, for reasons outlined earlier, *Cambists* dispute the relevance of the non-bank arbitrage function, equilibrium in the forward market is nevertheless restored in both formulations by arbitrage transactions equal and opposite to those of speculators. The main difference is that the *Cambists* postulate this as taking place automatically by the banks rather than by non-banks. *Cambists* recognise that banks do perform an equilibrating arbitrage role in the forward market. However, it is argued by Coulbois and Prissert (1974):

We think the difference to be essential for, according to the cambist theory, banks charge to their customers forward rates which simply reflect the interest rate differential, whereas arbitrageurs, according to the academic theory, operate under the incentive of an intrinsic premium (or discount). It follows from the cambist analysis that forward market equilibrium does not require the appearance of an intrinsic premium and that average forward rates are always at the level dictated by the interest rate differential which exists in the markets where banks are lenders or borrowers. Their profit consists of nothing else than the spread they apply to their customers between their buying and selling rates, both spot and forward.

But there is no important analytical difference between bank and non-bank arbitrage, and the two interpretations of the forward exchange mechanism do not differ in any significant respect. According to the *Cambist* formulation, equilibrium in the forward market (which is necessarily achieved at the *parity* level) is determined automatically and as a result of banks' spot covering of forward transactions with their customers. Non-bank arbitrage is not, according to this view, the equilibrating mechanism.

CONCLUSIONS

Overall the distinction between the *Cambist* and *structural* models is more apparent than real as far as the major analytical points of forward exchange analysis are concerned. The major conclusion common to both formulations may be summarised:

(1) The interest-parity condition is always maintained within the euro-currency markets, as within these markets all the necessary conditions for parity exist, e.g. homogeneous assets, similar status of the issuer of securities, total absence of exchange control and the same degree of 'political' risk (see Chapter 7). Under these conditions both formulations postulate a perfectly elastic arbitrage schedule at the parity level of the forward rate. However, the euro markets are essentially inter-bank markets with very limited covered arbitrage possibilities for non-banks. For the banks the arbitrage transactions are predominantly the counterpart of their forward transactions with customers at the latter's initiative.

(2) While the parity condition is always maintained within the euro market there is no unique direction of causation linking any two euro-currency interest rates and the corresponding forward exchange rate. At any one time an individual bank will quote a forward rate to a customer on the basis of two euro-currency interest rates, and at the same time quote a euro-currency rate based on the forward rate and the other euro-currency interest rate. To an individual bank, in conditions approximating to perfect competition, all prices are exogenously determined. But in the market as a whole all prices are endogenous.

(3) When comparing other interest rates between countries intrinsic premia/discounts are possible (and frequently observed) as the strict conditions for parity do not exist. In practice the bulk of non-bank-covered arbitrage takes place between heterogeneous markets (e.g. the euro-dollar market and U.K. treasury bills, etc.) and yet most forward exchange theory is based on the assumption of homogeneous securities. In this respect much of the theoretical analysis ignores what in practice are the most fruitful arbitrage possibilities for non-banks. The forward transactions involved in such arbitrage influence the forward rate, though, as the securities involved are not similar, the arbitrage schedule will be less than perfectly elastic.

(4) Both formulations of the determination of the forward exchange rate

agree that speculative positions are a necessary prerequisite for *net* spot covered capital movements.

(5) The strength of speculative pressure (measured by the elasticity of the speculators' schedule and the difference between the expected future spot rate and the parity level of the forward rate) determines the magnitude of covered spot capital movements.

(6) In the limiting case of complete certainty with respect to the future spot rate the forward rate is determined uniquely by speculators and equilibrating adjustments are made through interest rates.

(7) Except in the case of a perfectly elastic speculators' schedule, the effect of interest-rate changes on the covered interest-rate differential is partly offset in the short run by changes in the forward exchange rate.

There is therefore no inherent significant conflict between the two formulations. In particular the precise mechanism of arbitrage (the main difference between the two) has little analytical significance. The *structural* model may therefore be taken as a reasonable representation of the forces operating in the market. Nevertheless, it remains true that, except when there is heavy speculation in the forward market, it is uncovered rather than covered capital flows that affect domestic monetary conditions.

SELECTED BIBLIOGRAPHY

Brown, B. (1978) *Money, Hard and Soft* (London: Macmillan).
Coulbois, P., and Prissert, P. (1974) 'Forward Exchange, Short Term Capital Flows and Monetary Policy', *De Economist*, no. 4, 1974.
Prissert, P. (1974) *A Critical Examination of Forward Exchange Theory*, SUERF Reprint Series.

6

International Capital Movements: Theory and Evidence

In Chapter 2 the simple *IS/LM* paradigm was extended to incorporate the monetary effects of the balance of payments. While this paradigm, despite its many and well-known limitations, was found to be a useful general analytical framework, it is particularly weak in its representation of the theory of international capital movements. In particular, the notion of a stable *F* schedule implicitly assumes that: (i) capital flows in response to interest-rate *levels*; (ii) capital movements take place on an uncovered basis;[1] and (iii) domestic interest rates move independently of foreign interest rates so that a rise in the domestic rate induces a corresponding widening of the interest-rate differential against foreign assets. In this chapter we find that each of these assumptions is unwarranted both theoretically and empirically.

The object in this chapter is to review the theory and empirical evidence of international capital movements. Several empirical exercises are reported, though the purpose is not to offer a comprehensive survey, but to illustrate the models used and in particular the role of equilibrating mechanisms which tend to limit the response of capital to changes in interest rates. The empirical issues are important in that the response of capital to interest-rate changes is a key factor in international monetary interdependence.

Within the theoretical and empirical literature three general models may be identified: (i) a simple *flow* theory; (ii) a *portfolio stock-adjustment* model; and (iii) a hybrid *stock-adjustment-flow* model. The simple *flow* theory, incorporated in the analysis of Chapter 2, postulates a relationship between continuous capital flows and interest-rate differentials. It is implicit in this model that capital flows at a constant rate through time while a given interest-rate differential is maintained. On the other hand, *stock-adjustment* models are based upon equilibrium with respect to stocks of assets, and postulate that demands for domestic and foreign assets are for stocks rather than continuous flows. Equilibrium in these models is established when, at a given constellation of interest rates, tastes and degrees of risk and wealth, etc., wealth-holders are satisfied with the composition of their portfolio of wealth. The focus of attention is upon equilibrium holdings of stocks of assets at different interest-rate levels. The important corollary is that capital movements respond to *changes* in interest-rate differentials; a rise in the foreign rate of interest induces a once-for-all stock adjustment as wealth-holders rearrange their given portfolio (substituting foreign for domestic assets) in the light of the new circumstances. Once the finite portfolio adjustment has been made a new equilibrium is established even though interest-rate differentials may persist. The important theoretical and empirical difference between the two models is that the *stock-adjustment* model implies a single finite adjustment while the *flow* theory postulates a continuous and constant flow through time.

Stock-adjustment-flow models incorporate elements of both, though are based firmly in the tradition of the second in that they focus upon equilibrium in stocks of assets. However, these models incorporate a *flow* element through the effects of the growth in portfolios. Thus, while the major effect of a change in interest-rate differentials is the initial finite stock-adjustment, the pattern and volume of capital flows through time is also affected by the growth in portfolios. In particular, if an initial equilibrium is disturbed by a rise in the foreign interest rate, it is likely that a higher proportion of increments to wealth through time will be invested in foreign assets than at the previous set of interest rates. It is demonstrated later that both theory and the empirical evidence give stronger support for the two *stock-adjustment* models than the more traditional *flow* theory. However, if the stock-adjustment occurs with an extended time-lag (and the evidence supports this too) the adjustment may appear statistically as a flow. Thus if the adjustment were made over an extended period, and the proportion of the adjustment was the same in each period, the stable F schedule could be retained in the analysis even though the equation upon which it is based mis-specifies the basic theory.

PORTFOLIO BALANCE THEORY

Stock-adjustment models follow the earlier tradition established by Markowitz (1959) and Tobin (1958), who developed a theoretical framework to explain the rationality of diversified portfolios. In general, wealth-holders distribute their portfolios so as to maximise a utility function incorporating expected rates of return and risk. Other things being equal, portfolio compositions which increase the expected rate of return with a constant risk, or reduce risk with a given expected rate of return, are viewed as superior to alternative compositions. Portfolio selection is based upon the proposition that diversified are superior to concentrated portfolios, as they reduce risk at given expected rates of return on the total portfolio. This is because the variance is less. The benefit of a diversified portfolio can be secured through either a higher average rate of return or lower risk, or some combination of both. In terms of standard indifference analysis the exact composition of a wealth-holder's portfolio will therefore depend upon the size of the portfolio and the shape of the wealth-holder's indifference curve between rates of return and safety.

Grubel (1968) demonstrates that, with respect to international diversification, wealth-holders in different countries can, through increased diversification of their portfolios, reduce risk and/or raise the average rate of return simply by exchanging assets. Based upon a survey of rates of return on assets in eleven countries in the period 1959–66 it was established that portfolio diversification for an American investor would have yielded a higher rate of return and a lower variance than investment in the United States alone. Specifically, for the same variability in the rate of return on a purely standard U.S. portfolio, the average rate of return was raised from 7.5 per cent to 12.6 per cent. It follows that *gross* capital movements between countries are rational even with zero interest-rate differentials. In terms of Grubel's analysis the quantity of foreign assets demanded by a domestic wealth-holder is a function of: (i) total wealth (size of the portfolio); (ii) the interest-rate differential; (iii) the perceived risk differential on domestic and foreign assets; (iv) the R_2 of returns on domestic and foreign assets; (v) tastes; and (vi) the existing proportion of total assets invested in foreign assets. It follows that, in addition to interest-rate movements, *net* capital movements between countries may result from: (i) differential risks on foreign and domestic assets; (ii) different tastes of domestic and foreign wealth-holders; and (iii) different rates of growth of wealth portfolios of domestic and non-residents. Thus necessary ingredients in the analysis of international capital movements are the general advantage of diversified portfolios and the effect of the growth of portfolios. Both must be allowed for when considering the interest-rate sensitivity of international capital movements.

STOCK-ADJUSTMENT MODEL

In terms of empirical testing the essence of the *stock-adjustment-flow* model, based upon the portfolio-balance theory just described, is that the demand for foreign assets (securities, bonds, bank deposits, etc.) is a function of: (i) wealth; (ii) differential risks; (iii) expected rates of return on domestic and foreign assets; and (iv) other non-interest factors such as domestic credit controls, various controls on international capital movements and speculative capital movements on the basis of expected changes in exchange rates. For each constellation of these variables there is an equilibrium structure of portfolios with the portfolio mix maximising a utility function based upon risks and expected rates of return on domestic and foreign assets. In formal terms the basic equation with respect to the proportion of wealth held in foreign assets is:

$$\left(\frac{K^f}{W}\right) = f(i_d, i_f, R, W, Z).^2 \qquad (6.1)$$

Wealth is entered as an independent variable as the ratio may depend upon the total size of the portfolio. Multiplying by W, and assuming a linear function, the equilibrium demand for foreign assets becomes:

$$K^f = a \cdot W + b\,(Wi_d) + c \cdot (Wi_f) + d \cdot (WR) + e \cdot (W^2) + f(WZ) + u. \qquad (6.2)$$

The expected values of the coefficient are: $a > 0, b < 0, c > 0, d < 0, e \gtrless 0$ and $f \gtrless 0$. The stock-adjustment effect on the demand for foreign assets in a linearised first difference form of equation (6.2) becomes:

$$\Delta K^f = a \cdot \Delta W + b \cdot \Delta Wi_d + c \cdot \Delta Wi_f + d \cdot \Delta (WR) + e \cdot \Delta (W^2)$$
$$+ f \cdot \Delta (WZ) + u. \tag{6.3}$$

The W in each variable represents a scale factor, suggesting that, for a given coefficient, the magnitude of the capital flow response to a given change in the independent variable is determined by the size of the portfolio and is presumed therefore to increase through time. While the empirical research reported below differ in detail, equation (6.3) forms the basis of most of the tests reported.

The important aspect of equation (6.3) is that it is *changes* in interest rates, rather than levels, that influence capital movements through a stock-adjustment effect. In practice such an adjustment is unlikely to be made instantaneously and most tests incorporate a distributed lag on the independent variables. Thus a change in the relevant interest-rate differential induces a threefold effect upon international capital movements: (i) an immediate and substantial stock-adjustment as wealth-holders substitute foreign for domestic assets or vice-versa; (ii) a longer-term lagged effect of the stock-adjustment; and (iii) a smaller and continuing wealth effect as, with increasing portfolio size, wealth-holders distribute the increments to wealth differently as a result of the new interest-rate structure. Capital movements are therefore viewed as changes in stocks of foreign assets. This methodology is illustrated, for a rise in foreign interest rate, in Figure 6.1. The slope of the unbroken line reflects the continuous growth in domestic wealth-holders' portfolios. In the period OA interest rates are constant and the holding of foreign assets increases (capital outflow) as wealth rises. At time A the foreign

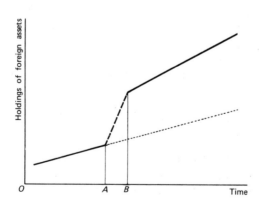

FIGURE 6.1   Stock-adjustment model

interest rate rises inducing a lagged stock-adjustment in period AB. After time B, with the new structure of interest rates held constant and the same growth of portfolios, holdings of foreign assets rise at a faster rate due to the higher foreign interest rate. Thus, a substantial capital outflow might be expected immediately following a rise in the foreign interest rate, followed by a smaller capital outflow associated with the rise in portfolio size.

A somewhat different approach, adopted for instance by Kouri and Porter (1974), is based upon a theoretical framework which views capital movements as a mechanism for eliminating excess supply or demand for money. The testable equation is:

$$K = a + b \, (\Delta NDA) + C \, (CAB) + d \, (\Delta y) + e \, (\Delta R) + f(D), \qquad (6.4)$$

with the major variables being: (i) changes in the domestic component of high-powered money (NDA); (ii) the current account balance (CAB); (iii) changes in domestic income (Y); (iv) the foreign interest rate (R); and (v) expectations with respect to exchange-rate movements. Each variable affects either the *ex ante* supply or demand for money, and the coefficient (b) is the *offset coefficient*; i.e. the extent to which a change in the domestic component of high-powered money is offset by capital movements.

PROBLEMS OF EMPIRICAL TESTING

While the general theoretical structure of the equations is reasonably well-established, with most analysts agreeing on a version of equation (6.3), there are formidable practical problems in empirical testing capital-flow equations. In the first place, several of the significant variables (notably perceived differential risk, expectations regarding movements in the future spot rate, and expected rates of return) are not immediately observable. With respect to speculation, three alternative methodologies are applied. The theoretically preferred, though in practice more difficult, method is to incorporate a specific model of expectations formation. A second approach is to adopt proxy measures of speculative activity such as particularly sharp movements in the forward exchange rate. However, such variables are usually also measuring other phenomena and are seldom good or exclusive indicators of speculation. A third method incorporates quantitative dummy variables in those periods where informed opinion (e.g. as discerned from central bank reports) indicates that speculative pressure was present. The main problem with this, however, is that it is difficult to indicate degrees of speculative activity.

A second general problem is the measurement of net wealth and its rate of growth. The quality of wealth data is frequently suspect, even when it is available at all, and hence various proxies have to be used as alternatives. The existence of capital and credit controls, and the implied rationing, is also a severe problem for empirical testing,[3] as transactors are moved off equilibrium supply and demand curves. This means that observed rates of interest do not equate the *ex ante* supply and demand for funds, and do not yield information about the supply and demand curves. Thus, if portfolios are not initially in equilibrium, movements in interest rates may not necessarily induce quantity adjustments.

But the most serious problem in testing equation (6.3), and particularly in interpreting the resulting coefficients, is the strong simultaneous equations bias. While exogenous changes in interest rates affect capital movements, these induced movements also have substantial effects upon interest rates. Thus observed *ex post* changes in interest-rate differentials are frequently smaller than *ex ante* changes. Similarly an exogenous change in interest rates in one country (notably the United States) may substantially affect interest rates elsewhere. This also means that if the capital account response to interest-rate changes is very high, substantial interest-rate differentials or changes in differentials will not be observed *ex post* as, with a high degree of integration, capital adjusts quickly to eliminate arbitrage differentials. It follows that observed interest-rate differentials become less significant in explaining capital movements the higher is the degree of international financial integration. While statistical techniques are available to overcome simultaneous equations bias, many of the reported results tend to understate the interest-rate sensitivity of capital movements.

STATISTICAL DETERMINANTS

The major statistical determinants in the equations reported below, and those found to be most significant are: (i) movements in interest rates and the forward premium; (ii) variables to capture speculative pressure; (iii) changes in policy instruments other than interest rates (e.g. reserve requirements), and policy-induced changes in the domestic component of high-powered money; (iv) proxy measures for wealth (a scale variable); (v) trade flows as a determinant of capital movements associated with trade credit; and (vi) various indicators of domestic credit conditions. The last-mentioned are frequently significant in situations where interest rates do not adequately reflect the demand for credit or extent of credit stringency as financial institutions maintain a degree of excess demand for credit at current interest rates. Capital movements in these circumstances may reflect changes in excess demand for credit rather than interest-rate differentials.

With respect to the dependent variable the main issue is the degree of disaggregation to be applied and the interpretation of the 'errors and omissions' component of the balance of payments. While some analysts have used the *net* capital balance a more appropriate methodology is to test separately for external claims and liabilities given that the responses of domestic and foreign wealth-holders may be different, and that the growth in the size of portfolios may not be the same.

THE EMPIRICAL RESULTS

In the remainder of this chapter a review is given of various empirical exercises published since 1971. The object is to illustrate the methodology and theory rather than to offer a comprehensive survey of the literature. Indeed, given the different models and methodologies applied, direct comparison of results is invalid.

(1) Branson and Hill (1971)

United States   The basic model tested was a version of equation (6.3), with allowance for the effect of the Voluntary Foreign Credit Restraint (VFCR) programme (a programme in the 1960s to limit capital outflows from the United States). The results of the equation, for the period 1960–70, are given as:

$$\Delta C_t^s = 203.1 + 51.7\Delta(W \cdot RT^{UK})_t - 85.3\Delta(W \cdot RT^{US})_{t-2} + 2378.0\Delta W_t$$
$$ (3.6) \quad (2.2) \qquad\qquad (2.0) \qquad\qquad\qquad (2.1)$$

$$ + 0.17\Delta X_t + 0.44\Delta X_{t-1}$$
$$ \quad (1.5) \qquad\quad (3.8) \qquad\qquad\qquad\qquad\qquad\qquad (6.5)$$

$$ - 392.3 IET1 - 606.8 DF1 - 213.1 DF2.$$
$$ \quad (2.0) \qquad\quad (5.2) \qquad\quad (3.2)$$

The symbols are explained in the note.[4] The equation for long-term portfolio claims on foreigners is:

$$\Delta C_t^1 = 233.5 + 50.7\Delta(W \cdot RED)_t + 31.0\Delta(W \cdot RED)_{t-1}$$
$$ (5.4) \quad (3.0) \qquad\qquad (1.9)$$

$$ - 44.9\Delta(W \cdot MI)_t - 735.6\Delta(WV^{US})_t$$
$$ \quad (1.9) \qquad\qquad (2.2) \qquad\qquad\qquad\qquad\qquad (6.6)$$

$$ + 5310.6\Delta W_t - 440.6 IET2$$
$$ \quad (4.0) \qquad\quad (5.0)$$

The U.S. velocity measure and credit-rationing index both play a significant role in explaining U.S. portfolio capital outflows and were included to reflect the fact that, when credit conditions tighten, the rise in interest rates is less than that necessary to eliminate excess demand for credit.

On the basis of similar equations for external liabilities (ΔL^s and ΔL^1) Table 6.1 gives the calculated stock-adjustment multipliers for changes in interest rates and velocities. The data give the magnitude (in $ million) of the capital account response to a 1 per cent change in interest rates, a 0.1 per cent change in U.S. and Canadian velocities and the U.S. credit-rationing index and a

INTERNATIONAL FINANCIAL INTEGRATION

TABLE 6.1 Stock-adjustment multipliers of changes in interest rates and velocities
$ million, + is inflow[a]

Capital-flow item		Interest rates and velocities								
Type	Mean quarterly flow 1960 I–1969 IV	RT^{US}	RT^{UK}	RT^{CN}	RED	RB^{UK}	MI	V^{US}	V^{UK}	V^{CN}
ΔC^s	210.8	257.6 (3)	−156.1 (2)							
ΔC^l	278.7				−247.0 (2)		13.6 (1)	222.2 (1)		
ΔL^s	552.4	1 176.7 (1)					79.4 (2)		−148.7 (2)	−353.7 (2)
ΔL^l	320.9				−216.6 (2)	−808.5 (2)		379.7 (1)	−133.8 (5)	
EO	255.5	1 131.3 (2)		−345.8 (1)	−628.8 (2)					
KA		2 565.6	−156.1	−345.8	−1 092.4	−808.5	93.0	601.9	−282.6	−353.7

[a] Multipliers are calculated for end-of-1969 values of scale variables:
W = $3.02 trillion in the multipliers for ΔC^s, ΔC^l, EO; G = $71.9 billion in the multipliers for ΔL^s, ΔL^l.

0.01 change in U.K. velocity; all are calculated on the basis of end-1969 wealth values. The stock-adjustment multiplier is calculated as: $(\Delta R \cdot W \cdot \text{coefficient})$. Thus for C^s a 1 per cent change in the U.S. interest rate gives: (85.3 × 3.02 trillion × 1.0) = $257.6, where 85.3 is the relevant coefficient in equation (6.5). To determine the total effect on the capital account (KA) of a given change in interest rates, etc., the magnitudes are summed vertically. Thus a 1 per cent change in U.S. interest rates induces a $2.6 billion stock-adjustment.

The continuing wealth effect of exogenous changes in the relevant variables, based upon the growth of portfolios, is given simply by: $(G \times SS)$, i.e. the growth rate of the portfolio of wealth (7 per cent in the United States) multiplied by the stock-shift multiplier given in Table 6.1. Thus a change in the U.S. interest rate induces an $18 million per annum (C_s) capital movement (258 × 0.07). Combining the two results, but assuming non-adjustment to the euro-dollar rate, the results indicate that a rise of 1 per cent in the U.S. interest rate at 1969 wealth levels induced a total stock-adjustment of $2.6 billion and a continuing wealth effect of $180 million per year. Monetary policy therefore has a powerful, though temporary, effect upon external reserves. On the other hand, if the euro-dollar rate adjusts fully to the U.S. domestic rate the stock-adjustment effect is reduced to $1.5 billion ($2.6 − $1.1 billion in the table), and the wealth effect is reduced to $77 million. In practice this would be the more likely outcome.

The adjustment to the euro-dollar rate noted is a good example of the simultaneous equations bias noted earlier. It is therefore difficult to interpret the coefficient on the U.S. domestic rate if this also influences the foreign rate (the euro-dollar rate in this example). The true effect of an exogenous rise in the U.S. rate is not given by $b \cdot (Wi_d)$, as in equation (6.7). The b coefficient in the basic equation

$$\Delta K^f = a \cdot \Delta W + b \cdot \Delta (Wi_d) + c \cdot \Delta \cdot (Wi_f) + u \qquad (6.7)$$

needs to be adjusted to a 'net' basis if changes in i_d induce offsetting changes in i_f. Equation (6.7) is adjusted by:

$$\Delta i_f = d\Delta i_d + e\Delta Z + u, \qquad (6.8)$$

where Z is other exogenous forces determining i_f. In this formulation (generally appropriate for the United States), i_d affects i_f but the reverse is not true. Thus while coefficient c in equation (6.7) gives an unbiased estimate, the coefficient b must be adjusted for d in equation (6.8). The total coefficient of Δi_d is therefore $(b) + (c) \cdot (d)$ which is necessarily smaller than (b) as (b) and (c) have opposite signs. This problem will be found in other results.

United Kingdom   The major determinants identified by Branson and Hill (1971) for the U.K. short-term capital account are: (i) the balance of trade; (ii) the U.K. velocity of circulation; (iii) the forward exchange rate (cost of forward cover); (iv) the U.S. Treasury bill rate; and (v) the euro-dollar rate. The two best equations are given as

TABLE 6.2   Equations explaining the net capital account of the United Kingdom[a]

	TB[b]	V(−1)[c]	C	RLA	RT[US]	RED	R^2	SE	N[d]	D–W
UK–1	−1.09	902.6	158.2		−742.7	174.9	0.78	242.5	36	1.79
	(3.8)[e]	(1.1)	(4.1)		(4.0)	(1.5)				
UK–2	−1.06	972.0	139.3	−105.0	−671.5	198.5	0.79	243.9	33	1.99
	(3.7)	(1.0)	(3.3)	(1.2)	(2.8)	(1.5)				

[a] Each row of the table represents a separate equation. The numbers not in parentheses are the estimated coefficients of changes (first-differences) in the variables listed across the top of the table in an equation explaining the net capital flow (inflow is +).

[b] Variables listed without superscripts are U.K. variables. Definitions of the independent variables listed here are:

TB = Trade balance RT^{US} = U.S. three-month bill rate
V = Velocity   RED = Three-month euro-dollar deposit rate
C = Cost of forward cover   RT = U.K. three-month bill rate
RLA = U.K. three-month local-authority rate

[c] (−1) indicates a variable lagged one quarter.
[d] N is the number of observations in the equation.
[e] Numbers in parentheses are the t-ratios of the estimated coefficients.

The trade balance tends to be offset by the capital account, and as the cost of forward cover in moving out of sterling rises the capital outflow is reduced. The euro-dollar rate coefficient is misleading in that it indicates a capital inflow as it rises. This is rather unsatisfactorily explained by Branson and Hill: 'euro dollar banks are in London and even if the rate increase is due to an increase in loan demand outside the UK, some of the funds drawn to London may stay in the UK'. Following the analysis of the link between the United States and the euro-dollar rate, the effect on the U.K. capital account of a 1 per cent rise in the U.S. rate is estimated at $570 million ($£743 - £175$ million) in equation UK–1 above.

The particularly interesting feature of equation (6.2) is that the U.K. interest rate enters with apparently the wrong sign. This is almost certainly due to the policy reaction of the U.K. authorities who adjusted interest rates in response to undesired capital flows. This was also found by Herring and Marston (1977).

(2) Herring and Marston (1977)

A similar *stock-adjustment-flow* model was used in an extensive study of the German capital account by Herring and Marston. One of the objects of the study was to determine the degree of monetary independence in a world of fixed exchange rates. The equations fitted for changes in Germany's external claims and liabilities over the period 1961–71 were somewhat more complex than those of Branson and Hill. They are included here to illustrate the equilibrating role of the forward exchange rate and the use of a model for simulation purposes.

The two basic equations are:[5]

$$\Delta L = 0.00165\,\Delta(W_f \cdot (i_g^* - i_s^* - f_p^*)) + 0.03794\,\Delta W_f$$
$$\quad\;\; (5.5) \qquad\qquad\qquad\qquad\qquad (10.8)$$

$$- 0.00050\,(W_f \cdot NOI) + 3.75\,SPEC - 0.000079\,\Delta(W_f \cdot S1)$$
$$\quad\;\; (-6.0) \qquad\qquad\quad (3.4) \qquad\qquad (-1.9)$$

$$- 0.000080\,\Delta(W_f \cdot S2) + 0.000126\,\Delta(W_f \cdot S4),$$
$$\quad\;\; (-1.9) \qquad\qquad\quad (3.1)$$

$$R^2 = 0.8534,\ DW = 2.10,\ SEE = 1.069. \tag{6.9}$$

$$\Delta C = 0.00274\,\Delta(W_g \cdot (i_g^* - i_s^* - f\!\bar{p}a)) + 0.00443\,\Delta(W_g \cdot i_g^*)$$
$$\quad\;\; (2.4) \qquad\qquad\qquad\qquad\qquad (3.4)$$

$$- 0.00767\,\Delta(W_g \cdot i_s^*) + 0.1712\,\Delta W_g - 0.00031\,\Delta(W_g^2)$$
$$\quad\;\; (-6.3) \qquad\qquad (2.6) \qquad\qquad (-4.7)$$

$$- 0.00102\,\Delta(W_g \cdot S1) - 0.00003\,\Delta(W_g \cdot S2) + 0.00108\,\Delta(W_g \cdot S4)$$
$$\quad\;\; (-1.8) \qquad\qquad\quad (-0.1) \qquad\qquad (2.3)$$

$$R^2 = 0.7308,\ DW = 1.97,\ SEE = 1.25. \tag{6.10}$$

The main conclusions of these equations may be summarised: (i) capital flows (changes in external assets and liabilities) were sensitive to changes in the covered interest-rate differential and the Bundesbank's forward market intervention; (ii) capital inflows were effectively constrained by the interest-rate ban on external liabilities, e.g. external liabilities were DM 3 billion lower in 1969 (4) on the basis of an estimated wealth factor of DM 6 trillion; (iii) the coefficient on W_g^2 in the claims equation is negative indicating that the German demand for foreign assets is not homogeneous with respect to wealth, and the desired proportion of external assets in the total portfolio declines as wealth rises; (iv) speculation was found to have a powerful effect on capital movements; and (v) the effect of equal changes in the German and foreign interest rates was asymmetrical and induced a net capital outflow. On the basis of the size of portfolios at the end of the period, a 1 per cent rise in the German interest rate, with *other things equal*, induced a capital inflow equivalent to 8 per cent of the volume of high-powered money in Germany, while an equal rise in the dollar rate induced an outflow corresponding to 12 per cent.

Incorporating the wealth effect in a similar way to Branson and Hill, and taking an 8 per cent p.a. growth in the size of the German portfolio, a simulation exercise for separate 1 per cent changes in the two interest rates and the forward premium yielded a cumulative impact on external reserves measured in DM billion over a period of four years as shown in Table 6.3. The simulations were based upon the two equations noted earlier and compare the effects of constraining the model to no adjustments in the other variables, with the outcome when one or both of the other two are allowed to adjust to the induced capital movement. It can be seen that: (i) the forward premium reacts in a powerful equilibrating manner (rising/falling with a rise in the dollar/German interest rate) which substantially reduces the impact of interest-rate changes on capital movements; and (ii) the effect on capital movements of a change in the dollar interest rate is also limited by equilibrating adjustments to the German interest rate induced by the initial

TABLE 6.3   Simulation results

	CUMULATIVE IMPACT ON EXTERNAL RESERVES OF:		
	1 % change in $i_{\$}$	*1 % change in* i_g	*1 % change in* f_p
Other two variables constant	−13.2	+11.6	−9.4
Other interest rate constant but forward premium adjusts[1]	− 6.3	+ 4.7	
Other two variables adjust[2]	− 3.5		

[1] forward premium adjusts by 0.733 %.
[2] forward premium adjusts by 0.52 % and i_g by 0.3 %.

capital movement. As noted earlier the two basic equations tend, for these reasons, to overestimate the true coefficients. The simulations also established that three-quarters of the total effect occurred within a year.

The distribution of the DM 13.2 billion between the stock-adjustment effect and the continuing wealth effect was DM 9.5 billion for the former and DM 3.6 billion for the latter. Again the evidence supports the theoretical proposition that the finite stock-adjustment effect dominates, and that a change in interest rates induces a sharp and immediate change in external reserves with only a comparatively small continuing effect.

OTHER STUDIES

Other notable empirical studies include Porter (1972); Kouri (1975), Kouri and Porter (1974); Hodjera (1973); Hodjera (1974) and Argy and Kouri (1974). For instance Porter found that changes in reserve requirements on German bank liabilities induced substantial offsetting capital flows; a rise in reserve requirements equivalent to DM 1 billion induced a capital inflow of over DM 600 million. Porter also found that changes in the euro-dollar rate had a greater impact on capital movements (DM 5.3 million) than equivalent changes in the German interest rate (DM 2.8 million). This was ascribed to different simultaneous equation biases with changes in the dollar rate having a greater effect upon the German rate than the reverse.

Kouri and Porter (1974) estimated policy *offset coefficients* for four countries: Germany 77 per cent, Australia 47 per cent, Italy 43 per cent and Netherlands 59 per cent. They also found that changes in income were significant in determining capital inflows which suggests that changes in income induce changes in the demand for money, part of which is met from external sources. This lends support to the theoretical notion that capital movements are at least in part a reflection of excess demand or supply for money.

Argy and Kouri (1974) tested the equation:

$$\Delta C = a + b \cdot \Delta NDA + C \cdot TB + d \cdot \Delta Y + e \cdot \Delta i_f + u, \qquad (6.11)$$

where C is the net capital inflow; NDA is the net domestic assets of the central bank (domestic component of high-powered money); TB is the current account balance and i_f is the euro-dollar rate. The values of the coefficients for three countries were:

	a	b	c	d	e
Italy	+87.33	−0.53	−1.01	+9.40	− 46.13
Netherlands	+99.49	−0.51	−0.93	+7.63	−120.50
Germany	−742.85	−0.91	−0.73	+0.73	−2030.83⁻

The results indicate significant *offset coefficients* (*b*), though all are less than unity. Thus domestic monetary policy retained some independence and the authors note that the authorities in each country were able to sterilise part of the domestic monetary effects of capital movements.

Beenstock (1978), applying a different methodology, concludes that, with respect to the United Kingdom, a 1 percentage point change in the *covered* interest-rate differential induces a once-for-all stock adjustment of £300 million in the capital account. The substantial offsetting effect of the forward exchange rate is indicated by the much smaller (£48 million) response to a 1 percentage point change in the *uncovered* differential.

Hutton (1977), in a model of capital flows and the forward exchange rate, estimates that a 1 per cent rise in U.K. interest rates induces a £100 million capital inflow. Hodjera (1971) estimates that the capital account response in the United Kingdom to a 1 percentage point change in the *covered* differential at £475 million but, as the forward rate adjusts to capital flows, the response to a similar change in the uncovered interest-rate differential is around £100 million. All of these estimates would now be substantially modified since the abolition of U.K. exchange control in 1979.

FORWARD EXCHANGE RATE

In Chapter 4 the extent to which the forward rate adjusts to offset changes in the uncovered interest differential is determined by the elasticities of the arbitrage and speculators' schedule for forward exchange; i.e. the interest-rate sensitivity of capital movements and the perceived degree of risk and risk-aversion of speculators in the forward market. In particular the elasticity of the speculators' schedule is a decisive determinant of the response of covered capital movements to interest-rate changes. Thus even if the elasticity of capital movements to covered interest-rate differentials is infinite, a low elasticity of the speculators' schedule limits the response of capital movements to changes in interest rates as the volume of forward exchange made available by speculators is small (see Chapter 4). Other things being equal, the more elastic is the speculators' schedule, the greater will be the volume of capital movements and the smaller will be the adjustment to the forward rate in response to changes in interest rates.

The empirical evidence indicates that the forward rate adjusts substantially to offset the effect on the covered differential of changes in interest rates. Herring and Marston (1977), for instance, produce a 0.73 percentage point equilibrating change in the forward premium of the Deutsche Mark for a 1 percentage point change in the euro-dollar date. Beenstock (1978) also calculated that equilibrating movements in the forward rate are substantial. For the United Kingdom, Beenstock (1978) estimates that 95 per cent of the variance in the forward rate is explained by arbitrage, i.e. capital flows dominate the determination of the forward rate. This suggests that the speculators' schedule is inelastic and that the volume of capital flows in response to changes in interest rates is severely limited by offsetting movements in forward exchange rates. The Beenstock evidence suggests that the arbitrageurs' schedule is less than infinitely elastic, and that the speculators' schedule for forward exchange tends to be inelastic. Both would indicate that interest-rate changes are not totally swamped by capital movements.

CONCLUSIONS

The results of the empirical exercises are consistent with the *stock-adjustment-flow* model of capital movements. Interest-rate changes have a finite stock-adjustment effect, and the continuing wealth effect tends to be comparatively small. The immediate policy implications are: (i) monetary policy is best suited for inducing a change in reserves rather than contributing to balance-of-payments adjustment; and (ii) in the absence of a stable F schedule in Chapter 2, a sustained capital inflow requires continuously rising interest rates. However, as noted by Willett and Forte (1969), the rise in interest rates would have to be greater in each subsequent period in order to offset the effect of increasing risks incurred by external holders of domestic assets. As the higher interest rate is also paid to existing holders, the balance-of-payments effect eventually becomes perverse as the annual interest payments to non-residents exceed the capital inflow.

The evidence also indicates that the effect of domestic monetary policy is partly offset by capital flows though in no case has an *offset coefficient* of unity been found. The implication is that some independence for monetary policy is possible with fixed exchange rates and, in practice, governments are able to sterilise part of the externally induced changes in high-powered money but only at the cost of substantial changes in external reserves.

With respect to the forward rate there is strong evidence that the extent of equilibrating adjustments in the forward rate is substantial and this limits the capital account response to interest-rate changes. It also implies that official intervention in the forward market is a potentially powerful policy mechanism for influencing the capital account (see Chapter 10). Overall, the evidence is inconsistent with a perfectly elastic F schedule.

SELECTED BIBLIOGRAPHY

Argy, V., and Kouri, P. (1974) 'Sterilisation Policies and the Volatility in International Reserves', in *National Monetary Policies and the International Financial System*, ed. R. Z. Aliber (Chicago: Chicago University Press).
Beenstock, M. (1977) 'Monetary Independence Under Fixed Exchange Rates: West Germany 1958–72', in Frowen, S., and others (eds) *Monetary Policy*

and Economic Activity in West Germany (Guildford: University of Surrey Press).

Beenstock, M. (1978) *The Foreign Exchanges* (London: Macmillan).

Branson, W. H., and Hill, R. D. (1971) *Capital Movements in the OECD Area: An Econometric Analysis*, Occasional Studies.

Grubel, H. G. (1968) 'Internationally Diversified Portfolios', *American Economic Review*, Dec 1968.

Herring, R. J., and Marston, R. C. (1977) *National Monetary Policies and International Financial Markets* (Amsterdam: North-Holland) chap. 6.

Hodjera, Z. (1971) 'Short Term Capital Movements of the UK, 1963–67', *Journal of Political Economy*, July/Aug 1971.

Hodjera, Z. (1973) 'International Short Term Capital Movements: Survey of Theory and Evidence', *IMF Staff Papers*, Nov 1973.

Hodjera, Z. (1974) 'Alternative Approaches in the Analysis of International Capital Movements: Case Study of Austria and France', *IMF Staff Papers*, Nov 1976.

Hutton, J. P. (1977) 'Model of Short Term Capital Movements, the Foreign Exchange Market and Official Intervention in the UK, 1963–70', *Review of Economic Studies*, Feb 1977.

Kouri, P. (1975) 'The Hypothesis of Offsetting Capital Flows: A Case Study of Germany', *Journal of Monetary Economics*, 1975.

Kouri, P., and Porter, M. (1974) 'International Capital Flows and Portfolio Equilibrium', *Journal of Political Economy*, May/June 1974.

Markowitz, H. M. (1959) *Portfolio Selection in Efficient Diversification of Investment* (New York: Wiley).

Porter, M. G. (1972) 'Capital Flows as an Offset to Monetary Policy: German Experience', *IMF Staff Papers*, July 1972.

Stern, R., and Leamer, E. E. (1970) *Quantitative International Economics* (Boston: Allyn & Bacon).

Tobin, J. (1958) 'Liquidity Preference and Behaviour Towards Risk', *Review of Economic Studies*, Feb 1958.

Willett, T., and Forte, F. (1969) 'Interest Rate Policy and External Balance', *Quarterly Journal of Economics*, May 1969.

7
International Arbitrage

Consideration is given in this chapter to empirical relationships between interest rates and forward exchange rates in different financial centres: Three-month forward premia and discounts of four currencies are shown in Charts 7.1 and 7.2. Each has experienced sharp fluctuations, associated with interest-rate movements and changing expectations about movements in the spot rate. Sterling was at a forward discount for most of the period after 1971, though, following a very sharp fall in U.K. interest rates, moved to a small premium towards the end of 1977 for the first time in close on six years.

Between 1964 and 1967 sterling was supported by official intervention in the forward market and the forward discount was maintained in a range 0.4 to 3.3 per cent and generally less than 1 per cent. This had the intended effect of maintaining the covered interest differential within plus or minus 1 percentage point (Chart 7.2). Immediately after support ceased, in November 1967, the forward discount widened markedly (from 1 per cent to close on 5 per cent) and the covered differential moved sharply against the United Kingdom. At one time in 1969 the negative differential peaked at over 5 percentage points.

Summarising the analysis of Chapters 4 and 5 we may identify the major factors that induce a widening of the forward discount: (i) covered capital outflows in response to movements in interest rates; (ii) automatic marking-down of the forward rate by foreign-exchange dealers in the light of changed interest-rate differentials; (iii) increased speculative forward sales of the currency; and (iv) changes in official intervention policy.

TYPES OF ARBITRAGE

When free of exchange-control regulations, investors who wish to hold funds in bank deposits make two choices: (i) the currency in which to hold their funds, and (ii) the location of the deposit. With respect to the second, an important distinction is made between domestic and euro-currency deposits. The distinction and significance of the euro-currency market are discussed in detail in Chapter 9. For the moment, a deposit in a domestic market occurs when the bank is located in the country issuing the currency of the deposit (e.g. a Deutsche Mark deposit held by a resident or non-resident at a bank in Germany). Investors may also hold funds in the euro-currency market which relates to bank deposits denominated in a currency other than the domestic currency of the bank. Thus Deutsche Mark deposits may be held at

CHART 7.1 Three-month forward exchange-rates premia (+), or discount (−) (per cent per annum)

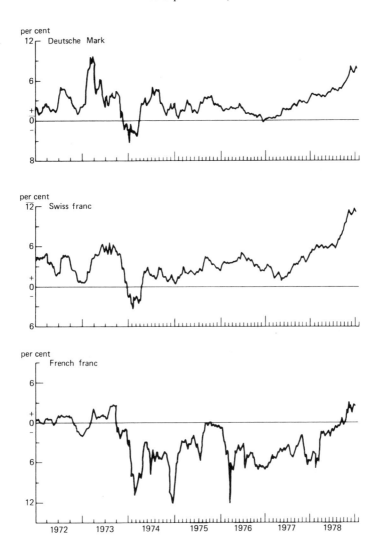

banks in London or Luxembourg, etc., and these are euro-DM deposits.

Given the variety of financial assets in national and international money and capital markets there is a multitude of potential arbitrage channels. As the forward exchange rate cannot adjust to all possibilities, potential profitable arbitrage on a covered basis is frequently possible, particularly when dissimilar securities are compared. Four broad arbitrage channels may be identified between: (i) assets in different countries, e.g. U.S. and U.K.

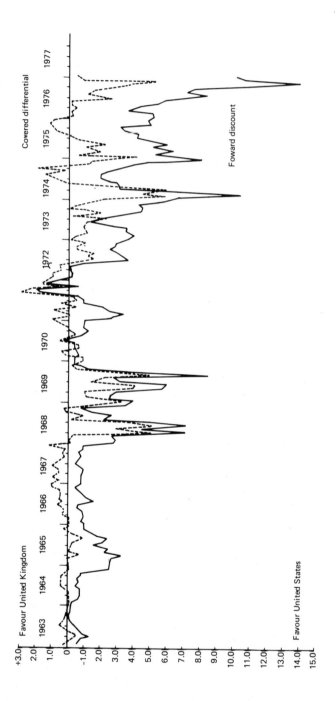

CHART 7.2   Sterling forward discount and covered interest-rate differential: U.K. and U.S. Treasury bills

Treasury bills; (ii) the domestic and euro market in the same currency, e.g. between bank deposits in Germany and euro-DM deposits; (iii) euro markets in different currencies; and (iv) the euro market in one currency and a domestic market in another. With respect to the last-mentioned, an important arbitrage channel in the case of the United Kingdom is between euro-dollar and U.K. local authority deposits. In each sector comparison may also be made between *homogeneous* (e.g. Treasury bills in two countries) and *heterogeneous* securities (e.g. arbitrage involving borrowing euro dollars to finance investment in U.K. finance-house deposits or even short-term government bonds).

Thus a multitude of interest rates gives rise to several arbitrage possibilities when *heterogeneous* assets are considered. In principle, however, providing there is no limit to the supply of arbitrage funds, and that investors in different countries have the same perception of the differential risks, etc., between different securities in the same country (e.g. German arbitrageurs place the same risk premium on inter-bank deposits compared with Treasury bills in both Germany and the United States as do U.S. arbitrageurs), profitable arbitrage opportunities tend to be competed away. But these are stringent requirements in practice. The interest-parity condition relates strictly to *homogeneous* securities such as euro-currency deposits in different currencies. In practice, international arbitrage frequently takes place on a covered basis between *heterogeneous* securities where covered differentials may be significant. In September 1977, for instance, while the covered interest differential between euro-dollar deposits and domestic inter-bank sterling was only 0.7 per cent, that between euro dollars and U.K. medium-term government bonds was 4.8 per cent. While non-resident investors who finance investment in U.K. bonds through borrowing in the euro-dollar market incur a non-exchange risk (bond prices might fall by the time repayment was due on euro-market borrowing) there was evidence of substantial arbitrage in this sector in 1977.

Before considering empirical relationships in detail, a distinction is made between what might be termed *global* and *partial* parity conditions. In the former case arbitrage ensures that: (i) the covered differential between different euro currencies is zero, i.e. the forward rate is at its parity level with respect to euro-currency interest rates; (ii) the covered differential between homogeneous securities (having the same maturity, sovereign and default risks, etc.) in different countries and currencies is zero, which in turn implies that: (iii) domestic inter-bank rates are approximately equal to euro-currency deposit rates in the same currency. *Global parity* requires free arbitrage uninhibited by exchange control and distortions to effective interest rates due, for instance, to differential reserve requirements on banks' domestic and external liabilities. Partial parity can exist as exchange control may prevent conditions (ii) and (iii) of the *global parity* condition, though cannot prevent the attainment of the first. Exchange control cannot inhibit interest parity or arbitrage within the euro-currency market as, within a country which is a euro-currency centre, a given degree of exchange-control and other regulations would never differentiate between bank deposits in different foreign currencies. In the United Kingdom, exchange-control limited U.K. residents ability to hold any foreign currency anywhere. But they did not prevent non-residents holding foreign-currency deposit at banks in London, and neither would any regulation ever be designed to limit non-residents' ability to switch the currency denomination of foreign-currency deposits at banks in the United Kingdom. Arbitrage *within* the euro-currency market is therefore uninhibited by official control.

Exchange control may prevent outward arbitrage with the result that the domestic inter-bank rate may be significantly lower than the euro-currency rate in the same currency. This would also mean that a covered interest-rate differential between homogeneous securities in two countries may be sustained as arbitrage is constrained by controls. Although exchange control cannot prevent non-resident holders of domestic currency from arbitraging out of domestic currency assets, it can prevent domestic residents taking advantage of covered interest-rate differentials in favour of foreign-currency investment.

EURO-CURRENCY AND DOMESTIC MARKETS

A major link between domestic and euro-currency interest rates in the same currency, and between different euro-currency interest rates and forward exchange rates, operates via arbitrage activity of banks. Most banks active in the euro-currency markets are branches or subsidiaries of large domestic banks, and in general there is a close association between the banks' euro-currency and forward exchange market operations. For these reasons banks are able to arbitrage easily between the domestic and euro-currency money markets, and such arbitrage in normal circumstances tends to eliminate profit opportunities. Arbitrage by banks is conducted on both sides of the balance-sheet. Funding can be undertaken in three markets: (i) the domestic money market; (ii) the euro-currency market of the domestic currency; or (iii) the euro-currency market of a foreign currency with the exchange risk eliminated by selling the borrowed currency forward at the prevailing forward exchange rate. Clearly, other things being equal, banks seek to minimise the cost of funds. Similarly, on the assets side funds may be deployed in the same three markets with, in the third case, the currency sold forward if it is different from that borrowed. The evidence strongly suggests that banks arbitrage between euro and domestic money markets on a large scale with forward cover taken when appropriate. For this reason, when arbitrage is free of control the *global parity* condition will normally be sustained.

Such arbitrage activity simultaneously determines the domestic inter-bank interest rate, the euro currency rate in the same currency, the euro rate in other currencies, and the relevant forward exchange rate. In the absence of exchange control, or other impediments to the free flow of arbitrage funds, profit opportunities are normally competed away.

Arbitrage determines euro-currency rates in the following manner. The supply and demand curves for euro-currency deposits (banks and non-banks) in a currency are given in Figure 7.1. The supply of funds by non-banks is presumed to be a rising function of the differential between the euro-currency deposit rate and the rate offered by banks in the domestic market of the currency (i_0). This is represented by the segment AB. There may be a positive supply below i_0 if, for any reason, non-banks have a preference for euro-currency over domestic deposits. The supply of funds to the euro market by banks is assumed to be a rising function of the differential between the euro-currency deposit rate and the banks' effective domestic borrowing rate (which incorporates the effect of reserve requirements, etc.). In the absence of exchange control the supply of funds by banks becomes infinitely elastic (BC) when the euro-market rate rises above the effective cost of funds in the domestic market (i_3). This is because at higher rates profits are earned by borrowing in the domestic market to finance lending in the euro segment of the same money market. Thus in Figure 7.1A the supply curve becomes infinitely elastic when the euro-currency deposit rate equals the effective cost of domestic funds (i_3). The rate of interest i_3 is higher than i_0 by virtue of reserve

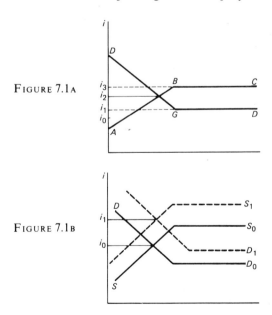

FIGURE 7.1A

FIGURE 7.1B

FIGURE 7.1 Supply and demand in the euro-currency market

requirements on domestic liabilities. Thus the effective cost of funds is given by $1(1 - r_d) \cdot i_0$, where r_d is the percentage reserve requirement on domestic liabilities.

The demand for euro-market funds by banks is a derived demand based upon the demand curve of non-bank borrowers which is assumed to be downward-sloping (DG). Domestic banks borrow in the euro market when the effective cost of such borrowing (i.e. allowing for any reserve requirements on external liabilities) is lower than the effective cost in the domestic market. The banks' demand for euro-market funds is likely to be infinitely elastic at the euro-currency rate at which the effective cost of borrowing in the two markets is the same. The interest rate at which it is profitable for domestic banks to borrow in the euro market depends, therefore, upon the domestic interest rate and the level of reserve requirements on domestic and external liabilities. The effective cost of internal and external funding is the same when:

$$\left(\frac{1}{1-r_d}\right) \cdot i_d = \left(\frac{1}{1-r_f}\right) \cdot i_e,$$

where r_d and r_f are percentage reserve requirements on domestic and external liabilities and i_d and i_e are the domestic and corresponding euro-currency interest rates. When the left-hand term exceeds the right-hand term bank funding is cheaper in the euro market of the domestic currency and vice versa. If the two are not the same, banks switch the source of funding which, given the infinitely elastic demand for funds noted above, induces equilibrating movements in domestic and euro-market rates. There is, therefore, a unique equilibrium relationship between the interest-rate differential and the differential between reserve requirements on domestic and external liabilities.

In Figure 7.1A, i_3 is the euro-currency interest rate which is equivalent to the effective cost of domestic funding. But providing there are also reserve requirements on external liabilities, it will be profitable for domestic banks to borrow in the euro market only if the euro-currency interest rate is below this level. In Figure 7.1A the critical interest rate is i_1, such that $1/(1 - r_f) \cdot i_1 = i_3$, where r_f is the percentage reserve requirement on banks' external liabilities.

As $i_1 > i_0$ Figure 7.1A implicitly assumes that reserve requirements are higher against domestic than external liabilities. In general the relationship between domestic and corresponding euro-currency interest rates is determined, in the absence of exchange control, by the level of reserve requirements on banks' domestic and external liabilities. Differential reserve requirements may be applied as a means of discouraging capital inflows (see Chapters 8 and 11). If reserve requirements are substantially higher on banks' external liabilities (which include borrowing from the euro market) than domestic liabilities, the domestic interest rate may rise significantly above the corresponding euro-currency rate. In fact the opposite is the more usual pattern.

It follows that, irrespective of the supply of and demand for euro-market funds by non-banks, the euro-currency interest rate is constrained within the range $i_1 i_3$ in Figure 7.1A by arbitrage by banks. It also follows that such arbitrage will, in normal circumstances, keep the banks' domestic and corresponding euro-market deposit rates in close alignment. If, from an initial equilibrium, the domestic rate moved above the euro rate the supply curve of funds to the euro market would shift to the left, and the demand curve to the right inducing a rise in the euro-currency interest rate. Conversely, for a fall in the domestic rate. As noted in Figure 7.1B, equilibrium may be restored by a rise in the euro-currency interest rate without inducing a substantial volume of actual arbitrage funds to be switched between the markets.

The close relationship between U.S. and euro-dollar interest rates after 1974 is seen in Chart 7.3 (the earlier period is discussed later in this chapter). One empirical exercise[2] indicates that between January 1975 and March 1978 the differential between the three-month euro-dollar rate and the effective cost of U.S. bank borrowing in the domestic market averaged 0.07 percentage point. However in 1973, when arbitrage was constrained by controls on capital outflows from the United Kingdom, the differential averaged 0.48 p.p. (and much larger in some earlier years).

EURO-CURRENCY AND FORWARD RATES

However, banks are not restricted to a single currency on either side of the balance-sheet. With a bank eliminating the exchange-rate risk in the forward market the effective cost of foreign currency borrowing equals the interest rate in the foreign currency euro market *plus* that currency's forward premium or *minus* its forward discount against the currency of the banks' assets. With forward cover taken banks should be indifferent between different euro currencies both as a source of funding and as a market for investment. Therefore in equilibrium (zero arbitrage profit opportunities) the interest-parity condition should be fulfilled within the euro-currency markets. This is simply because, with forward cover euro-currency markets in different currencies are effectively perfect substitutes. The interest-parity condition is not fulfilled when, for example, the euro-DM rate is 6 per cent, the euro-dollar rate is 8 per cent and the forward discount of the dollar is, say, 3 per cent. In this case banks could profit by borrowing euro dollars at 8 per cent, selling dollars spot for Deutsche Marks and placing the funds on deposit in the euro-DM market at 6 per cent and simultaneously buying dollars forward at a 3 per cent discount. The rate of return on invested funds is 6 per cent but the effective cost of funds is only 5 per cent. Such arbitrage with a fixed spot rate would: (i) raise the euro-dollar rate; (ii) lower the euro-DM rate; and (iii) through increased purchases of forward dollars would narrow the dollar's forward discount. This would continue until the parity condition is attained.

It follows that bank arbitrage on both sides of the balance-sheet could, in a

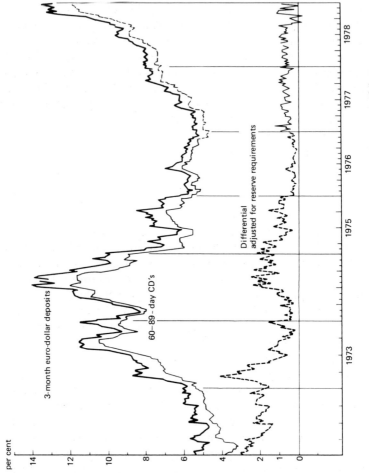

CHART 7.3   Euro-dollar and U.S. money market rates (%)

situation where an initial equilibrium parity position was disturbed by, for instance, a change in the forward rate, induce equilibrating movements in: (i) two euro-currency interest rates; (ii) two domestic interest rates; and (iii) the forward exchange rate. This is illustrated in Table 7.2 (p. 98).

EMPIRICAL RELATIONSHIPS

The tables and charts in this chapter give a selection of arbitrage relationships between dollar, Deutsche Mark and sterling securities and bank deposits. The comparisons including sterling interest rates are interesting in that they demonstrate the effect of controls on capital outflows. On the other hand, Deutsche Mark comparisons include a period (1971–3) when various measures were adopted by the German monetary authorities to inhibit capital inflows into Germany, and the post-1973 period when there have been no exchange-control regulations in force to prevent completely free arbitrage.

The main conclusions of the data may be briefly summarised:

(1) Subject to measurement error the interest-parity condition has invariably been maintained within the euro markets even in periods of exchange control and when uncovered interest differentials have at times been substantial. Thus forward premia/discounts invariably equal uncovered differentials between euro-currency interest rate. The necessary conditions for interest parity are therefore fulfilled within the euro markets.

(2) Since January 1974, after the complete abolition of controls on capital inflows, *global parity* has been achieved between Deutsche Mark and dollar securities. Thus, for instance, the domestic inter-bank rate and the euro-DM deposit rate have been approximately the same throughout the period (Chart 7.4), whereas during the period of exchange control substantial differentials emerged. Also, the euro-dollar rate has been approximately equal to the euro-DM rate plus the forward DM premium. This has also been true in the case of the Netherlands guilder and Swiss franc as both countries have had virtually no effective exchange control since 1974.

(3) In the case of sterling and the French franc (both the United Kingdom and France have had extensive exchange control regulations to inhibit capital outflows though they were abolished in the United Kingdom in 1979) *global parity* has frequently not been achieved. Thus the interest-rate differential between the euro and domestic segments of the sterling and French franc money markets (Chart 7.4) has frequently been substantial, with exchange control preventing U.K. and French residents taking advantage of higher interest rates in the euro market. Also, covered differentials between U.K. and U.S. Treasury bills (Chart 7.2) and U.K. domestic interest rates and the euro-dollar rate have frequently been substantially against the United Kingdom. While significant potential

CHART 7.4   Domestic short-term and euro-currency interest rates

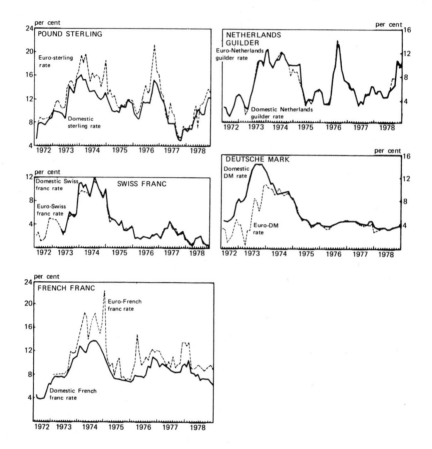

arbitrage profits have been available they have not been taken because of
the constraint of exchange control. This would not be expected since the
abolition of exchange control in the United Kingdom in October 1979.
(4) In general, movements in the forward rate tend, even in the exchange-
control case, to narrow arbitrage possibilities between national securities
in that the covered interest rate differential has usually been less than the
uncovered differential (Chart 7.2, p. 80). Overall, though not in each and
every month, changes in the uncovered differential have induced offsetting
movements in the forward discount. A systematic analysis of the 1960s by
Herring and Marston (1977) concluded that adjustments in the forward
exchange rate afforded a significant degree of insulation to European
countries from movements in dollar interest rates. For instance, the
cumulative capital outflow from Germany induced by a 1 percentage point

rise in the euro-dollar rate was more than 50 per cent lower after allowance was made for equilibrating adjustments in the forward exchange rate. Over the estimating period a 1 percentage point rise in the euro-dollar rate induced, on average, a 0.73 percentage point equilibrating adjustment to the forward exchange rate.

(5) When exchange control inhibits capital outflows (as was the case in the United Kingdom prior to 1979 and in France) large covered differentials against domestic assets have tended to be associated with wide forward discounts rather than substantial uncovered differentials (Chart 7.2). Thus domestic interest rates tend not to reflect the forward discount when the latter is particularly wide and when exchange control prevents arbitrage both from the domestic to the euro segment of a money market, and from domestic to foreign currency assets. The implication is that speculative pressure in the forward market (causing a wide discount) did not induce a sufficient outflow from U.K. domestic securities to eliminate the negative covered interest-rate differential associated with the wide forward discount.

Exchange control offers a degree of insulation to the spot exchange rate and domestic interest rates from the spot capital outflows that would otherwise result from the effect on covered interest differentials of forward speculation.

The major observation from the data is that while the parity condition is invariably satisfied within the euro-currency markets, this is not the case when comparison is made between even *homogeneous* securities between countries when one of the countries has applied various forms of exchange control. Using monthly data, the evidence is summarised for the period April 1974 to June 1978 in Table 7.1 in terms of the magnitude of the deviation (percentage points) from parity for different pairs of securities. The difference between countries with exchange control on capital outflows (the United Kingdom), and those without controls (Germany in the case above though also

TABLE 7.1   Deviations from parity

	Average deviation	Minimum[1] deviation	Maximum[1] deviation	Range
Euros (£ and $)	0.08	—	0.44	0.44
Euro $ and U.K. inter-bank rate	1.90	0.11	5.16	5.05
U.K. and U.S. Treasury bills	1.50	0.15	5.64	5.55
Euro $ and Frankfurt inter-bank rate[2]	0.38	0.05	0.73	0.68
U.S. and German Treasury bills	0.52	0.02	1.15	1.30

[1] Average of three lowest or highest.

[2] Since January 1974.

Switzerland, Netherlands and the United States) is clear; *global* parity is maintained in the latter case while only *partial* parity is secured in the former.

Exchange control may, though need not necessarily, cause some of the elements of *global parity* to be suspended, and the form of non-parity depends largely upon whether exchange control is designed to limit capital inflows (as in Germany in the period 1971–4) or outflows (as in France and until 1979 the United Kingdom). The mechanisms and rationale of controls are considered in more detail in Chapters 8 and 11, but for the moment we note that controls on outflows have three main implications: (i) domestic residents are unable to purchase foreign currency for investment overseas and hence are unable to take advantage of interest-rate differentials (covered or uncovered) against the domestic currency; (ii) limits are placed on the ability of non-residents to borrow the domestic currency; and (iii) domestic residents are unable to switch from the domestic to the euro-currency segment of their currency's money markets. Thus, until the end of 1979 U.K. residents were unable to deposit in the euro-sterling market in Paris simply because, without such a prohibition, the uncontrolled euro segment would be an effective 'leak' in the exchange-control system designed to prevent residents switching from domestic to foreign currency. Without such control there would be no limit to the supply of domestic funds to the euro market and the potential for conversion to foreign currency.

Interest-rate differentials are influenced by different forms of exchange-control and differential-reserve requirements on banks domestic and external liabilities. In the case where there is no exchange control there is normally no reason why the conditions of *global parity* should not be fulfilled between strictly *homogeneous* assets. But deviations from *global parity* may occur from time to time, even in the absence of exchange control, because of changes in investors' perception of non-exchange risks associated with different locations of investment. An example occurred in the middle of 1974 in the euro-dollar market. After February of that year, when the U.S. capital restraint programme was ended, there were no official regulations preventing U.S. banks and non-bank residents placing funds either in the euro-dollar or other foreign money markets. The immediate impact of the abolition of controls was a substantial narrowing of the domestic/euro-dollar differential (Chart 7.3, p. 86) to a level considered an appropriate reflection of the differential risk associated with U.S. and European banks. In the middle of 1974 the euro markets faced a confidence crisis (partly associated with the failure of the Herstatt Bank), and funds were withdrawn from the market. As a result the differential against U.S. interest rates widened markedly. Although there were no exchange controls to prevent arbitrage from the New York to the euro-dollar money market, the differential widened to a peak of $2\frac{1}{2}$ percentage points. As confidence was restored the differential narrowed and remained around 0.3 percentage point thereafter.

Thus with a constant risk premium the absence of exchange control would normally create a *global parity* condition. On the other hand, controls on capital outflows imply that while the euro-currency rate will not fall below the domestic interest rate (as otherwise banks would borrow in the euro market to finance domestic lending, and external investors would switch funds from the euro market to the domestic market) the interest rate in the euro market may rise significantly above the domestic rate (e.g. sterling in 1973, 1974 and 1976 and French franc in 1973, 1974 and 1976). Controls on outflows also imply that a covered interest differential against (but not in favour of) the domestic currency can be sustained. Nevertheless, a substantial positive differential between the euro and domestic interest rate may be limited by arbitrage by non-resident holders of the currency who are not subject to exchange control.

Controls on capital inflows imply the reverse; while the covered differential between euro currencies will not diverge markedly from zero, the euro-currency rate may be significantly below the corresponding domestic rate as non-residents hold the currency only in the euro segment of the money market. This is clearly noted in the case of DM interest rates in the period 1972–4 (Charts 7.4 and 7.5). For similar reasons, a positive covered interest-rate differential between domestic and foreign interest rates is sustainable as was the case with the Deutsche Mark when, in 1973, the positive differential between the Frankfurt inter-bank rate and the euro-dollar rate averaged 7 percentage points and peaked at 10 percentage points (Chart 7.5). On the other hand, a covered differential against the domestic money market will not be sustained if exchange-control limits inflows but not outflows. The central point in the analysis of the effect of exchange control is simply that the volume of arbitrage funds able to take advantage of covered (or uncovered) interest differentials is strictly limited.

The extent of deviation from *global parity* when exchange-control limits capital outflows depends largely upon why an exogenous change in the covered differential has taken place. This is because the forward exchange rate is more flexible than the uncovered interest-rate differential. Thus the forward exchange rate is more able to adjust to autonomous changes in the uncovered interest differential than vice versa. It can be seen in Chart 7.2 (p. 80) (which relates to a period when exchange controls were in force in the United Kingdom) that: (i) the uncovered differential fluctuates less than the forward exchange rate; and (ii) the negative covered differential is widest when the forward discount is wide. Therefore, a wide-covered differential may emerge between domestic securities when there is substantial autonomous (e.g. speculative) pressure on the forward rate as the 'allowable' capital outflow is less than that needed to induce a change in interest rates to restore *global parity*.

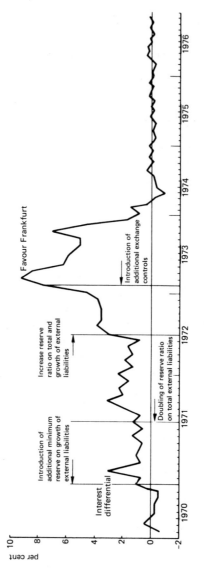

CHART 7.5 Deutsche Mark domestic/euro differential

As *partial parity* always exists within the euro market, the corollary is that when the forward discount is wide a substantial gap emerges between the domestic inter-bank rate and the corresponding euro-currency rate, e.g. in the sterling markets in 1974 and 1976 (Chart 7.4, p. 88). The gap was sustainable as exchange control prevented domestic residents taking advantage of the higher rates in the euro market but also, as the supply of funds to a euro market is limited when the country of issue has imposed exchange control, external holders of the currency are inhibited by the rigidity of the euro market (e.g. large minimum deposits and narrow range of maturities, etc.).[3] Indeed, the euro-sterling and French franc markets have been little more than adjuncts to the forward exchange market rather than true deposit markets.

In formal terms, *global parity* in a situation of exchange control on capital outflows requires either: (i) no strong speculative pressure in the forward market, or (ii) speculative pressure where the expected future spot rate is close to the parity level of the forward rate. The effect of exchange control is to limit the supply of arbitrage funds to A_1 rather than A_0. For the forward exchange rate to be determined at its parity level in these circumstances the speculators' schedule must intersect the arbitrage schedule in the elastic segment of the latter (e.g. when the speculators' schedule is S_0 rather than S_1 in Figure 7.2). With S_1 the forward exchange rate is determined close to its parity level when arbitrage is not inhibited by exchange control (i.e. at E_2 along A_0), but not when exchange control is imposed (e.g. E_1 along A_1).

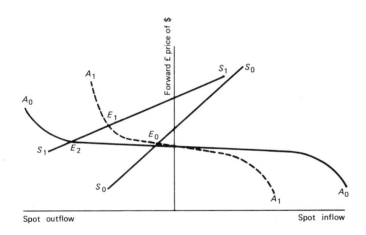

FIGURE 7.2 The parity condition

CONTROL ON CAPITAL INFLOWS

Much of the analysis of the previous section applies in reverse when exchange control is designed to inhibit capital inflows (e.g. as in Germany in the period 1971–4). In this period the measures to limit spot capital inflows took the form of additional reserve requirements on German banks' external liabilities rather than a direct prohibition on receiving external funds.[4] As a result non-resident Deutsche Mark deposits could be held only in either the unregulated euro-DM market, or at German banks at a low interest rate to compensate for the banks' higher reserve requirement. The effect was to cause the euro-DM interest rate to fall substantially below the domestic money market rate in Frankfurt. The reserve requirement on external liabilities meant also that it was not profitable for German banks to borrow in the euro-DM market despite the substantially lower interest rate there compared with inter-bank rates in the German money market. This is illustrated in Charts 7.4 and 7.5. However, to prevent German non-banks borrowing in the euro-DM market at a lower interest rate than in Germany (which would have circumvented the effect of the measures to limit capital inflows), 'reserve requirements' on such borrowing were also applied in the form of the *Bardepot* (this is discussed, along with a general analysis of reserve requirements on external bank liabilities, in Chapter 11).

Discriminatory reserve requirements on German banks' external liabilities were also imposed in January 1978 in order to discourage capital inflows. A reserve requirement of 95 per cent was placed upon increases in external liabilities and, as in 1973, the euro-DM rate fell below interest rates in the German money market. However, unlike in 1973, the euro-DM rate was quickly aligned with domestic rates largely because, unlike 1973, no reserve requirements were placed upon non-bank borrowing in the euro-DM market and hence non-banks could effectively arbitrage between the euro and domestic segments of the DM market.

GLOBAL AND PARTIAL PARITY

We may summarise the analysis with respect to why the parity condition is invariably fulfilled within the euro-currency markets, irrespective of the exchange-control regime, but not always between securities in different countries. When parity is not achieved in the latter case the analysis needs to explain why arbitrage is limited between: (i) the domestic and the euro segments of the same money market; and (ii) the national money market and foreign currency markets. Four broad types of explanation apart from measurement error,[5] may be offered: (i) the banks' forward exchange mechanism; (ii) transactions costs; (iii) limited supply of arbitrage funds; and (iv) market imperfections.

The first has already been discussed in detail. In conditions in the foreign exchange market which approximate to perfect competition, the forward rate quoted by any bank cannot deviate from the differential between the respective euro-currency interest rates. Banks in competition are able to provide customers with forward dollars against sterling without risk to themselves by borrowing euro-sterling, selling spot for dollars and depositing in the euro-dollar market. The 'cost' to the bank is the difference between the two euro-currency interest rates and this determines the forward rate quoted. Competition between banks ensures that profits are kept to a competitive minimum and, as the banks' marginal cost of forward transactions is low, the commission will also be small. Thus the forward-exchange mechanism ensures parity in the euro-currency markets. Indeed in some cases the condition becomes a tautology as forward quotations are calculated by traders as the difference between relevant euro-currency interest rates, and euro-currency rates are calculated on the basis of the euro-dollar rate and the relevant currency's forward premium. For instance, if a bank in France is offered a (euro)-sterling deposit it will in all probability: (i) sell sterling spot for dollars; (ii) buy sterling forward to cover its exchange-rate risk; and (iii) invest the dollar proceeds of the spot sale in the euro-dollar market. The rate of interest a competitive bank offers on sterling deposits is therefore determined by the rate of interest it receives on its own euro-dollar deposits plus the forward discount on sterling. This is particularly true for those small euro-currency markets (all except the U.S. dollar, Deutsche Mark and Swiss franc) that are little more than adjuncts to banks' foreign exchange operations.

If exchange control inhibits capital outflows, banks are unable to finance the spot counterpart of forward transactions in the domestic money market, and hence the forward exchange mechanism need not imply parity between national money market. Nevertheless, without exchange control, the mechanism is a sufficient condition for *global parity* between inter-bank interest rates as banks can choose to finance the spot counterpart of forward transactions in either the domestic or euro segment of the money markets.

Arbitrage transactions are clearly not costless and tend to be greater for non-banks than banks. When arbitrage between different currencies also involves securities traded in domestic markets, not only are foreign exchange costs incurred (difference between buying and selling prices and any commission charges, etc.), but similar costs in buying and selling the securities. Arbitrage by banks in the euro-currency market involves only foreign-exchange market costs and are conducted at finer interest rates than applicable to non-banks. The effect of different transaction costs is to create a wider band of neutral arbitrage possibilities in the case of securities in different domestic markets than with euro-currency interest rates. Thus, it would be expected that the average covered differential between, say, U.S. and Germany Treasury bill rates would be greater than between euro-dollar and DM rates. Indeed, Frenkel and Levich (1975) demonstrate that when allowance is made for transactions costs, most of the apparent arbitrage possibilities between reasonably homogeneous national securities disappear. Even when comparison is made between U.K. and U.S. Treasury bills they estimate that 85 per cent of potential covered arbitrage profits is eliminated when all transactions costs are considered. However, while the neutral band would be wider with securities than with inter-bank deposits, and foreign-exchange

96 INTERNATIONAL FINANCIAL INTEGRATION

transactions costs tend to rise at times of uncertainty in the exchange markets, higher costs cannot explain the particularly wide-covered differential (in excess of 3 per cent) sometimes observed between U.S. and U.K. Treasury bills in Chart 7.2 (p. 80). An explanation is still needed for the sometimes substantial covered differentials outside the neutral band.

Clearly any limit to the supply of arbitrage funds is a sufficient condition for a covered interest-rate differential to be sustained, as the flow of funds may cease before the respective exchange and interest rates adjust to parity levels. One reason why the supply of funds might be limited is exchange control. It is largely this that explains the difference between the covered differential (average and maximum) observed earlier between U.S./U.K. and U.S./German Treasury bills. Thus, as noted earlier, when considering the period before the abolition of U.K. exchange control, when the forward discount was wide the supply of arbitrage funds from the United Kingdom was limited and insufficient in relation to the size of the London and New York money markets to induce the necessary changes in U.K. and U.S. interest rates. Also, given the limited supply of arbitrage funds, any short-term impact on U.K. interest rates could be offset by the monetary authorities. In the euro market, on the other hand, the volume of funds is substantial and banks are always and instantaneously able to borrow in one to deposit in another, if small, temporary covered differentials emerge. Thus an important factor preventing *global parity* is the effect of exchange control in limiting the supply of arbitrage funds in situations where, because of a wide forward discount, the required adjustment to domestic interest rates is substantial.

Finally, market imperfections may account for the absence of *global parity* which imply that the securities being compared are not strictly homogeneous. The interest-parity formulation is ultimately based on the proposition that, unless markets can be segregated, identical products cannot sell for different prices. For the parity condition to apply between securities in two countries they must be identical in all significant respects. In three major respects apparently homogeneous securities (e.g. Treasury bills in different countries and deposits at banks in different countries) may be differentiated. First, the fact that the securities are issued in different countries introduces an element of what bankers term *sovereign risk*. There is a residual risk that, before a security comes to maturity, the host government might impose exchange control which prevents the repatriation of funds. This would not apply between euro-currency deposits of different currencies at banks in the same country, as exchange control would not differentiate between particular currencies. Second, forward cover removes only the exchange-rate risk while the credit-standing and hence default-risk of the issuers might vary between the two countries. The financial difficulties of New York City indicate that the apparently most secure issuers may default and, as already noted, the sharp widening of the euro-dollar and U.S. Certificate of Deposit interest-rate differential in 1974 was associated with increasing doubts about the viability and security of euro-market banks. A sustained covered interest differential may therefore reflect a non-exchange-rate risk premium. Third, particular institutional characteristics (such as certain assets being eligible reserve assets for banks) may differentiate apparently similar securities issued in different countries.

Overall, the predominant reason for non-parity between similar securities is usually associated with the limitations on the supply of arbitrage funds due to the effect of exchange control. It follows that non-parity is more likely to emerge when speculative pressure induces a comparatively wide forward discount. When arbitrage occurs between heterogeneous securities the issue of investors' portfolio balance will limit the volume of arbitrage and sustain a covered interest-rate differential.

DYNAMIC ADJUSTMENTS

The system of euro-currency and domestic interest rates, together with the spot and forward exchange rate, make up a 'mobile' in which an exogenous change in any one variable induces arbitrage and equilibrating movements in the other variables. The effect of the exogenous change is generalised through the relevant money markets until a new equilibrium is attained in which parity is always restored in the euro market and, subject to exchange control, a new *global parity* condition is usually established. Which interest or foreign-exchange rates change, and by how much, depends critically upon the flexibility of the rates, the causes and strength of the initial disturbance to equilibrium, the relative size of the different markets and the relevant elasticities of supply and demand in each market. Thus in a fixed (spot) exchange-rate system, if the forward rate is uniquely determined either by speculation or official intervention, all dynamic adjustments occur through interest rates. There would in this case be a fixed relationship between different euro-currency interest rates and domestic interest rates in a *global parity* situation. The interdependence of national interest rates is greatest in this situation. Which interest-rate adjustments dominate in this case depends crucially upon the elasticity of supply and demand for funds in the relevant markets. In general, the higher the elasticities of demand for funds in the markets between which arbitrage is taking place, the greater will be the volume of capital flows as a substantial flow is needed to induce changes in interest rates. Thus a greater degree of independence of national interest rates is achieved in large countries, and where the elasticity of demand for funds is high. For this reason interest rates in small European countries have frequently been dominated by monetary policy in the United States as a given capital flow is large in relation to the European money market compared with that of the United States. Also given the size and sophistication of the U.S. money market, the elasticity of demand for funds is relatively high.

On the other hand, if the forward rate is flexible the degree of interest-rate

INTERNATIONAL FINANCIAL INTEGRATION

TABLE 7.2   Dynamic

	Exogenous change:	Forward sterling discount[1] widens	Rise in euro-sterling interest rate
IMPACT EFFECT	Arithmetic effect	– forward discount widens	– euro £ rate rise against domestic rate
	Impact on covered interest-rate differential	– against £ in domestic and euro markets	– in favour of euro £
PRIMARY ARBITRAGE EFFECT ON:	International capital flows	– U.K. to U.S. markets[2] – U.K. to euro $ – euro £ to euro $ – banks borrow euro £ to sell spot for $[4]	– (U.K. to euro £)[2] – (U.S. to euro £) – euro $ to euro £ – banks borrow euro $ to sell spot for £[5]
	Foreign-exchange-market transactions	– £ spot sales for $ – £ forward purchases	– £ spot purchases – £ forward sales
	Spot exchange rate	– £ depreciates	– £ appreciates[6]
	Sterling forward discount[1]	– narrows (offset to initial exo-genous change)	– widens
	Interest rates	– euro £ rises – domestic £ rises – euro $ declines – (domestic $ declines)	– euro £ declines – (domestic £ rises) – euro $ rises – (domestic $ rises)
EQUILIBRIUM EFFECTS	U.S. domestic interest rate	– (declines)	– (rises)
	Euro-dollar rate	– (declines)	– rises
	Sterling spot rate	– declines	– rises
	Sterling forward discount[1]	– narrows	– widens
	U.K. domestic interest rate	– (rises)	– (rises)
	Euro- sterling rate	– rises	– declines

( ) Small, if any, change.   [1] %.   [2] By external holders of sterling.   [3] Spot rises with forward exchange rate constant.   [4] If the arbitrageur is able to borrow euro sterling before the forward exchange rate and/or euro-currency interest rates move to the covered interest-parity arbitrage adjustments

Rise in U.K. domestic interest rate	Rise in spot sterling exchange rate	Rise in U.S. domestic interest rate	Rise in euro-dollar interest rate
– domestic £ interest rate rises against euro £ rate	– £ forward discount widens[1, 3]	– domestic $ interest rate rises against euro $ rate	– euro $ interest rate rises against domestic $ rate
– in favour of domestic sterling	– against £ in domestic and euro markets	– against £ in domestic and euro markets	– against £ in euro and domestic markets in favour of euro £
– U.S. to U.K. markets – euro £ to domestic £ – banks borrow euro $ to sell spot for £[5]	– U.K. to U.S. markets – U.K. to euro $[2] – euro £ to euro $ – banks borrow euro £ to sell spot for $[4]	– U.K. to U.S. markets[2] – euro $ to U.S. – euro £ to U.S. $ – banks borrow euro $ to switch to U.S.[5]	– U.S. to euro $ – euro £ to euro $ – banks borrow euro £ to sell for £[4] – banks borrow in U.S.
– £ spot purchases – £ forward sales	– £ spot sales – £ forward purchases	– $ spot purchases – $ forward sales	– $ spot purchases – $ forward sales
– £ appreciate[6]	– £ depreciates	– $ appreciates[6]	– $ appreciates
– widens	– narrows	– narrows	– narrows
– euro £ rises – domestic £ declines – euro $ rises – (domestic $ falls)	– euro £ rises – domestic £ rises – euro $ declines – domestic $ declines	– euro £ rises – domestic £ rises – euro $ rises – domestic $ declines	– euro £ rises – domestic £ rises – euro $ declines – domestic $ rises
(rises) – rises – rises	– (declines) – declines – declines	– declines – rises – declines	– rises – declines – declines
– widens	– narrows	– narrows	– narrows
– declines	– rises	– rises	– rises
– rises	– rises	– rises	– rises

level.   [5] If the arbitrageur is able to borrow euro dollars before the forward exchange rate and/or euro-currency interest rates move to the covered interest-parity level.   [6] Including effect on uncovered capital movements.

linkage is also determined by the elasticity of supply of forward exchange. If this is high, substantial changes in quantity are required to influence the price and hence the greater the extent of interest-rate changes induced by the counterpart spot capital flows. On the other hand, if the elasticity of supply is low the forward exchange rate adjusts substantially, the volume of capital movements is small and hence little impact is made on interest rates after an exogenous disturbance to equilibrium.

The system of dynamic adjustments implicit in the analysis is outlined in Table 7.2 where the effect of an exogenous disturbance to an initial equilibrium is considered in terms of: (i) an impact effect; (ii) primary arbitrage effects; and (iii) final equilibrating changes. All rates are assumed to be flexible and exchange control limits capital outflows by U.K. residents. As substantial capital movements take place on an uncovered basis the effects of these flows are also incorporated. Equilibrium is assumed to be restored through the effect of capital movements, though in practice these may be small if exchange dealers' quotations respond immediately to a non-parity condition. Also, as many of the changes would in practice occur simultaneously, the schema is not to be interpreted in a sequential manner but as a general indication and summary of the major potential arbitrage channels.

Thus, within the interest-parity 'mobile' the concept of causality must be treated with caution. Any exogenous disturbance to equilibrium (interest-parity condition) will induce *simultaneous* changes in the spot rate, forward rate and the two interest rates until parity is restored. It is not appropriate, under these circumstances, to say that causality runs from the forward rate to euro-currency interest rates or vice versa, as an exogenous disturbance will *simultaneously* affect each variable in the 'mobile'. It also means that, when the *global-parity* condition is fulfilled, the spot and forward rates and euro-currency and domestic interest rates are all simultaneously determined. Thus in the partial analysis of Chapter 4 the domestic and foreign interest rates cannot in reality be taken as *given* with the adjustment to a disturbance being made solely by the forward exchange rate. In a sense there is no separate theory of the determination of the forward exchange rate. It is determined simultaneously with the spot rate and relevant interest rates and is therefore influenced by any factor which impinges initially upon any variable in the parity 'mobile'. The inference of causality in a mutually determined system is fraught with practical and methodological problems.

CONCLUDING REMARKS

A distinction has been made between *global* and *partial parity* with the empirical evidence strongly supporting the interest-parity theorem. This is clearly demonstrated within the euro-currency markets as the necessary and sufficient conditions for parity (homogeneous securities, absence of exchange control to limit the volume of arbitrage flows, etc.) exist within these markets.

In some cases the parity condition is effectively a tautology. But exchange control may limit the volume of arbitrage funds to and from national markets and prevent *global parity* being achieved. In these circumstances significant *covered* interest-rate differentials tend to emerge when autonomous pressure in the forward market creates a wide forward discount. It has also been noted that, from time to time, *global parity* may also not be observed because of changes in investors' perceived risk associated with apparently similar assets in different countries.

Global or *partial* parity (particularly the latter) may be attained with a relatively small volume of net spot capital flows when only a limited volume of speculation in the forward market is taking place and when dealers making the market respond quickly to intrinsic covered premia/discounts. In this latter case *partial parity* may be attained almost instantaneously without spot capital flows.

Overall the evidence lends support to the interest-parity theorem, particularly within the euro markets where arbitrage is dominated by banks. But, as all variables in the model are determined simultaneously, it is inappropriate to regard it in any way as a *theory* of the forward exchange rate. The interest-parity formulation is not inconsistent with the *structural* model of the forward exchange rate outlined in Chapter 4. Nor does it preclude autonomous speculative pressure having a powerful influence on the forward rate. It indicates that, when appropriate securities are compared, the elasticity of the arbitrage schedule is high. But this does not imply that the volume of capital flows in response to interest-rate movements is substantial. The capital flow response is determined also by the elasticity of the speculators' schedule and the evidence indicates that this is low.

The evidence indicates that, in the absence of controls, arbitrage by banks on both sides of the balance-sheet limits the extent to which domestic and corresponding euro-currency rates, and euro-currency rates in different currencies can differ. The former limit is set by differential reserve requirements on banks' domestic and external liabilities, while the latter is related directly to the forward exchange premium. In turn the forward premium is constrained by bank arbitrage between the maximum interest-rate differential between two currencies. This is determined by the differential reserve requirements between domestic and external liabilities in the two countries. Overall, the analysis suggests that euro-currency markets are an integral part of the corresponding domestic money markets and, given the arbitrage activities of banks, are not independent of domestic money markets. This is discussed further in Chapter 9.

Abolition of U.K. Exchange Control

The remnants of exchange control on capital outflows were removed on 24 October 1979 after forty years. This followed a gradual easing over the previous two years. This could prove to be one of the most significant changes in the monetary environment of the United Kingdom since 1945, and it certainly increases the extent to which the country is financially integrated into the international money markets. In terms of the analysis of Chapter 7 one of the immediate implications of the abolition of exchange control is that the structure of arbitrage relationships involving sterling interest rates has been substantially extended as domestic residents (previously only non-resident holders of sterling) may freely arbitrage between domestic sterling, the euro-sterling and other euro and foreign money markets. In principle there is no reason why the *global parity* condition (which requires free arbitrage uninhibited by exchange control) should not apply to the sterling money markets. Thus, the abolition of exchange control means that significant divergencies should not emerge between euro-sterling interest rates and domestic inter-bank rates, and the covered differential between domestic and foreign currency interest rates should fluctuate narrowly around zero. This implies that domestic interest rates are likely to be even more influenced by interest-rate trends in international money markets, and also influenced to a greater extent by movements in the sterling forward exchange rate.

One of the major implications of the abolition of exchange control is that U.K. residents can now legally hold euro- (foreign) currency deposits at banks in London. In practice, given the nature of the market, this is likely to be of practical relevance only for large companies and investors. It follows that, providing both sides to a financial transaction agree, there is no legal reason why purely domestic transactions could not be conducted in foreign currency through the transfer of foreign currency bank deposits in London. Under some, admittedly unlikely circumstances, foreign currency could displace domestic currency as a medium of exchange and other monetary functions. The spectre of uncontrolled inflation might be one condition for such a displacement to occur.

While this is unlikely for small transactions, it could be feasible for large depositors who, for some reason, find it convenient to maintain large bank balances in foreign currency. An interest-rate incentive to this development could emerge. As noted earlier, within the euro-currency markets the forward premium is approximately equal to interest-rate differentials. But because of the competitive advantage of euro markets over domestic money markets (partly due to the absence of compulsory reserve requirements), the euro-currency deposit rate is usually slightly above the corresponding domestic interest rate. It follows that, for given levels of the forward premium, banks can offer a higher interest rate on foreign currency deposits than on domestic currency deposits.

The United Kingdom is now almost unique in the world as a country which simultaneously has no exchange control but also exempts domestic banks from reserve requirements on foreign currency business. In general, the largest euro-market centres have exchange control (e.g. the United Kingdom until October 1979, France, Belgium/Luxembourg) which prevents domestic residents maintaining foreign currency bank balances. On the other hand, countries which are free of exchange control (notably Germany) are not significant euro-market centres as the normal reserve requirements on domestic currency liabilities apply also to foreign currency business as no distinction is made. Thus, in principle, there could develop an interest-rate incentive for foreign currency to displace sterling for some purely domestic business.

MONETARY POLICY

The abolition of exchange control also has important implications for the conduct of U.K. monetary policy in several dimensions.[1] In effect, by strengthening the offshore component of the sterling money and credit markets, a pre-1971 situation has been re-created. Throughout the 1960s, prior to Competition and Credit Control, the non-controlled sector of the U.K. banking system expanded substantially. Credit demand that, for various reasons, could not be satisfied from within the controlled sector (mainly the clearing banks) could be met from banks outside the system of monetary controls. It was for reasons of equity and the efficiency of monetary and credit control that, in 1971, a wider range of institutions were brought within the traditional control mechanism. In this way, for instance, a shortage of reserve assets in the controlled sector could not be circumvented simply by switching credit demand to non-controlled banks.

The abolition of exchange control may have transformed the U.K. monetary system. By enabling funds to be drawn from the domestic to the euro sector of the sterling money market the credit capacity of the sterling banking sector need no longer be constrained by policy measures directed at domestic banks. It is in this sense that the weakness of the pre-1971 regime were re-created by the abolition of exchange control.

SELECTED BIBLIOGRAPHY

Aliber, R. Z. (1973) 'The Interest Rate Parity Theorem: A Reinterpretation', *Journal of Political Economy*, Nov/Dec 1973.

Branson, W. H. (1969) 'Minimum Covered Interest Rate Differential Needed for International Arbitrage Activity', *Journal of Political Economy*, Dec 1969.

Dufey, G., and Giddy, I. (1978) *The International Money Market* (Englewood Cliffs, N.J.: Prentice-Hall).

Frenkel, J., and Levich, R. M. (1975) 'Covered Interest Arbitrage: Unexploited Profits?', *Journal of Political Economy*, Apr 1975.

Herring, R., and Marston, R. (1977) *National Monetary Policies and International Financial Markets*, chaps 3 and 4 (Amsterdam: North-Holland).

Johnston, R. B. (1979) 'Some Aspects of the Determination of Euro Currency Interest Rates', *Bank of England Quarterly Bulletin*, Mar 1979.

Llewellyn, D. T. (1979) 'End of Exchange Control: Monetary Implications', *The Banker*, Dec 1979.

Marston, R. (1974) *American Monetary Policy and the Structure of the Euro Dollar Market*, Studies in International Finance, No. 34 (Princeton University Press).

Marston, R. (1976) 'Interest Arbitrage in the Euro Currency Markets', *European Economic Review*, Jan 1976.

Officer, L. H., and Willett, T. D. (1970) 'The Covered Arbitrage Schedule: Critical Survey of Recent Developments', *Journal of Money, Credit and Banking*, May 1970.

8
The Policy Options

Speculative and interest arbitrage capital movements may clearly have a powerful impact upon the domestic economy through their effect on domestic monetary conditions and the exchange rate. The interest-rate sensitivity of capital movements also affects the power of stabilisation policy in general and the degree of monetary policy independence in particular. In view of this, monetary authorities have frequently sought to devise policy measures to influence capital movements and offset their undesired consequences. In this chapter an outline is given of the broad policy options available to monetary authorities faced with undesired capital inflows. The focus of attention is on the issue of monetary control and hence upon measures to discourage capital inflows. We shall not consider the more general measures of exchange control which many governments, notably those of the United Kingdom, France and Italy, have imposed to limit long-term direct and portfolio capital outflows.

At several times in the past thirty years governments have moved to limit capital inflows. Indeed during the 1960s it became increasingly apparent to monetary authorities that fixed exchange rates, freedom of international capital movements and an independent monetary policy were incompatible. At various times during the fixed-exchange-rate period of the 1960s domestic monetary management was seriously undermined by substantial capital inflows (both speculative and based on interest-rate differentials associated with differences in the stance of monetary policy in different countries). The first response, throughout the decade but notably at the turn of the 1960s, was to erect a battery of controls and other measures to prevent these inflows. As these introduced their own peculiar distortions, and became increasingly ineffective, the system of fixed exchange rates was eventually disbanded after thirty years. Prior to that Germany had on two occasions (1969 and 1971) resorted unilaterally to a floating exchange rate in response to substantial capital inflows.

For most of the period after the adoption of generalised floating exchange rates in 1973, and contrary to the experience of the previous decade, deliberate measures to ward off capital inflows have been limited. However, in the final months of 1977 international money markets were dominated by substantial speculative pressure against the dollar associated with the large U.S. current account deficit and growth of the U.S. money supply. It has been estimated that Germany received a DM 10 billion inflow in the month to mid-December! The countries subject to the resultant inflow (mainly Germany, Switzerland, the United Kingdom and Japan) were therefore faced with the prospect of either allowing their currencies to appreciate or accepting a sharp growth of the domestic money supply, neither of which was desired. To avoid both possibilities these countries had three basic options: (1) to offset the internal monetary effect by conventional domestic monetary policy measures; (2) to liberalise capital outflow controls (relevant for the United Kingdom and Japan); and/or (3) to adopt measures to limit the inflow into their domestic money markets.

The four countries mentioned responded in different ways. The U.K. authorities, concerned at the money-supply implications of the inflow, responded at the end of October by allowing sterling to appreciate as the supposed beneficial effect of this on domestic inflation was seen as an advantage. Controls on capital inflows were also considered to be impractical. Switzerland acted by banning forward sales of Swiss francs with a maturity of less than ten days by Swiss banks to non-residents. This was because such sales were believed to be a mechanism for circumventing the existing negative interest rate on deposits by non-residents at Swiss banks. On the other hand, the German and Japanese authorities responded by measures designed to prevent capital inflows into the domestic money market. In November 1977 the Bank of Japan imposed a reserve requirement ratio on non-resident deposits in yen at domestic banks (50 per cent of any increase in such deposits above their average levels during October) and.a ban on foreign purchases of short-term government bonds. Similarly, in December the Bundesbank also acted to control the inflows with a series of measures akin to those adopted in the early 1970s, which included increased compulsory reserve requirements on existing external liabilities of domestic banks, a 100 per cent reserve requirement on increases in external liabilities after 1 January 1978, and a ban on non-resident purchases of domestic securities with a 2–4-year maturity.

OPTIONS AVAILABLE

Faced with a capital inflow monetary authorities have four broad policy options most of which, at various times, have been taken by European countries:

(1) Control the euro-currency market.
(2) Allow an automatic adjustment to:
    (i) domestic monetary conditions or
    (ii) the exchange rate.
(3) Influence the pattern of capital movements through:
    (i) spot exchange-rate mechanisms
    (ii) forward exchange-rate policy
    (iii) interest-rate measures
    (iv) specific measures directed at banks

    (v) similar measures directed at non-bank financial institutions
    (vi) direct primary measures and/or
(4) Offset the external and/or domestic effects of the capital inflow.

In the first option it might be envisaged that, as the euro-currency markets are frequently the institutional mechanism of international capital movements and have undoubtedly contributed to the increased mobility of capital between countries and currencies, monetary authorities might seek to control and limit the operation of the markets. This is discussed in Chapter 9 where considerable scepticism is entertained. The second broad option is simply to allow capital inflows to increase the domestic money supply (with a fixed exchange rate) or induce an appreciation of a floating exchange rate. While both may contribute towards appropriate balance-of-payments adjustment in the long run, they frequently do not appeal to governments, either because they view capital movements as temporary and volatile (and not necessarily reflecting fundamental economic conditions), or because they seek to delay balance-of-payments adjustment. Allowing the money supply to rise is tantamount to accepting that monetary policy is determined externally and a rising exchange rate is frequently resisted on domestic employment grounds. A compromise, attempted in various ways by France, Netherlands, Belgium, Italy and the United Kingdom, is to adopt a split or two-tier exchange market whereby capital account transactions are directed through a free *financial* exchange market (where there may be no official intervention and the spot rate finds its own level), while all other transactions are conducted through a *commercial* market where the exchange rate is supported by official intervention. This amounts to a fixed exchange rate for current account transactions and a floating rate for capital movements. In order to prevent arbitrage between the two markets, exchange-control procedures are required to effectively keep the two markets separate.

    The third broad option is to influence the pattern of capital movements and, within this category, six broad types of measure are noted in Table 8.1. A detailed analysis of some of these particular measures is given in later chapters. Broadly such measures are designed to: (i) discourage or prevent non-residents acquiring domestic bank deposits; (ii) restrict overseas borrowing by domestic residents; and/or (iii) limit the access of non-residents to domestic securities.

    The final broad policy option is to accept the market-determined pattern of capital movements but adopt specific measures to *offset* or *sterilise* both the internal and external consequences. Domestically, it implies a general monetary policy to 'mop up' the domestic liquidity effects of any inflow by, for instance, sales of public-sector debt to the non-banks. This strategy necessitates a flexible monetary policy to cope with potentially volatile international flows. On the external side, a series of offset mechanisms are available such as central bank 'swaps', automatic recycling, etc., which in

TABLE 8.1 Policy options

SUMMARY OF OPTIONS

	MARKET MECHANISMS	CONTROL MECHANISMS
(1) AUTOMATIC	– Allow domestic money supply to rise – Exchange-rate appreciation	
(2) INTEREST-RATE MEASURES	– Interest-rate differentials – Special 'taxes'/commissions on interest payments on external deposits – Internal/external interest-rate difference – 'Operation Twist'	– Direct limitation on interest rates allowed on external bank deposits
(3) SPOT EXCHANGE-RATE SYSTEMS	– Split/two-tier exchange – Crawling peg	– Exchange-control element of two-tier exchange market
(4) FORWARD EXCHANGE-RATE POLICY	– Open-market policy – Forward support for a 'closed' market – Official guarantee for foreign-currency debts of public-sector agencies	– restrictions on use of forward cover for traders – Limitation on banks sales of forward domestic currency to non-residents
(5) BANKING MEASURES	– Reserve requirements less than 100 per cent (a) gross external liabilities (b) net external liabilities (c) on level of liabilities (d) on changes in liabilities	– 100 per cent reserve requirements on external liabilities – Prohibition on acceptance of external deposits (in either domestic or foreign currency) – Ceiling on gross or net external liabilities – Switching/conversion limits from foreign to domestic currency – Matching regulations (balancing external assets and liabilities) – Restriction on repatriation of external assets – Control of term structure of external liabilities – Penalties on 'excess' external liabilities – Instructions to repay external liabilities – Freeze on external liabilities in excess of specified amount – Control over transfer to external accounts
(6) NON-BANK FINANCIAL INSTITUTIONS	– Reserve requirements on external liabilities	– Limits on overseas borrowing – Other mechanisms from (5) above

TABLE 8.1 (*contd*)

	MARKET MECHANISMS	CONTROL MECHANISMS
(7) DIRECT PRIMARY MEASURES	– Withholding tax on dividends to non-residents – *Bardepot* mechanism	– Prohibition on foreign-currency borrowing for internal use – Prohibition on advance payments for imports/exports – Controls on inter-company transfers and credit – Control of foreign purchases of domestic money market assets, securities and real estate – Rules to ensure conversion into foreign currency of loans raised by non-residents on domestic money markets – Non-convertibility of bank-notes remitted from overseas
(8) INTERNAL OFFSET MECHANISMS	– Open-market operations – Reserve requirements on banks domestic liabilities – Central bank swap mechanisms with banks	– Credit restrictions – Limit banks' access to central bank facilities
(9) EXTERNAL OFFSET MECHANISMS	– Inter-bank central bank swaps	– Liberalise controls on capital outflows – Official debt repayments – Ease restrictions on lending to non-residents

effect return the reserves lost by the country suffering a capital outflow. There is also an option in some cases to accelerate public-sector external debt repayments.

MARKET V CONTROL MECHANISMS

Examples of the type of measures that have been applied under each category are given in Table 8.1. When considering measures to influence the pattern of capital flows, a distinction is made between policies which rely predominantly on market forces as opposed to direct control. The former involves policy manipulation of the determinants of capital movements. Direct-control mechanisms, on the other hand, involve regulations which prevent capital flows following the pattern that would occur on the basis of market variables. These would include measures that directly limit capital inflows in response to an inward interest-rate differential or expectation of an exchange-rate appreciation. Table 8.1 lists the main measures adopted at various times during the 1960s and early 1970s in Western Europe and Japan, and are divided between the two broad mechanisms. Although each country tends to have a bias towards one mechanism rather than the other, there was a tendency for countries (including a reluctant Germany) to rely increasingly on direct control.

Direct-control mechanisms tended to become more extensive in the late 1960s and early 1970s. They involved such measures as limits an external borrowing by banks and non-banks and requirements that a certain proportion of external liabilities must be paid off. At one time in Germany a 'penalty' on banks' excess external liabilities was imposed with each financial institution's rediscount quota (borrowing capacity) at the central bank being reduced by the amount of any external liabilities in excess of stipulated levels. Many European countries also imposed ceilings on banks' domestic credit in order to reduce the incentive for banks to seek external funds to switch into domestic currency to increase domestic lending. Many European countries have also at times directly limited the extent of bank switching of foreign currency liabilities into domestic currency. On occasion controls were specifically designed to limit speculative, while allowing non-speculative, flows by imposing different regulations on the maturity of banks' external liabilities with less stringent controls applied as the maturity lengthens. In addition, Swiss banks agreed in August 1971 to limit the conversion into Swiss francs of U.S. dollar inflows that appeared to be of a speculative nature. The Swiss authorities also require non-resident borrowers of Swiss francs on the domestic bond market to convert the SWF proceeds into foreign currency. This, in effect, induces a net capital outflow.

Direct primary measures became more common during the 1960s as controls and measures directed at banks and other financial institutions were gradually circumvented. A particularly good example was the imposition of the *Bardepot* by the monetary authorities in Germany in 1972. As banks had been increasingly constrained in accepting external funds an inevitable process of financial *disintermediation* occurred as commercial and industrial enterprises borrowed directly in foreign money markets. To offset this the Bundesbank responded by placing reserve requirements on these enterprises and in effect treated them like banks. The *Bardepot* required 40 per cent (later 50 per cent) of funds borrowed externally to be placed interest-free on deposit at the central bank which in effect required enterprises to borrow (and pay interest upon) double the amount that could profitably be utilised. Other direct-control mechanisms are noted in Table 8.1 (p. 109).

Except where banks are expressly prohibited from paying interest on external deposits, interest-rate measures are essentially market orientated. A major problem with their use, however, is the potential conflict between internal and external requirements. 'Operation Twist', attempted in the United States in the early 1960s, was a technique which in principle alleviated this conflict. By raising short-term relative to long-term rates, a short-term capital inflow may be induced without dampening domestic investment. It necessarily assumes that open-market operations can change the term structure of interest rates and that short-term rates are exclusively applicable to external capital flows, while long-term rates are relevant for domestic investment. Other governments have manipulated the interest-rate mechanism in the face of a conflict between internal and external requirements by raising interest rates as an anti-inflation measure, while imposing a special withholding tax on the interest payable to non-residents.

THE MEASURES IN PRACTICE

Measures specifically designed to influence the pattern of capital movements for domestic monetary management reasons were frequent during the 1960s.[1] Indeed, for some countries (Germany and Switzerland in particular) policy measures with respect to capital movements were regarded as an integral part of domestic monetary policy.

The main policy measures adopted at various times during the 1960s by many European governments were: (i) currency swaps between the central bank and commercial banks; (ii) reserve requirements on external liabilities of domestic banks; (iii) limitations on the effective interest rate that could be paid by banks on deposits by non-residents; (iv) direct limitation on the size of banks' *net* external liabilities (i.e. the extent of switching external funds into domestic currency); and (v) discouragement to non-residents in acquiring domestic assets.

Currency swaps (whereby the central bank sells foreign currency spot to the commercial banks for domestic currency and buys the currency forward from the banks) is a form of forward exchange market intervention. It is a positive encouragement to the banks to increase their external assets (financed by giving up domestic currency to the central bank) as the central bank agrees to buy back the foreign currency at a favourable price. In so doing it induces a preferential covered interest-rate differential to the banks for foreign rather than domestic investment. This technique was used extensively by the German, Netherlands and Swiss monetary authorities, both to encourage capital outflows *per se*, and to neutralise the domestic monetary consequences of capital inflows (see Chapter 10).

Reserve requirements on external liabilities reduce the profitability to the banks of accepting external deposit (as they freeze a proportion of the funds received), and may be placed on *gross* or *net* external liabilities and upon either *levels* or *increases* above stipulated levels. External liabilities (deposits) may be in either domestic or foreign currency (the latter being euro-currency deposits). With respect to external liabilities denominated in domestic currency (e.g. non-resident holders of DM deposits at banks in Germany) reserve requirement on *gross* liabilities are necessary to discourage capital inflows. A foreign currency liability, on the other hand, represents a net capital inflow only to the extent that banks sell the foreign currency for domestic currency. Therefore, reserve requirements on the banks *net* foreign currency liabilities suffice to discourage capital inflows.

Although several countries imposed such measures intermittently during the 1960s, a barrage of controls was established in the early 1970s. The process tended to escalate both within each country (as more and more measures were needed in the face of substantial capital inflows) and between countries as controls in one deflected capital to other countries. In a sense, Europe experienced a process of *competitive exchange control* in the face of the weakness of the dollar, and the Smithsonian multilateral exchange-rate adjustments needed to be buttressed by measures to prevent capital flows from the United States to Europe. Ultimately, the measures proved ineffective and governments ceased to support exchange rates at rigid levels. Thus the attempt to resist the conflict between fixed exchange rates and domestic monetary control was first made by restricting capital flows. But eventually, as controls became more extensive, the conflict was removed by adopting floating exchange rates. It became increasingly apparent that the extensive use of such capital account measures was introducing distortions to international transactions that were never intended. They were also becoming internationally competitive and offsetting, and needed to be made more intensive and extensive within each country as initial and limited measures were gradually circumvented. The period after generalised floating exchange rates has been generally more free of controls to limit capital inflows though, as already noted, Germany, Switzerland and Japan did adopt measures to limit the upward pressure on their currencies in 1977 and 1978.

CONCLUSIONS

The broad policy options have been outlined. Throughout the post-war period the monetary authorities have applied measures to limit capital inflows. On the domestic side the measures amounted to an attempt at pursuing an independent monetary policy under circumstances where it tended to be undermined by substantial capital flows. On the external side the policies were designed to limit either changes in the reserves or movements in the exchange rate. Exchange control, and other policies relating to capital flows, have been attempts to resolve a basic conflict of internal and external monetary policy. This conflict can be alleviated to the extent that high interest rates required for domestic reasons do not induce offsetting capital inflows. It is in this context that monetary authorities have frequently sought to limit such flows. In the final analysis capital account policies are an attempt to retain a degree of monetary independence in a system of fixed exchange rates and a high degree of international capital mobility. Also, in a floating exchange-rate regime they may be used to limit movements in exchange rates due to capital flows.

SELECTED BIBLIOGRAPHY

Katz, S. I. (1969) *External Surpluses, Capital Flows and Credit Policy*, Princeton Essays in International Finance, No. 22 (Princeton University Press).

Mills, R. H. (1972) 'Regulation on Short Term Capital Movements', Recent Techniques in Selected Countries', *Federal Reserve Board Discussion Paper* (Washington, D.C.).

O.E.C.D. (1972) *Economic Outlook* (1972) pp. 71–7.

9
Euro-currency Markets and their Control

A substantial proportion of international capital movements takes place through the euro-currency markets, and from time to time policy-makers contemplate direct policy measures to limit the role and power of the markets to contribute to international capital movements. Such measures envisage restricting the *institutions* which create the markets rather than altering the fundamental forces making for international capital transfers. Implicit in the argument must be the notion that the markets add to the volume of world credit and capital movements *compared with what would be the case if the markets did not exist*. If, on the other hand, the euro-currency markets are simply alternative mechanisms or channels for credit creation and capital movements that would occur in some other way, control of the markets would have little rationale.

Broadly speaking, international capital and money flows may follow three patterns: (i) directly from one country to another as when banks in the United States make loans to borrowers in other countries; (ii) from surplus sectors in one country to a euro-currency market and in turn to deficit sectors in other countries; and (iii) from surplus units in one country to deficit units *in the same country* again via the euro-currency market. This last pattern will occur if the euro-currency market is in some sense a more 'efficient' financial inter-mediation mechanism than the domestic financial system. One possibility, therefore, is that the intermediation of the euro-currency markets may simply alter the channel of capital and credit flows rather than increase the total. For instance, channel (ii) may, and almost certainly does to some extent, divert funds from channel (i), and hence controlling this mechanism will not necessarily reduce the total flow of funds and credit availability in the world economy.

Since the early days of the euro-currency markets there have been calls for some form of control based on the notion that they are money and credit mechanisms outside the immediate sphere of influence of domestic monetary authorities. As such, it is claimed, domestic monetary measures may be frustrated and offset by transactions in these uncontrolled markets. In the 1960s, at times of currency unrest, there were frequent calls for control. The markets were also seen as a mechanism through which the effect of monetary policy in the United States was transmitted to Europe via U.S. banks borrowing in the euro-dollar market to offset domestic liquidity constraints. Indeed, it was sometimes the case that through this mechanism the induced rise in interest rates in the euro-dollar market, and hence in domestic money markets in Europe, was greater than that in the United States. But this was a reflection of the rigidities created by the combination of Regulation Q in the United States and controls on capital outflows from the United States.

Ultimately, policy-makers may be concerned at five main features of the euro markets: (i) their contribution to the growth of international liquidity; (ii) their ability to add to the total volume of world credit; (iii) their contribution to world net liquidity (in that euro banks engaged in maturity transformation and hence add to net liquidity);[1] (iv) the undermining of domestic monetary policy through capital movements via the markets; and (v) the facilities offered for exchange-market speculation and the instability of exchange rates. Before considering the broader issue of credit creation through the euro markets, a brief review of the mechanics of the markets is offered.

NATURE OF THE MARKET[2]

Although the markets are made by banks a more appropriate methodology of analysis is that of non-bank financial intermediation. In other words, the euro-currency markets stand with respect to domestic money and credit markets in very much the same way as do non-bank financial intermediaries within a country stand with respect to the banking system. The analysis is very similar in both cases and raises similar issues with respect to credit creation. Basically a euro-currency market is a market in interest-bearing bank deposits denominated in currencies other than the domestic currency of the banks involved.[3] The euro-dollar market is a market in U.S. bank deposits. Being generally subject to no official regulations (such as compulsory reserve requirements) the margin between deposit and lending rates tends to be narrower in the euro market than in the corresponding domestic money market (see Chart 9.1), and it is from this that the markets derive their competitive strength *vis-à-vis* domestic banking systems. This 'competitive advantage' over their domestic counterparts derives largely from: the absence of officially imposed reserve requirements on banks' foreign currency liabilities, the absence of interest-rate regulation, the economies of scale derived in international business, the more competitive structure of the market, the absence of regulatory expenses such as deposit insurance, a less-constrained asset structure in the absence of official regulations, and the fact that euro banks are not involved in the expensive money transmission process and hence are able to operate with lower fixed costs. The banks may also be located in areas where taxation is low. The most important element is the absence of official regulation (especially the absence of compulsory reserve requirements). Together, these enable euro banks to offer higher deposit rates and lower borrowing rates to non-bank customers.

In the absence of exchange controls it would be expected that arbitrage

CHART 9.1   Domestic and euro-dollar borrowing and lending rates, 1974–6

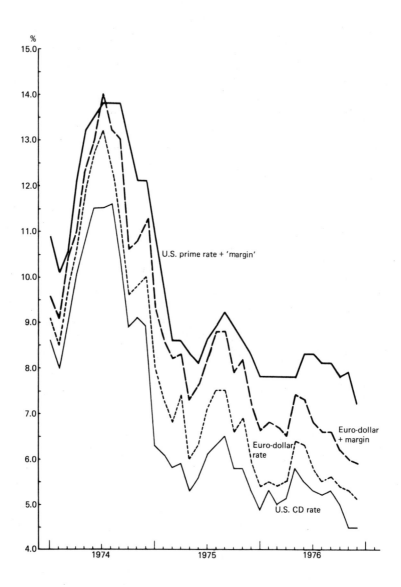

would ensure that dollar interest rates would lie in the following descending order: (i) domestic U.S. banks' prime lending rate plus 'margin';[4] (ii) euro-dollar rate (London Inter-Bank Offered Rate – LIBOR) plus euro-credit lending margin; (iii) euro-dollar deposit rate; and (iv) the U.S. domestic Certificate of Deposit rate. This is precisely the pattern that emerges in the post-1974 period as indicated in Chart 9.1. Throughout this period the two basic features of the euro-dollar market (smaller margins and lower lending and higher deposits rates) in a sense 'justifying its existence', have been maintained.

However, these arbitrage relationships need not hold in a situation where capital controls prevent funds flowing from the United States. This represents the position in the period 1965–74. In 1965 the U.S. authorities instituted a voluntary programme aimed at protecting the balance of payments by limiting the acquisition of foreign assets by U.S. banks and non-banks. In this period euro-dollar rates could rise substantially above both CD rates and the adjusted prime rate as in 1966, 1969 and 1971 (see Chart 13.1, p. 187) while exchange control prevented U.S. resident banks and non-banks arbitraging by borrowing in the United States to invest in the euro-dollar market. Similarly, non-resident borrowers could not take advantage of substantially lower U.S. interest rates, and hence relatively high euro rates could be sustained for considerable periods. On the other hand, U.S. interest rates (the CD rate in particular) set an effective floor to the euro-dollar rate as foreigners were always free to invest in the U.S. money market.

It was during this period of capital controls that banks in the United States used the euro-dollar market as a major source of funds when, constrained by Regulation Q,[5] the rise in domestic interest rates made it difficult to borrow in the United States. This was particularly powerful in 1966 and 1968, but most dramatically in 1969, when interest rates on commercial paper and U.S. Treasury bills rose substantially, and to levels higher than the then maximum allowed to be paid by banks on CDs under Regulation Q. The result was a massive liquidation by non-bank holders of CDs from a peak of $24 billion at the end of 1968 to $11 billion a year later. To secure funds for domestic lending business, U.S. banks therefore borrowed heavily in the euro-dollar market as reflected in a $7 billion rise to ($12.8 billion) in their liabilities against their overseas branches during 1969. Such borrowing, which had a substantial effect on the euro-dollar rate (Chart 13.1, p. 187), was feasible as Regulation Q could not apply in the euro-dollar market, and at that time there were no required reserves to be maintained against bank borrowing from their foreign branches or other foreign banks. While such bank borrowing was substantial (and took the euro-dollar rate at one time to close to 2 percentage points above the adjusted prime rate and close to 4 percentage points over the commercial paper rate) the effect was to induce U.S. banks to compete with each other for funds already available within the U.S. domestic banking system. Through such borrowing tight monetary policy in the United States was spread, via the

euro-dollar market and capital flows, to Europe. The subsequent repayment
of such borrowing (U.S. banks' liabilities to foreign branches fell from $12.8
billion at the end of 1969 to $1.5 billion in June 1971) induced an equally
dramatic fall in euro-dollar and European interest rates (Chart 13.1).

The differential between the domestic CD and the euro-dollar interest rate
since the abolition of U.S. capital controls in February 1974 is indicated in
Chart 7.4, p. 88. The immediate impact of the abolition of capital controls
was a substantial narrowing of the differential between the euro-dollar rate
and the U.S. domestic rate until the middle months of 1974. Following the
international banking difficulties associated with the closure of Herstatt bank
the differential widened temporarily to a peak of 2.5 percentage points in
August as confidence in the euro markets was strained and funds were
transferred to the United States. The differential narrowed sharply during
1975 and remained around 0.3 percentage point thereafter.

The normal pattern of interest rates noted in Chart 9.1 also means that, in
principle, the euro market may at times intermediate between surplus and
deficit sectors *within the same country*. Thus prime depositors in a country
might at times secure a higher deposit rate in the euro market than in their
domestic market (e.g. the euro-dollar deposit rate is higher than the U.S.
Certificate of Deposit rate) while prime borrowers might be able to borrow
more cheaply in the euro than in the domestic bank credit market. In this way
sectors or firms in financial surplus in the United States might indirectly
finance deficit sectors in the United States through the intermediation of the
euro-dollar market. It is essentially this competitive pattern of interest rates
that accounts for the euro-dollar market's survival and continuous growth. It
also follows that the viability of the markets would be severely strained by any
measures (such as compulsory reserve requirements) which would undermine
this interest-rate structure.

SUPPLY AND DEMAND FOR FUNDS

The supply of funds to the euro-(dollar) market may, as noted by Swoboda,[6]
be from three distinct categories of wealth-holders: (i) those who, when
deposit rates at banks in the United States and the euro-dollar market are
equal, prefer to hold euro-dollar deposits because of political considerations
or the convenience of time, knowledge of the banks, and general convenience
of conducting banking business in Europe rather than in the United States; (ii)
those wealth-holders who regard euro-dollar and U.S. bank deposits as
perfect substitutes; and (iii) those whose preference is, other things being
equal, for U.S. bank deposits. Similar considerations apply to borrowers. On
balance, category (iii) seems to dominate and hence deposit rates in the euro
market tend to be marginally higher than in New York. This is largely because
of a slightly higher perceived risk associated with euro-market deposits due to
the absence of a clearly defined lender of last resort, and less secure source of

funds than exists for banks operating in their own national market. Also, there is a greater sovereign risk in that a depositor in the euro-dollar market is subject to two potential exchange-control risks: (i) the Federal Reserve might conceivably block the accounts of non-residents and euro banks held in the United States (and hence London banks might be unable to repay a deposit on maturity); and (ii) the Bank of England might restrict payment by euro banks in London. While neither might be very likely the residual risk remains, whereas deposits in New York are subject only to the first-mentioned risk.

The non-banks supply and demand curves for euro-currency funds are depicted in Figure 9.1; both become very elastic as interest rates in the euro-market approach corresponding interest rates in the United States. The lending rate of banks in the United States places an effective ceiling on the euro-dollar markets' lending rate; if the latter were to move above the former borrowers with access to both markets would borrow in the United States. Similarly, in normal circumstances the domestic bank deposit rate in the United States sets an effective floor to the euro-dollar deposit rate as if the latter falls below this funds are transferred to banks in the United States, and such arbitrage would tend to lower the domestic and raise the euro-dollar deposit rates.

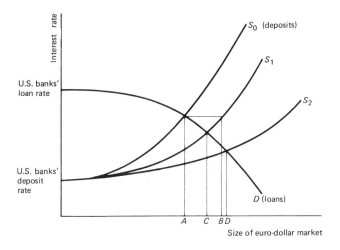

FIGURE 9.1   Supply and demand for euro dollars

It was noted earlier that the appropriate methodology when analysing the euro-currency market is that of non-bank financial intermediation. A euro bank can make new loans only to the extent that it receives a deposit, and when it makes a loan it loses reserves automatically. A transfer of deposits from a bank in New York to a euro bank may induce: (i) an increase in the total volume of world credit as the lending capacity of the euro bank is increased while that of the New York bank is not decreased;[7] (ii) an increased

SCHEMA 9.1   The euro-currency market

Stage 1

U.S. BANK ($m.)

Liabilities	Assets
Demand deposits	
− 1m. (*A*)	
+ 1m. Euro bank I	
Net change 0	0

EURO BANK I

Liabilities	Assets
Time deposits	*Demand deposits*
+ 1m. (*A*)	+ 1m. (demand deposit
	at U.S. bank)
Net change + 1m.	+ 1m.

Stage 2

U.S. BANK ($m.)

Liabilities	Assets
Demand deposits	
− 1m. Euro bank I	
+ 1m. Euro bank II	
Net change 0	0

EURO BANK I

Liabilities	Assets
	− 1m. (demand deposit
	at U.S. bank)
	+ 1m. (time deposit at
	Euro bank II)
Net change 0	0

EURO BANK II

Liabilities	Assets
+ 1m. (time deposit of	+ 1m. (demand deposit
Euro bank I)	at U.S. bank)
Net change + 1m.	+ 1m.

Stage 3

EURO BANK II ($m.)

	Liabilities	Assets
		− 1m. (demand deposit at U.S. bank)
		+ 1m. (commercial loan)
Net change	0	0

U.S. BANK

	Liabilities	Assets
Demand deposits		
	− 1m. Euro bank II	
	+ 1m. commercial borrower	
	− 1m. commercial borrower	
	+ 1m. Banque de France	
Net change	0	0

From G. L. Bell (1973).

velocity of circulation of money; (iii) a multiple increase in credit to the extent that, until interest-rate differentials adjust, a proportion of funds loaned by the euro bank might be subsequently redeposited in the euro-currency market; or (iv) merely a change in the location of credit rather than the total in that borrowing from a euro bank may be an alternative to a U.S. bank which in turn is unable to extend credit elsewhere. Each of these possibilities has a direct parallel in the process of financial intermediation by NBFIs in domestic economies. These points may be appreciated by noting the basic operating details of the market.

MECHANICS OF THE MARKET

The basic mechanics of the euro-dollar market are described in Schema 9.1. The essential point is that the euro-dollar market is in truth an adjunct to the New York money market, and frequently euro-dollar market transactions have a counterpart in the Federal Funds market (inter-bank market in the United States). Thus Corporation *A* holds $1 million on deposit at a bank in New York and decides to switch that dollar deposit to a bank (Euro bank I) in London. The corporation's *time* deposit is allowed to mature and the *demand* deposit is transferred to a bank in London. The balance-sheet positions are described in Stage 1 of the schema. At this point there has been no direct effect on the U.S. money supply or volume of bank deposits[8] as there has been only a change in the ownership of U.S. bank deposits. But the volume of world dollar deposits has risen by $1 million as the U.S. bank has not lost deposits, while the euro bank has gained deposits. For this to be sustainable there must be a willingness by non-banks to hold an increased volume of bank deposits either in the euro-dollar market or within the U.S. domestic banking system. Without this increased demand an initial shift from *time* deposits at banks in the United States to deposits at euro banks creates an excess supply of dollar bank deposits in total. In the final equilibrium, unless directly or indirectly the intermediation of the euro-dollar market induces a net increase in the demand for dollar bank deposits, there will be subsequent adjustments within the euro market and domestic banking system to offset the initial effect on aggregate deposits of the original shift to the euro-dollar market.

Having received funds, Euro bank I will seek to on-lend the deposit, as it is paying interest to the depositor but receiving no interest from the U.S. bank on its *demand* deposit. If Euro bank I on-lends in the inter-bank market to Euro bank II there is a further change in the ownership of U.S. bank deposits (Stage 2), though again no change in the total; and a further \$1 million increase in the world volume of dollar bank deposits. If, at Stage 3, Euro bank II lends to a corporate borrower in France, which in turn sells dollars spot for French francs and the Banque de France buys the dollars to prevent an upward appreciation of the franc, the bank deposit in the United States is transferred to the Banque de France. The key to the issue of whether there is a multiple increase in euro-market credit on the basis of an initial exogenous deposit in the market is the portfolio decision of the ultimate receiver of the dollar deposit – in this case the Banque de France. If it subsequently deposits in the euro-dollar market the process is repeated and a *multiple* creation of euro-market credit occurs. Indeed, the Banque de France could itself experience a multiple increase in foreign-exchange reserve if the exact chain of events was repeated. Whether or not this occurs depends upon how quickly interest rates adjust in New York and the euro-dollar market. In practice they adjust quickly and hence the redeposit ratio and euro-market multiplier are low. On the other hand, if the Banque de France holds its dollar deposit in the United States (see Chapter 12 for a detailed discussion) the expansion in the gross size of the euro market comes to an end.

The net result of the transactions described has been: (i) no change in the U.S. money supply;[9] (ii) a rise in the volume of high-powered money and money supply in France; (iii) an increased volume of world credit (the euro-market loan to the French corporation;[10] (iv) a rise in the world volume of dollar bank deposits; and (v) a rise in foreign-exchange reserves of the Banque de France. There has been a rise in the total volume of world credit as the transfer of funds from the United States to the euro-dollar market raises the lending capacity of euro banks without reducing that of the U.S. banking system. In other words, although the euro market is made by banks, the relevant analysis is that which is traditionally applied to non-bank financial intermediaries within a purely domestic system. The essential point is that, although there may be several transactions in the euro-dollar market, the dollars in no sense ever leave the U.S. banking system. The euro-dollar market is an offshore market in U.S. bank deposits. For this reason the ability of banks in the United States to raise their aggregate lending potential by borrowing from the euro-dollar market is limited as, in effect, the banks are competing for funds already within the U.S. banking system. However, to the extent that the reserve requirements on U.S. banks external liabilities are lower than on domestic liabilities, the lending capacity of domestic banks is increased by the freeing of reserves.

MULTIPLE CREDIT CREATION

This leads to consideration of whether, as traditionally argued within domestic banking systems, there may be a *multiple* creation of credit and deposits on the basis of an initial transfer of funds to the market. An important distinction must be drawn between *pyramiding* (inter-bank deposits) and genuine *credit creation*. The bulk of euro-currency market transactions is between banks with one bank in effect passing on deposits to another as described above. While this may produce a substantial pyramiding of deposits it will have little economic significance as aggregate demand is unaffected just as is the case with domestic inter-bank borrowing and lending. On the other hand, a genuine *multiple* creation of credit can occur if any proportion of the ultimate loan to a non-bank borrower is directly or indirectly placed back in the market. This process is well-established in standard textbook analyses of domestic banking systems as, bank deposits being money, a high proportion of funds loaned are presumed to be redeposited within the banking system. The size of the domestic bank credit multiplier in these models is determined, among other factors, by the size of the banks' reserve ratio. There may also be a multiple creation of domestic credit on the basis of an initial transfer of funds to a non-bank financial intermediary if the increased credit induces any redepositing of funds at the NBFI. While the theoretical process may be similar for banks and NBFIs the leakages are assumed to be greater in the latter case.

There is a direct parallel in the euro-currency markets. In Figure 9.1 (p. 119) an initial new deposit (shift in the supply curve) of (AB) causes an immediate adjustment to interest rates (determined by the elasticity of demand for euro dollars) and a partially offsetting movement along the supply curve. The net increase in the size of the market is AC and the 'multiplier' is less than unity.[11] However, if funds are redeposited there may be a multiplier of greater than unity (in Figure 9.1 this implies a subsequent shift in the supply curve to S_2). Such redepositing may be by the central banks who acquire the dollars being sold for domestic currency by the non-bank borrower though, in 1971, central banks in the Group of Ten countries agreed to refrain from depositing in the market. In figure 9.1 the multiplier is AC/AB, i.e. < 1 with no redepositing and AD/AB, i.e. > 1 with redeposits.

On the face of it, it might appear that the standard bank-credit multiplier analysis could be applied to the euro-currency market where the value of the multiplier would be given by:

$$K = \left(\frac{1}{1-(1-e)\cdot d} \right),$$

where e is the reserve ratio of the euro-(dollar) market (euro banks demand deposits at banks in America), and d is the redeposit ratio (the proportion of funds loaned to non-banks that is directly or indirectly redeposited in the euro market). An initial deposit of funds in the market raises, by an equal amount, the reserves of euro banks at banks in America as described in Schema 9.1 (p. 120) above. Clearly, the ultimate value of the multiplier is determined by the value of e and d. The smaller is e and the larger is d the greater is the multiplier. In fact reserves of euro banks are low (and the ratio to euro deposits has been on a trend decline) as: the maturity of euro-banks' assets and liabilities is fairly closely matched, there is no legal compulsion to maintain reserves, maturities of liabilities tend to be fixed and, given that banks reserves in their domestic currency against domestic liabilities are often high, these excess reserves may serve as indirect reserves for euro-currency business.

Thus the value of the multiplier could be high as the basic reserve ratio is low. But the evidence indicates a low multiplier. For instance, assuming redeposits of funds by central banks, Hewson and Sakakibara (1974) estimate the multiplier at around 1.45.[12] This implies that the redeposit ratio is low, i.e. the leakages from the market are high. This may not be surprising given that borrowers of funds almost certainly switch into domestic currency with the ultimate recipients of funds tending to maintain bank deposits predominantly within their own domestic banking systems. If the dollars sold by euro-market borrowers are purchased by central banks the key issue becomes the portfolio preference of central banks as between deposits in the euro-dollar market and the other alternative forms of holding dollar assets.

In the final analysis the standard multiplier analysis as applied to domestic banking systems is not a fruitful approach to the analysis of credit creation in the euro-currency market as there is no clearly defined reserve base in the euro markets, the reserve ratio is clearly not constant, and, the leakages are high (redeposit ratio low) as interest rates adjust quickly. Indeed, portfolio balance theories of banking behaviour question the usefulness of the traditional multiplier concept even when applied to domestic banking systems and the determination of the money supply within a purely national economy. Within the U.K. banking system the concept of a multiple creation or destruction of bank deposits on the basis of exogenous changes in reserves has long ceased to be a useful representation of the money-supply process. The substantial growth experienced in the euro-dollar market is associated not with a high internal multiplier but with a similar rapid growth in monetary and financial aggregates in the United States. Thus, in line with standard portfolio balance theory, all markets share in the distribution of any increase in the total supply of dollar assets and, through a learning process and a strong competitive position, the euro-dollar market has tended to increase its share of the total. This is similar reasoning to that applied to the growth of non-bank financial intermediaries within domestic financial systems. Thus as the leakages are high and, because interest rates adjust quickly a continuous flow of funds from the United States is unlikely, the concept of an internal multiplier is of limited value and, in any case, is likely to be low. The centrepiece of the analysis should be the elasticity of the supply and demand curves for euro-currency funds, rather than the concept of a multiplier.

THE NBFI ANALOGY EXTENDED

The analysis of the credit potential of the euro markets is similar to that of non-bank financial intermediaries within a domestic financial system. It is useful, therefore, to review the analytical framework of non-bank financial intermediation as it yields relevant insights into the operation of the euro-currency markets. A transfer of funds from a bank to an NBFI (and the subsequent on-lending) adds to the total volume of credit, rather than substitutes for credit that would otherwise have been provided by the banks, only when one or more of the following conditions are satisfied: (i) NBFIs, because of their 'efficiency', are able to offer credit at lower interest rates than are banks and credit demand is interest sensitive; (ii) banks are either unable or unwilling to complete in the credit markets of NBFIs; (iii) banks ration credit and cause an excess demand for credit at current interest rates which can be absorbed by NBFIs; (iv) the profit-maximising level of bank credit is constrained by an officially imposed limitation on bank reserves; and/or (v) the banking system is not fully competitive with the result that profits are excessive and derive from an uncompetitively wide differential between deposit and lending interest rates. If both banks and NBFIs are fully competitive, in that their interest-rate structures are such as to eliminate excess demand for credit, NBFIs may increase credit only to the extent that, at their lower interest rates, the demand for credit is raised. Without this, any expansion of NBFI credit must be at the expense of credit that would otherwise have been given elsewhere.

It follows, therefore, that NBFIs add to the *total* volume of credit only to the extent that either there is excess demand for credit at prevailing interest rates, or their lower interest rates stimulate increased demand.

Precisely similar arguments apply to the credit effects of the euro-currency markets, bearing in mind that these markets may be taken to be fully competitive with no excess demand at prevailing interest rates, and that U.S. banks do compete in the same credit markets as euro banks.

WORLD CREDIT EFFECT

The effect of euro-dollar market transactions upon the total volume of world credit (and hence what some commentators believe to be the market's inflationary potential) is complex and cannot be measured simply in terms of the volume of euro-dollar market lending itself. In particular allowance has to be made for the fact that some of this credit demand may have been switched from alternative sources, and hence is not a net increase in world demand for credit. Also the effect upon the lending capacity of banks in the U.S. and other national banking systems must be considered. An important issue, therefore, and particularly relevant to the question of whether the euro markets should be officially regulated in order to control the volume of world credit, is the extent to which the euro markets add to the total volume of world credit and availability of funds, or simply provide alternative channels for credit that would otherwise have been extended through other means.

In general a flow of funds to the euro dollar market may add to the total volume of world credit if:

(1) The demand for credit is sensitive to the lower lending interest rates charged by euro banks compared with lending rates in national banking systems (see Chart 9.1, p. 116).

(2) The competitive strength of euro banks forces domestic bank lending rates to be lower than would otherwise have been the case, and again the demand for credit is interest-sensitive.

(3) Borrowing from the euro-dollar market, with the funds switched into some other currency, induces a rise in the external component of high-powered money through central-bank foreign-exchange-market intervention, and this increases the lending capacity of domestic banks in the country experiencing the capital inflow. This increases the total volume of credit in the country to the extent that: (i) the borrowing from the euro-dollar market is not an alternative to borrowing from domestic banks; and (ii) there is a demand for credit in the country which is not being met because domestic banks are inhibited by a shortage of reserves.

(4) Similarly, if U.S. residents are borrowing in the euro-dollar market in a situation where there is an excess demand for credit at prevailing interest rates in the United States. Also, in principle, some U.S. borrowers may have access to' euro-market credit who would not have been able to borrow from banks in the United States because of the latter's higher creditworthyness criteria.

(5) Euro banks may, through competitive pressures, actually generate a demand for credit that would not otherwise have existed. Some analysts have maintained, for instance, that in the early 1970s euro banks were at times inducing developing countries to borrow in the markets on a larger scale than they had initially intended.

(6) Countries in need of external finance may not have access to national

banking systems (e.g. in the United States) because of official restraints on external lending by domestic banks. In the period 1963–74, for instance, most countries did not have access to the U.S. market because of restrictions placed on external lending by banks in the United States.

(7) The volume of world credit may be increased to the extent that capital flows through the euro markets from countries where the banking system has an excess supply of funds to those with an excess demand. However, the euro markets add to the total volume of world credit in this way only to the extent that such flows would not have occurred except for the intermediary role of the euro-currency markets.

In effect, and abstracting from the complications of borrowers and lenders through the euro-dollar market frequently being in different countries, the euro-dollar market may add to the total volume of credit in much the same way as, within a national monetary system, non-bank financial intermediaries add to the total volume of domestic credit.

On the other hand, the euro-dollar market may be an alternative channel for credit that would otherwise have occurred in a different way. Thus, because of their competitive strength, euro banks may cause borrowers to switch their demand from banks in the United States which, because there is no excess demand for credit, are unable to find alternative borrowers. Also, in a situation where U.S. banks have no excess reserves, euro-market borrowers might otherwise have attempted to borrow from banks in the United States and, in order to prevent interest rates rising, the Federal Reserve might in these circumstances have increased the reserves and the lending capacity of the U.S. banking system. In both cases, the existence of euro-dollar market lending does not add to the volume of credit that would have existed without the euro market.

GEOGRAPHICAL PATTERNS

When considering the effect of euro-dollar market lending upon the volume of world credit the precise geographical pattern of financial flows through the market must also be considered. The analysis is outlined in Table 9.1, which summarises the effect upon the volume of credit resulting from a series of financial flows through the euro-dollar market. Three countries (X, Y and the $U.S.$) are considered, and borrowers may be either banks (subscript B) or non-banks (subscript NB). In each case the assumption is made that central banks intervene in the foreign-exchange market to hold exchange rates constant. It follows, therefore, that the external component of high-powered money in countries X and Y is affected by such financial flows. While, in competitive financial systems, there is doubt about the concept of the bank credit multiplier, for expositional purposes the notion is retained in the sections to follow.

TABLE 9.1 Credit effect of financial flows through the euro-dollar market

Funds flow from bank deposits in country:	Via euro-dollar market to:	Banks (B) or non-banks (NB) in country:	EFFECT OF FLOWS UPON VOLUME OF CREDIT			
			in country X	in country Y	in the U.S.	in the world
(1) X		$U.S._B$	minus	n.a.	zero[1]	minus
(2) X		$U.S._{NB}$	minus	n.a.	zero/plus	minus
(3) X		Y_B	minus	plus	zero	zero/plus/minus
(4) X		Y_{NB}	minus	zero/plus	zero	zero/plus/minus
(5) U.S.		$U.S._B$	n.a.	n.a.	zero[1]	zero
(6) U.S.		$U.S._{NB}$	n.a.	n.a.	zero/plus	zero/plus
(7) U.S.		Y_B	n.a.	plus	zero	plus
(8) U.S.		Y_{NB}	n.a.	zero/plus	zero	zero/plus

[1] There might be some slight rise in bank credit in the United States by virtue of the fact that, since 1978, U.S. banks are not required to keep reserves against borrowings from their overseas branches. In 1969, in order to limit U.S. bank borrowing from overseas branches, a 10% reserve requirement was placed on increases in such borrowing over stipulated amounts (Regulation M). This was raised to 20% in 1971, lowered to 8% in 1973, to 4% in 1976 and to zero in 1978. In effect, U.S. banks can now transform reserve-bearing deposits into reserve-free liabilities and hence free reserves. The lending capacity of banks is thereby raised.

Case (1)   A flow of funds from banks in country X to the euro-dollar market may induce a multiple reduction in bank lending in country X if initially the banks had no excess reserves. This is because the capital outflow induces the central bank to buy the domestic currency being sold for dollars, which as a counterpart has a reduction in the reserves of banks in country X at the central bank. However, the United States being a reserve currency centre (see Chapter 12), there is no change in the volume of high-powered money or total bank deposits in the United States. While the dollar reserves of the central bank of country X are reduced, the U.S. banking system is automatically insulated from such capital flows. Thus, although U.S. banks may borrow from the euro-dollar market, there is no change in the total volume of bank deposits or high-powered money in the United States. As noted earlier, U.S. bank borrowing in the euro-dollar market simply changes the ownership of bank reserves and deposits. On balance, therefore, the volume of world credit is likely to be reduced by these transactions.

Case (2)   As in the previous example, high-powered money is reduced in country X and remains unchanged in the United States. The credit potential of the U.S. banking system is unaffected. If the euro-dollar funds are borrowed by non-banks in the United States the total volume of credit in the United States is unchanged if the funds are used to repay existing bank credit, or rises if the borrowing would not otherwise have been made elsewhere or there previously existed a degree of excess demand for credit. The total volume of credit extended to U.S. residents may rise, therefore, as the lending capacity of the euro market is increased without impairing that of banks in the United States. On balance, however, there is a potential reduction in the world volume of credit as, through the series of transactions noted, there may be a *multiple* contraction in country X but a single rise in the volume of credit extended to the United States.

Case (3)   The euro-dollar market may intermediate between surplus and deficit sectors in countries X and Y. If banks in country Y borrow funds supplied to the euro-dollar market by surplus sectors in country X, there are equal and opposite changes in the external components of high-powered money in the two countries. Again the U.S. banking system is insulated as dollar reserves are simply switched from central bank X to central bank Y. The effect upon the volume of world credit depends upon the relative value of the bank credit multipliers in the two countries, and upon the strength of demand for credit in each. Credit may expand in country Y only if there is currently an excess demand at prevailing interest rates, or if the inflow causes interest rates to fall and the demand for credit is interest elastic. Also, if the financial flows result from a situation of excess supply in country X and excess demand in Y, the volume of world credit will likely rise as high-powered money is being switched to banking systems with a greater credit potential. In this case credit expands in country Y but remains unchanged in X. On the other hand, if the flow of funds is the result of interest–rate differentials associated with differences in inflation, or because currency Y is expected to appreciate, the financial flow might conceivably be from a country with an excess demand for credit to one whose banking system already has excess reserves. In this case the volume of world credit is likely to contract.

Case (4)   Similar considerations apply as in case (3) except that, when the borrowing is made by non-banks in country Y, the use of funds needs to be considered. Total credit is unchanged in Y if euro-market borrowing represents an alternative to domestic borrowing, but is increased (and possibly by a multiple) if there previously existed an excess demand for credit that the domestic banking system could not satisfy.

Case (5)   A non-bank in the United States transfers a deposit from Chase Manhattan in New York to a euro bank which keeps its account at Chemical Bank in New York. If Chase borrows from the euro market it is seeking to regain the reserves initially lost to the Chemical Bank. The transactions change only the ownership of bank reserves and deposits in the United States.

Case (6)   Again there are no changes anywhere in the volume of high-powered money. However, as the euro-dollar market's lending potential is raised while that of banks in the United States is not impaired (as the deposits are never lost to the U.S. banking system) there will be a net rise in the volume of credit extended to U.S. non-banks if the borrowing represents credit that would not otherwise have been made available in the United States. On the other hand, if there is initially no excess demand for credit in the United States the euro-dollar borrowing by U.S. non-banks changes in the pattern of credit supply but not the total.

Cases (7) and (8)   If funds transferred from deposits at U.S. banks to euro banks are borrowed by banks in country Y (case (7)) there is no effect upon credit potential in the United States, but that of the banking system in country Y is raised. The extent of any rise in the volume of credit depends upon the demand for credit. If the funds are borrowed by non-banks in Y, again high-powered money is increased as the borrower converts the proceeds into domestic currency. Whether the total volume of credit is affected again depends upon the strength of demand and the elasticity of demand with respect to any changes in interest rates that might occur in country Y.[13]

In the final analysis the effect of euro-dollar market transactions is complex and depends upon: (i) the geographical pattern of financial flows; (ii) the reasons for the flows; (iii) the extent of any excess demand for credit in national banking systems; (iv) the sensitivity of credit demand to interest-rate changes; and (v) whether the exchange rate is fixed or floating. Throughout the analysis fixed exchange rates were assumed and hence, unless the central bank offsets changes in the external component of high-powered money, capital flows affect high-powered money in all countries except the United States. If, on the other hand, exchange rates are freely floating all national monetary systems are assumed to be insulated from the effects of balance-of-payments flows. The credit effects in countries X and Y are, therefore, very much smaller when central banks do not intervene in the exchange markets.

Overall, there must be a presumption that at least some of the credit generated in the euro-dollar market is simply an alternative to credit that would otherwise have been provided through other channels.

THE ISSUE OF CONTROL

Given the importance of international capital movements it might appear reasonable that one of the major mechanisms of capital movements should be subject to some form of official control. Indeed, the market's strength derives largely from the absence of control. It is undoubtedly the case that, at times, euro-currency transactions do 'finance' speculation in the foreign-exchange market. It is also true, as demonstrated above, that the market can be a mechanism for adding to the volume of world credit. Through the efficiency of the market, and increased convenience it offers to interest arbitrageurs, the international mobility of capital is also increased and, therefore, problems of domestic monetary management may be accentuated. It might, therefore, seem illogical that monetary controls are applied to the domestic operation of banks, while their euro-currency business remains largely unregulated.

That having been said, however, it does not follow that international capital movements by arbitrageurs and speculation in the foreign-exchange market would cease if in some way the euro-currency markets were disbanded. While the euro-currency markets facilitate the flow of funds between countries, this is not to imply that they somehow *cause* them. Substantial capital flows were a serious problem to policy-makers in the 1920s and 1930s, long before euro-currency markets came into existence. Thus, while the markets may in practice be a vehicle for capital movements, in the absence of comprehensive exchange control (which would also have to encompass the problem of leads and lags in the financing of international trade), substantial capital flows would always be possible between national money markets. The earlier analysis also indicated that while the euro-currency markets potentially add to the volume of world credit, the magnitude needs to be kept in proportion as: (i) the internal credit multiplier is almost certainly small, and (ii) a proportion of the credit generated in the markets is likely to be an alternative to other forms, such as credit from domestic institutions and from the national banking systems of other countries. In Chapter 12 we note the empirical evidence which suggests that capital inflows (however financed) that increase the external component of high-powered money induce some offsetting reduction in commercial banks' borrowing of reserves from the central bank. In this sense changes in the total volume of high-powered money through the external component are partly, and automatically, offset by compensating changes in the domestic component. This suggests that the money supply is at least in part demand- rather than supply-determined, and that there is only limited excess demand for credit in domestic banking systems.

The case for control of the markets on these grounds (i.e. as a means of controlling world credit) is far from overwhelming. But even if it were, there is considerable doubt about whether effective controls could be established. The most likely measures for serious consideration are: (i) internationally agreed reserve requirements applied to euro banks; (ii) specified capital/deposit ratios,[14] which in general declined in the period 1971–5; (iii) open-market operations in the market conducted either by central banks or the BIS; (iv) more stringent agreement among central banks not to deposit funds in the market (as agreed by the Group of Ten in 1971); and (v) generalised application of the U.S. authorities' Regulation M.[15] The essence of all these moves would be to either make euro banking unprofitable (by removing the interest-rate advantage noted in Figure 9.1, p. 119) or to limit the supply of funds.

The most likely measure would be the imposition of compulsory reserve requirements on euro banks which would force the banks to offer a lower deposit rate and/or charge a higher lending interest rate. Clearly there is some level of reserve requirements that would eliminate the competitive advantage of euro banks noted in Chart 9.1, p. 116. However, the difficulty of such a move derives from the fact that there is no central bank or monetary authority with effective jurisdiction over the markets. It is undoubtedly possible for any individual central bank to require banks located in its country to maintain compulsory reserve requirements against their foreign currency liabilities, just as all central banks do on banks' domestic business. Indeed, some central banks do impose such reserve requirements with the result that the euro- currency business of banks in these countries is comparatively small (e.g. Germany). But the rapid growth of offshore financial centres (such as in the Caribbean, the Far East and Bahrain) testifies to the fact that, to be effective in limiting the size of the euro markets, such reserve requirements would need to be imposed by monetary authorities in all countries. The location of the markets has proved to be very flexible and they could move to any country which did not impose reserve requirements. Thus, in the absence of a universal agreement to subject banks' foreign-currency business to a common set of reserve requirements, this form of control is probably not feasible. There will always be some monetary authorities which, in order to gain the tax revenue and employment advantages of having the markets located in their country, will not impose such controls.

It might be possible to extend the agreement on limiting direct central bank deposits in the euro-currency market though, with competitive interest rates, the market is an attractive form of holding external reserves especially for developing countries. There may also be scope to establish agreements between central banks to govern the operations between central banks and their commercial banks (e.g. with respect to swap facilities). But as this is an important technique of domestic monetary policy in some countries (see Chapter 10) such an agreement is unlikely. Another possibility would be to develop techniques of open-market operations in the markets through, for instance, the Bank for International Settlements. Thus the BIS might borrow funds in the market and, in effect, withdraw liquidity. However, even if a strategy could be agreed, it would be unlikely to have a significant effect upon liquidity as the induced upward movement of euro-market interest rates would attract funds from domestic money markets. In other words, while open-market operations would undoubtedly have an effect upon euro-currency interest rates, the effect upon the volume of funds in the market would likely be very limited. There simply is not a fixed quantity in the market a proportion of which can be absorbed by, say, the BIS. Such operations would, through arbitrage, also have a significant impact upon domestic interest rates. Any effect upon the volume of credit would derive from this interest-rate effect.

An altogether different approach would be to remove some of the competitive disadvantages of banks in the United States. This might be done by the Federal Reserve eliminating, or substantially lowering, reserve requirements on *time* deposits, paying interest to the banks on their reserves, and/or ending all remaining restrictions on the payment of interest on domestic bank deposits. In effect, the interest-rate and general competitive advantage of the euro markets could be reduced not by penalising these markets by extending domestic control mechanisms, but by easing restrictions on the domestic banking system.

CONCLUSIONS

While the effect upon the total volume of world credit of financial flows through the euro-currency markets may be exaggerated, the efficiency and convenience of the markets undoubtedly does have significant credit effects. By creating a convenient institutional framework the markets almost certainly do contribute to increased capital flows between countries and exchange-market speculation. In the process the markets do raise the degree of integration between different money centres. The markets act as a financial intermediary and, as such, intermediate the maturity preferences of surplus and deficit sectors in the world economy (sometimes within the same country). Their role in the recycling of OPEC surpluses has been important since 1973,[16] and have enabled OPEC to acquire relatively short-term assets while enabling deficit countries (sectors) to secure long-term liabilities. They have also minimised for OPEC the sovereign risks associated with direct lending to deficit countries. The markets have an important inter-bank segment which offers a convenient and efficient means for banks to adjust their liquidity positions in both foreign and domestic currency. They are also a means of enabling banks to offer forward-exchange facilities to their customers by offering the banks a convenient mechanism for avoiding exchange-rate risk.

But all this is far from arguing that, without the markets, such flows would cease. In many ways the markets provide a convenient channel for flows that, in their absence, would occur in other ways. Thus the main conclusions of the analysis may be briefly summarised: (i) the convenience and efficiency of the market does increase the access to funds by borrowers, interest arbitrageurs and speculators, and as such the euro markets involve an institutional mechanism which facilitates the international flow of funds on a larger scale than would otherwise occur; but (ii) much of the credit and capital movements passing through the markets would occur in the absence of the markets; (iii) the internal credit creating capacity of the markets is probably small; and (iv) given the markets' flexibility (particularly with respect to location), effective control of the markets is not feasible. In the final analysis, the effect upon the volume of world credit is complex and depends, *inter alia* upon the precise geographical pattern of the financial flows through the markets.

The universal application of control mechanisms (such as compulsory reserve requirements in line with those in domestic markets) would undoubtedly impair the competitive position of the euro markets. But in themselves they would not alter the aggregate demand for world credit; existing borrowers would still seek funding. If such demand were switched to the U.S. banking system the initial excess demand for bank credit would induce a rise in U.S. interest rates. The Federal Reserve would then have two broad options: (1) it could ease the pressure on interest rates by supplying bank reserves to enable the banks to meet the increased credit demands; or (ii) it could refuse to increase the lending capacity of domestic banks by failing to increase the supply of bank reserves. In the first case, euro-market controls would only have an effect upon the aggregate volume of world credit to the extent that credit demand was sensitive to the previous small difference in interest rates between the euro and domestic segments of the dollar bank credit market.

In the second case the total volume of U.S. bank credit is constrained by the availability of reserves. While alternative intermediation channels might emerge, the rise in domestic interest rates needed to eliminate the excess demand for bank credit might be substantial and politically unacceptable. Again, the effect of the controls is seen to be dependent upon the interest-rate sensitivity of the demand for credit. It is also apparent that the world credit effect of the euro markets is determined largely by the stance of monetary policy in the major financial centres. In general the markets reflect monetary and credit conditions in the world economy rather than cause them. The euro markets are offshore components of domestic money and credit markets, and their growth reflects the preference for depositors and lenders to move out of purely national money markets into these external markets. This in turn is associated with the efficiency of the markets due, in part, to the absence of the control mechanisms applied to domestic banks. However, the *domestic* and *euro* segments of money markets are, in the absence of exchange control and distortions such as the now largely inoperative Regulation Q in the United States, highly integrated. If there is a high degree of substitutability between the *euro* and *domestic* segments of money markets, and if a competitive equilibrium exists between them, monetary policy directed at domestic markets will affect not only domestic monetary and credit conditions but also the availability of credit in all external markets. The relationship between the *euro* and *domestic* money market is strictly analogous to that between, say, member and non-member banks of the U.S. Federal Reserve System. Because of the power of arbitrage, and the highly integrated system, the behaviour of non-members' balance-sheets reflects almost identically that of member banks. Thus, while U.S. monetary policy measures may have their immediate impact upon member banks, this is generalised throughout the U.S. banking system as, within a highly integrated national financial system, significant interest-rate differentials between different components cannot be sustained. Similarly, credit conditions are also generalised through an integrated system.

The same applies to the euro-currency markets. It follows, therefore, that the euro markets reflect the monetary policy stance of governments throughout the world. They are a reflection of monetary and credit conditions determined by policy and, as such, cannot be regarded as a significant independent factor in world inflation, etc. Within this broad analytical framework, exchange-rate fluctuations, the growth of international liquidity and domestic monetary aggregates, international financial flows, etc., are a reflection of monetary policy particularly, though by no means exclusively, in the United States. Much of the instability that is attributed to the eurocurrency markets is in truth a reflection of divergent monetary policies between countries and the reserve currency role of the U.S. dollar. The euro markets mirror domestic monetary conditions rather than cause them in any significant way.

SELECTED BIBLIOGRAPHY

Bell, G. L. (1973) *The EuroDollar Market and the International Financial System* (London: Macmillan).
Brown, B. (1978) *Money, Hard and Soft* (London: Macmillan).
Clendenning, E. W. (1970) *The Euro Dollar Market* (Oxford: Clarendon Press).

Dufey, G., and Giddy, I. (1978) *The International Money Market* (Englewood Cliffs, N.J.: Prentice-Hall, 1978) pp. 48–77.

Einzig, P., and Quinn, B. S. (1977) *The EuroDollar System* (London: Macmillan).

Giddy, I. H., and Dufey, G. and Min, S. (1975) 'Interest Rates in the U.S. and Euro Dollar Markets', *Weltwirtschaftliches Archiv*, pp. 51–68.

Johnston, R. B. (1979) 'Some Aspects of the Determination of Euro Currency Interest Rates', *Bank of England Quarterly Bulletin*, Mar 1979.

Hewson, J., and Sakakibara, E. (1974) 'Euro Dollar Multiplier: A Portfolio Approach', *IMF Staff Papers*, July 1974.

Klopstock, F. (1968) *The Euro Dollar Market: Some Unresolved Issues*, Essays in International Finance, No. 65 (Princeton University Press).

Llewellyn, D. T. (1979) 'Do Building Societies take Deposits from Banks?', *Lloyds Bank Review*, Jan 1979.

Mayer, H. (1976) 'The BIS Concept of the Eurocurrency Market', *Euromoney*, May 1976.

McKenzie, G. W. (1976) *Economics of the Euro Currency System* (London: Macmillan).

McKinnon, R. I. *The Euro Currency Market*, Essays in International Finance, No. 125 (Princeton University Press).

Stem, C. M., *et al.* (1976) *Eurocurrencies and the International Monetary System* (Washington: American Enterprise Institute for Public Policy Research).

Swoboda, A. K. (1968) *The Euro Dollar Market: An Interpretation*, Essays in International Finance, No. 64 (Princeton University Press).

Willms, M. (1978) 'Money Creation in the Euro Currency Market', *Weltwirtschafliches Archiv*, pp. 201–30.

10
Forward Exchange Policy

In earlier chapters the forward exchange rate, and its relation to the spot rate, was viewed as a key element in international arbitrage. A significant proportion of international capital transfers is conducted on a covered basis, and the forward market is an important medium for exchange-market speculation.

INSTRUMENT OF POLICY

Intervention by central banks in the forward exchange market is, therefore, a potentially attractive policy instrument. By buying or selling its currency in the forward market the central bank may influence the forward rate and hence arbitrage calculations and capital flows. Such intervention has been used in some countries (e.g. Germany, the Netherlands, Switzerland) as a regular technique of domestic monetary policy. It has proved to be a convenient means of influencing domestic monetary conditions through capital movements when purely domestic operations are constrained by, for instance, the absence of an active market in government debt.

The immediate rationale of official intervention in the forward market is to influence the forward rate. In so doing the central bank may have any one of several objectives in mind.

(1) It may seek to influence spot arbitrage capital movements, which in turn is calculated to have a desired impact on the domestic money supply, interest rates, the balance of payments, external reserves or the spot exchange rate. Thus, by minimising a forward discount (or widening a forward premium) through official forward purchases of domestic currency, capital out-flows/inflows are expected to be less/greater than without intervention. Several European central banks have intervened in the forward market (sometimes by offering banks a preferential forward premium) in order to reduce the domestic money supply by buying domestic currency spot for foreign currency from domestic banks, and simultaneously buying the foreign currency forward. In the process the central bank simultaneously reduces the volume of high-powered money and the balance-of-payments surplus. The forward rate offered must clearly be such as to make it profitable for the banks to engage in the transaction. In this way a central bank may influence the pattern of capital flows without changing domestic interest rates.

(2) Intervention may also be designed to reduce the volume of spot speculation by the confidence effect that may derive from a narrower forward discount.

(3) Central bank intervention via *swaps* is also at times motivated by a desire to minimise spot sales of the domestic currency. The Bank of England, for instance, has stated that at times it has intervened in the *swap* market by simultaneously buying sterling spot and selling it forward. The rationale is that by depressing the forward rate close to, or below, the market's expected future spot rate, potential speculative profits of private speculators in the forward market are reduced. This means that the banks spot covering of their forward purchases of sterling is eliminated.

Einzig (1961) and Bloomfield (1964) have described the motives and mechanics of forward-market intervention in detail, and Einzig notes that such intervention dates back to the 1860s and was not uncommon in the 1920s and 1930s. The U.S. authorities, for instance, engaged in forward transactions in the 1960s in order to limit the decline in the U.S. gold stock. In Germany, Switzerland and the Netherlands such intervention (usually in the form of *swaps*) has at times been an integral part of domestic monetary policy designed to influence domestic liquidity conditions in the face of acute balance-of-payments surpluses. At times in Germany the dollars sold to the banks could be used to finance foreign currency loans to domestic customers which removed the necessity of borrowing overseas. In the process the international business of domestic banks was encouraged. This last motive was at times in the mind of the Italian authorities in similar transactions. In Belgium, on the other hand, the objective has at times been to ease the Government's financing difficulties associated with large budget deficits but a limited domestic capital market. Domestic banks might, for instance, borrow dollars and lend the proceeds to the Treasury which in turn sold them spot for Belgian francs and simultaneously bought them forward from the central bank.

A different kind of forward market policy has been used by the U.K. Treasury under the *Exchange Cover Scheme* (ECS). In order to encourage public corporations and local authorities to finance their deficits by borrowing foreign currency (which eases pressure on spot sterling, and boosts the United Kingdom's external foreign currency reserves) the Treasury agrees under the ECS to guarantee the borrower the sterling value of the foreign currency debt. This removes the risk to the borrower that the sterling value of the debt rises if, over the maturity of the loan, sterling depreciates or the currency borrowed appreciates. While no explicit forward transaction actually takes place, it is analogous to forward market intervention in a restricted market. The exchange-rate risk is, in effect, shifted to the Treasury and the tax-payer.

Thus, the mechanisms and motives of intervention in the forward market have been numerous and varied. The main concern of this chapter, however, is with the effect of intervention on capital movements motivated by a desire to influence domestic monetary conditions and the spot exchange rate.

TECHNIQUES OF INTERVENTION

Intervention may be either *discretionary* (where the central bank intervenes intermittently) or *continuous* and designed to effectively peg the forward rate within a fairly narrow range as in the United Kingdom in the period 1945–51 and 1964–7. In the extreme case, where the forward rate is pegged, the central bank stands prepared to supply an infinite volume of forward foreign or domestic currency. As noted in Table 8.1 (p. 108) intervention may also be in a *closed* or *open* market and may be *outright* or in the form of *swaps*. In a closed market the central bank offers forward facilities for a limited number of transactors and types of transaction, while open-market intervention does not make such distinctions. In Germany and Switzerland, for instance, the central banks may deal only with banks for certain purposes, and the forward rate offered by the central bank may diverge from that prevailing in the open market. An *outright* forward transaction by the central bank simply requires the central bank to buy/sell the forward currency being offered/demanded by the banks, but without any spot counterpart transaction. In *swap* transactions, on the other hand, the central bank simultaneously buys/sells currency forward and sells/buys it spot. In the period of continuous intervention (1964–7) the Bank of England engaged in *outright* forward deals. Thus banks would offer their customers the forward rate offered to them by the Bank of England. Thus a forward sale of dollars by the banks to their customers would not induce spot covering by the banks (spot purchase of dollars) as they could immediately cover their open forward position by securing a forward purchase of dollars from the Bank of England. In this way the Bank of England alleviated pressure on spot sterling which would otherwise have resulted from the banks spot covering of their customers speculative forward sales of sterling. In the post-1973 period, on the other hand, currency *swaps* have been the main method used by the Bank of England. The two techniques are discussed in more detail in the Appendix to this chapter.

In a currency *swap* the motive of the central bank might be to reduce domestic liquidity. In this case it sells foreign currency for domestic currency spot and buys back the foreign currency forward at an agreed forward rate. If the covered interest-rate differential based upon the open-market forward rate is such as to induce a capital inflow, the central bank may discourage this by agreeing to sell back the domestic currency sold spot by the banks to the central bank at a sufficient discount against the open market forward rate to make it attractive for the banks to deal with the central bank. Thus, the *closed* market premium must be smaller than that in the *open* market. The required premium is, of course, determined by interest-rate differentials.

MONETARY POLICY TECHNIQUE

As a technique of monetary policy *swaps* may be used to reduce the volume of domestic high-powered money. By buying domestic currency spot and selling it forward the central bank engineers: (i) a reduction in the volume of high-powered money as banks switch from domestic currency to foreign currency at the central bank; (ii) a wider forward discount on domestic currency due to increased net sales in the forward market; and, therefore, (iii) a higher euro-currency interest rate in the currency concerned and, through arbitrage, higher domestic interest rates. This is a useful technique in countries (e.g. Switzerland and the Netherlands) where domestic operations of the central bank are constrained. However, the rise in interest rates, to the extent that it attracts uncovered capital flows, tends to undermine the effect upon domestic high-powered money.

THE BASIC MODEL

The analysis of forward market intervention is demonstrated in Figure 10.1 in terms of the formal model given in Chapter 4 (p. 40). For a given arbitrageurs' schedule AA, and the central bank's capital flow target (assumed to be designed to limit capital outflows), the required volume of intervention depends upon the nature of speculators' expectations. For a given capital-flow target the more depreciated is the expected future spot rate (and the greater confidence with which this expectation is held) the greater is the required volume of intervention. The volume of capital flows at each forward rate is given by the arbitrageurs' schedule AA, and intervention must therefore produce the appropriate rate for the capital-flow target. The spot exchange rate is X_0, and hence the domestic interest rate is higher than the foreign rate as the parity forward rate (P_0) is at a discount. Assuming central bank

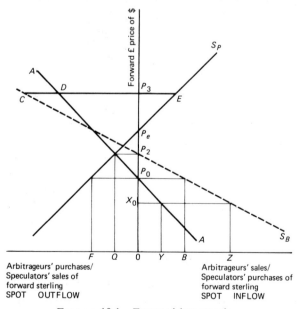

FIGURE 10.1   Forward intervention

intervention does not cause private speculators and arbitrageurs to change their market behaviour, the required volume of central bank forward sales/purchases is given by the schedule S_B for each forward rate. Without intervention the forward rate is determined at P_2 with a spot capital outflow $0Q$. If the desired capital flow is zero a market forward rate of P_0 is necessary. At P_0 arbitrageurs' transactions are zero but there is an excess supply of forward sterling $(0F)$ by private speculators. This excess supply has to be offset by equal $(0B)$ forward purchases by the central bank to prevent the forward rate moving from P_0. Alternatively, if the target capital outflow is P_3D a forward rate of P_3 must be induced at which rate there is excess demand for forward sterling of DE. This requires an equal (P_3C) volume of forward sales of domestic currency by the central bank. Only if the capital-flow target is equal to that produced at the market forward rate (i.e. $0Q$ at P_2) is central bank intervention not required.

The S_B schedule, therefore, defines the volume of forward transactions by the central bank required at each target level of the forward rate which, given the arbitrageurs' schedule, determines the volume of spot capital flows. As implied in Figure 10.1 the central bank almost invariably incurs open speculative positions opposite to those being taken by private speculators! It can easily be verified that, in Figure 10.1, the more inelastic is the speculators' schedule (S_P) the more inelastic becomes the central bank schedule (S_B). This means that: (i) a smaller volume of official intervention is needed for a given target effect on spot capital flows; and (ii) a smaller proportion of official deals are with speculators and a larger proportion are with arbitrageurs. Forward intervention therefore becomes a potential powerful means of influencing capital flows and the spot rate when the speculators' schedule is inelastic.

The profit-and-loss calculation for the central bank is complex even if the spot rate does not change during the maturity of its forward contracts. The central bank makes profits if it buys domestic currency at a forward discount. It makes losses if: (i) it *buys* domestic currency forward at a *premium* (i.e. at a rate below X_0 in Figure 10.1), which is necessary if it seeks a capital inflow in excess of $0Y$ which requires forward purchases in excess of $(0Z)$, or (ii) *sells* domestic currency forward at a *discount* (i.e. if it desires a capital outflow in excess of $0Q$). Outside the range of capital flows QY the central bank incurs losses on its forward transactions which may or may not be a significant consideration for the central bank. If interest rates are in favour (against) the domestic country, intervention is profitable to the central bank only to the extent that it reduces the forward discount (premium) that would exist without intervention, but without turning a discount into a premium. In Figure 10.1 this means that intervention is profitable while it operates at forward rates between P_2 and X_0.

EMPIRICAL EVIDENCE

Econometric investigation of official forward intervention is made difficult by the absence of data on the volume of central bank transactions. What evidence there is, however, suggests that intervention has a powerful effect upon spot capital flows, as a substantial proportion of official forward purchases of domestic currency have a market counterpart in arbitrage rather than speculative forward sales. One of the key issues in determining the effect of intervention is the elasticity of the arbitrage and speculation schedules in the forward market (see Chapter 4). If the speculators' schedule is inelastic (because of high perceived risk or risk-aversion by speculators) the forward rate adjusts substantially to changes in interest rates in the absence of intervention. This means that changes in interest rates are likely to have only a small effect upon the capital account, as the effect upon the *covered* differential is quickly and substantially offset by equilibrating movements in the forward rate. It follows that forward intervention, by preventing the forward rate adjusting, can be a powerful mechanism for inducing capital movements.

Beenstock (1978) estimates (for the period prior to the abolition of U.K. exchange control) that 95 per cent of the variance in the forward sterling rate is explained by arbitrage transactions. This also implies that 95 per cent of official forward sales of sterling would be reflected in equal and opposite spot market transactions with arbitrageurs. The implication is that the speculators' schedule is inelastic, as speculators are not prepared to incur the risk of supplying the counterpart forward exchange to arbitrageurs. Beenstock suggests that, over his estimating period, if the U.K. interest rate is raised by 1 per cent, an initial capital inflow of $1.9 billion is induced. But this is reduced to $0.1 billion by a substantial equilibrating movement in the forward discount. However, if this is accompanied by official forward intervention of $1.8 billion (95 per cent of $1.9 billion) the impact effect of the interest-rate change is not offset. Similarly, in the case of German Bundesbank purchases of forward exchange DM 100 have an estimated spot counterpart of DM 96.8.

The evidence seems to suggest that: (i) the speculators' schedule is frequently inelastic and that, therefore, (ii) forward intervention can have a powerful effect upon the capital account, as the central bank supplies the counterpart forward exchange to arbitrageurs which is not being provided by private speculators.

SPOT AND FORWARD INTERVENTION[1]

The authorities have the option of intervening in either the spot and/or forward markets. If the objective is to secure control over the domestic monetary base four possible alternative intervention strategies are possible, bearing in mind that maturing forward contracts of the central bank affect the monetary base in the same way as does intervention in the spot market:

(1) Fixed spot and forward rates;
(2) Fixed spot and floating forward rate;

(3) Floating forward and spot rates; and
(4) Fixed forward and floating spot rate with intervention in the spot market restricted to offsetting the domestic monetary effect of the central banks maturing forward contracts:

In the first structure the central bank stands prepared to provide an infinite volume of both spot and forward currency. As argued in earlier chapters, the money supply becomes endogenous through the balance of payments, and equilibrium is restored through money supply and interest-rate changes induced by capital flows. In this case there are no equilibrating movements in either the forward or the spot rate and the adjustment falls entirely on interest rates. In the second case the money supply is again endogenous through reserve flows. But equilibrating movements in the forward rate are possible; if the covered differential induces a spot inflow and a rise in the money supply, forward sales of domestic currency by arbitrageurs induce an equilibrating depreciation of the forward rate.

The third strategy involves no intervention in either market with both rates freely floating. A balance-of-payments deficit induces a depreciation of the spot rate and, if the elasticity of expectations is greater than zero, the forward rate is also likely to depreciate. Equilibrium is restored when the net depreciation of the spot and forward rates has induced a capital inflow and a sustainable structure of the current and capital accounts. The money supply is not influenced by external transactions, as there is no change in the external component of high-powered money due to the domestic monetary counterpart of either spot market intervention or of maturing forward contracts of the central bank.

The fourth alternative implies two intervention rules: (i) intervention in the forward market to peg the forward rate at a fixed level; and (ii) intervention in the spot market to offset the monetary effect of maturing forward commitments of the central bank. Forward sales of domestic currency by the central bank have no immediate effect upon high-powered money, but induce an expansion when the contract matures and domestic bank balances are increased. By restricting spot intervention to offsetting the monetary effects of forward maturities, high-powered money is insulated from the effect of external transactions. If the balance of payments is in deficit, and at current interest rates the central bank is buying domestic currency forward (implying a spot capital inflow), the spot rate will depreciate. This means that, with a fixed forward rate, the forward discount (premium) narrows (widens) and the covered interest-rate differential moves in the country's favour. This induces equilibrating capital movements. The advantage of this intervention strategy over that of a floating spot and forward rate is that, in the latter case, if the elasticity of expectations is greater than zero the degree of fluctuation in spot rates will be greater than when the forward rate is pegged. In the freely floating-rate case the forward rate depreciates with the spot rate and hence equilibrating movements in the forward *discount* are less. The required volume

144   INTERNATIONAL FINANCIAL INTEGRATION

of capital flows materialises only when the spot rate has depreciated by an amount required to produce the required *net* narrowing of the forward rate. The problem with the fourth strategy is, however, that if the spot rate is declining and the central bank is buying its currency forward it incurs losses to the extent that it is buying from speculators (see discussion below). Also, forward speculative sales of the currency may become substantial in such a situation. Nevertheless, it is an intervention strategy with the advantage over the floating spot rate case of smaller fluctuations in the spot rate.

BANK OF ENGLAND EXPERIENCE

The policy of the British monetary authorities has varied substantially in the post-war period with five subperiods identified: (1) 1945–51 when the forward rate was pegged at $\frac{3}{8}$ cents above or below the par spot rate; (2) 1951–64 when the forward rate was left free with the exception of occasional intervention (e.g. 1957); (3) in the period 1964–7 there was very substantial support of the forward rate by the Bank of England in the face of, at times, substantial pressure on the spot rate; (4) after the formal devaluation of the spot rate in 1967 forward intervention was ended (partly because of the apparent losses made by the Bank of England in buying forward sterling prior to the substantial devaluation of the spot rate); and (5) in the post-1973 period the Bank of England has occasionally engaged in swap transactions of a 'bear-squeeze' variety. The last-mentioned implies the opposite strategy to that adopted in the 1964–7 period. In the earlier period the Bank was a heavy and persistent buyer of forward sterling, while the bear-squeeze involves forward sales of sterling. The effect of intervention on the forward discount is seen in Chart 7.3 (p. 86). Over the period as a whole the Bank of England has been both a seller and purchaser of forward sterling even though, in both periods, the objective was to indirectly support the spot exchange rate.

In the period 1951–64, and in evidence to the Radcliffe committee of inquiry, the authorities were sceptical about official forward intervention. The prevailing opinion was that support of forward sterling simply enabled speculators to finance forward transactions at virtually zero cost, and that this increased the volume of forward speculative sales. Clearly, the closer the forward rate is to the current spot rate the cheaper it is to finance speculation, and the greater the potential speculative profits if the domestic currency is subsequently devalued. If the spot rate is not subsequently devalued, speculators are able to cover their position by buying domestic currency spot (to meet their forward commitments) at a rate close to the forward rate they contracted to supply domestic currency. The official policy changed dramatically in November 1964 and, until November 1967, the Bank of England continuously purchased forward sterling to prevent the forward rate falling to a substantial discount. The rationale of the policy was to: (1) retain a loyal clientele of existing non-resident holders of sterling (exchange control at that time limited U.K. residents' ability to sell sterling spot); (2) reduce speculative spot sales of sterling through the hoped-for confidence effect of the Bank being seen to be a purchaser of domestic currency; (3) induce covered spot capital inflows by an appropriate covered interest differential; and (4) support spot sterling without the necessity of totally subjecting domestic interest-rate policy to external requirements. The arguments in favour of such almost unlimited intervention, and the nature of the profits and losses to the central bank, are discussed in a later section. However, as noted by Tew (1977), '[the policy] ended up, in the weeks preceding devaluation, by affording almost unlimited opportunities for bear speculation, with the Bank of England not daring to withdraw its support in the forward market lest this be taken to imply that the British authorities had taken the decision to devalue'.

BEAR-SQUEEZE

In contrast the Bank of England has on occasions in the post-1973 period intervened in a different way. It has, at various times, attempted to *widen* the forward discount by simultaneously buying spot and selling forward sterling. This has the effect of raising euro-sterling interest rates and the spot rate, and making 'short positions' in sterling more expensive. The Bank of England, in so doing, hopes to discourage private speculative spot sales by itself forcing down the forward rate (raising euro-sterling rates) to near to the future spot rate expected by speculators. The rationale of the bear-squeeze has been explained succinctly by the Bank of England:

> When commercial banks outside the United Kingdom (and therefore not subject to UK exchange control) expect the spot rate to fall sharply, they may decide to 'borrow' sterling through a swap transaction (i.e. simultaneously buying spot and selling forward sterling – normally against US dollars), and then sell the sterling proceeds spot; alternatively, they may finance an earlier sale of spot sterling by such 'borrowing'. These operators hope that, at some future date, they will be able to buy sterling more cheaply than the forward rate deriving from the swap deal, and thus make a profit. However, the Bank can sometimes discourage such business by borrowing sterling themselves in a similar fashion, thereby depressing the forward rate close to, or below, the future rate expected by the market. In this case, the possibility of profit to commercial banks is reduced; so fewer banks would sell spot sterling while others, short of sterling, might prefer to buy spot sterling rather than incur the increased cost of borrowing sterling through a swap deal.[2]

The rise in the euro-sterling interest rate and in the spot rate might also 'punish' speculators who are forced to borrow sterling at high euro-sterling rates in order to close short positions in the currency and at a disadvantageous spot rate. The precise mechanisms of intervention are described in the Appendix to this chapter.

SUPPORTING FORWARD STERLING: 1964-7

The rationale of forward operations may be conveniently summarised by considering the pros and cons of the Bank of England's policy of supporting forward sterling in the period 1964-7. In this period the spot rate was fixed at $2.8 = £1 though there were, at times, expectations that the rate would be devalued to a new fixed level. Extensive exchange control also prohibited resident capital outflows. In the face of a weak balance-of-payments position, and speculative sentiment frequently against sterling, the Bank of England purchased substantial amounts of forward sterling. The object of the exercise was essentially to alleviate pressure on the spot exchange rate and over the period the forward discount generally did not exceed 3 per cent. Immediately after support ceased in 1967, the forward discount went to 8 per cent.

The arguments in favour of the policy may be summarised:

(1) By minimising the forward discount a favourable covered interest differential to attract non-resident spot purchases of sterling could be achieved without the necessity of high domestic interest rates.
(2) Intervention might also reduce hedging of existing non-resident holdings of sterling in the spot market. Without intervention the forward discount might have induced existing holders of sterling to protect the foreign currency value of their sterling investments by selling sterling spot for foreign currency as forward protection would have been expensive with a wide forward discount. By offering forward protection at a low cost the Bank hoped that the need for spot protection would be reduced.
(3) Similarly, such a policy almost certainly shifted some speculation that would otherwise have been conducted in the spot market into the forward market. As already noted the potential profit from forward speculation (if the spot rate is subsequently devalued) is reduced the wider is the forward discount. Speculative profits derive from the difference between the forward rate and the new spot rate, and the closer is the forward rate to the new spot rate the smaller are speculators' profits. Conversely, the wider is the forward discount the greater are speculators' losses if the spot rate is not devalued, as speculators have eventually to buy spot sterling (to meet forward commitments) with a larger volume of foreign currency than is received at the maturity of the forward contract. On both counts forward support operations are likely to shift some speculation from the spot to the forward market. There is an immediate reduction in pressure in the spot market and saving of foreign exchange reserves. There is no ultimate loss either (in fact the Bank of England makes a profit) if sterling is not subsequently devalued as, at the time of maturity, although the Bank of England pays out foreign currency, the speculator has also to buy sterling spot to meet his side of the contract. However, as noted below, for the same reason the policy is also likely to increase the total volume of forward

speculation as well as shifting it from the spot market, and this imposes a cost on the Bank of England *if the spot rate is devalued.*

(4) The policy might also reduce the combined volume of spot and forward speculative sales of sterling if the fact of intervention induces favourable confidence effects. Given that the Bank of England's forward commitments were not published, there might be such a net favourable effect if confidence would otherwise have been weakened through a wide forward discount and declining external reserves.

(5) Intervention also removed the necessity of the banks covering in the spot market the forward speculative sales of their customers. In a situation where the banks could not easily match these speculative forward sales in the forward market they would reduce their own open position by selling sterling spot for foreign currency to match their own forward sales of foreign currency to customers (Chapter 5). With the Bank of England agreeing to provide the banks with the forward foreign currency such spot covering became unnecessary.

(6) Intervention might also have a significant positive effect on external reserves through the leads and lags of foreign trade financing. A wide forward discount on domestic currency induces, through the covered interest-rate arbitrage mechanism, foreign buyers of British exports to borrow sterling to pay the exporter and cover the commitment by buying sterling forward at a low price. The receipt of foreign currency for exports is therefore delayed. Conversely, a wide discount makes it profitable for U.K. importers to borrow sterling, sell spot for foreign currency to make payment to the foreign exporter rather than borrow foreign currency and cover forward at a high price. The foreign currency payment is therefore accelerated. On both counts the United Kingdom's external reserves are adversely affected by a wide forward discount.

(7) Finally, it is relevant to note that, providing the spot rate is not devalued, the Bank of England makes a profit in foreign currency terms providing the forward rate is supported at a discount to the spot rate. Over the three-year period such profits to the Bank of England were not insignificant.

On the other hand, the Bank's intervention policy had its critics. In particular they argued that there were dangers in such a policy:

(1) The Bank of England would incur a substantial loss if the spot rate were devalued while the Bank of England had forward commitments to supply foreign currency. This is discussed below.

(2) Forward intervention may also induce the authorities to delay an inevitable devaluation as forward intervention may be used to support an untenable spot rate. This may be because a reduction in reserves is perceived more dramatically than a rise in the central bank's forward commitments, and the authorities may delay a devaluation to avoid the loss that it would incur on its forward commitments.

(3) Similarly, critics argued that the type of forward intervention practised removed the necessity of the monetary adjustment and higher domestic interest rates that were appropriate for a deficit country.

(4) As noted earlier, forward intervention makes forward speculation cheap and may thereby induce a straight increase in the combined volume of forward and spot speculation, as well as shifting speculative sales from the spot to the forward market. However, this imposes a burden only to the extent that the spot rate is subsequently devalued. Indeed, without such a devaluation there may be virtue in such an effect in that the Bank of England makes a profit while it supports the forward rate at a discount to the spot rate.

(5) Intervention was also criticised on the basis of 'bad banking', in that forward commitments to supply foreign currency might exceed the central banks' holding of foreign currency. However, forward sales of foreign currency to arbitrageurs are matched by receipts of foreign currency due to the spot inflow. Also, commitments to speculatiors would be matched on maturity by spot purchases of domestic currency by speculators. The real problem in this respect, therefore, is the extent to which the foreign currency receipts due to the capital inflow have already been utilised and the loss incurred by the Bank of England if spot sterling is devalued.

THE COSTS OF DEVALUATION

An immediate implication of forward exchange market intervention is that the central bank exposes itself to an exchange-rate risk, in that the spot rate may change while it has forward commitments. According to official statistics the Bank of England incurred a £356 million 'loss' when sterling was devalued in November 1967 and the Bank had bought sterling forward to minimise the forward discount. However, the true loss is not an easy figure to determine.

There is no real loss on the Bank of England's forward purchases of sterling from arbitrageurs as there had previously been a spot receipt of foreign currency. Thus, had the Bank been supplying forward sterling at the old spot rate it would be required to deliver the same volume of foreign currency at the maturity of the forward contract as had been received spot at the time of the capital inflow. In sterling terms the value of the forward commitment was raised, but so too was the value of the central bank's foreign currency reserves.

On the face of it the real loss is sustained on forward purchases from speculators as the Bank of England is committed to supply foreign currency at the old forward rate, which is now appreciated against the new spot rate at which speculators' purchase spot sterling to fulfil their side of the forward bargain. The Bank of England therefore delivers more foreign currency than it receives from speculators.

But even this calculation is not straightforward as the analysis must consider the effect of intervention itself upon the combined volume of spot and forward speculative sales of domestic currency. The appropriate comparison is not between the loss on the forward contracts with speculators and a zero loss, but with the *net* loss of foreign exchange associated with speculative *spot* sales of sterling when there is no forward intervention by the central bank. The central bank incurs a foreign currency loss if it buys spot sterling from speculators and subsequently the spot rate is devalued. This is because speculators repurchase the same volume of sterling with less foreign currency after the devaluation.

Thus the foreign currency loss incurred by the central bank when intervention is restricted to the spot market, and where the central bank has sold foreign currency spot to speculators, is given by:

$$\left[S_1 \times \left(\frac{e}{1+e} \right) \right],$$

where S_1 is the volume of spot speculative sales which are reversed after devaluation, and e is the percentage devaluation. When, on the other hand, the central bank intervenes in both the spot and forward markets, and spot and forward sales of foreign currency are made to speculators, the foreign currency loss to the central bank is given by:

$$\left[F \times \left(\frac{d}{1+d} \right) \right] + \left[S_0 \times \left(\frac{e}{1+e} \right) \right],$$

where F is the volume of forward commitments to speculators, S_0 is the volume of spot sales of domestic currency by speculators, and d is the percentage devaluation of the spot rate against the previous forward rate. Clearly, there are losses incurred on the forward contracts but this is at least partly offset by the fact that d is less than e (unless the forward rate was supported at the old spot rate), and in all probability S_0 is less than S_1. It could be that the loss incurred with forward intervention is less than without it, if the volume of forward commitments is small and the effect of intervention in the forward market is to induce a large reduction in the volume of spot speculative sales of domestic currency.

Whether or not the true losses are greater with forward intervention depends critically upon the effect of intervention on the combined volume of spot and forward speculation. If support of the forward rate induces: (i) a smaller volume of combined spot and forward sales of domestic currency, or (ii) spot speculators to switch to the forward market with the forward rate supported at a discount to the spot rate, the central bank incurs a smaller loss with intervention than without even though it incurs a loss on its actual forward commitments to speculators. The effect of intervention upon speculation is therefore the key issue. For purposes of the analysis, speculators may be divided into three groups: (i) those who speculate in *either* the spot *or* forward market dependent upon whether speculation in the forward market is cheap (i.e. when the forward rate is supported at a narrow discount); (ii) those who only speculate in the forward market and only when the discount is narrow; and (iii) those who speculate only in the spot market but whose expectations are affected by forward intervention by the central bank. With respect to (i), intervention will increase the volume of speculation in the forward market as the narrow forward discount makes the potential profits great and the loss (if the spot rate is not devalued) comparatively small. However, the true loss occurs only in category (ii) as in case (i) speculation has simply been switched from the spot to the forward market. But the central bank's loss is reduced to the extent that forward intervention induces: (i) a transfer of speculative selling from the spot to the forward market and the forward rate is supported at a discount (i.e. $d < e$); and (ii) a smaller volume of spot or forward speculation because intervention has a positive effect on confidence in the spot rate. The central bank also makes profits on its forward commitments in the periods when the spot rate is not devalued and speculators are forced to cover their commitments at a spot rate appreciated against the forward rate. If forward intervention shifts speculators from the spot to the forward market the gain when the spot rate is not devalued is not only the profit made on the forward deals, but also the absence of the temporary loss of foreign currency reserves when speculative spot sales of domestic currency are made.

A distinction is also made between *financial* and *real* costs. The former are only costs to the central bank and represent payment to other domestic residents. Thus, if the speculators were domestic residents only a transfer of income is involved. But *real* costs (overseas claim on domestic resources) are involved when the speculators are non-residents and the payments from the central bank are paid abroad.

CONCLUSIONS

Intervention in the forward exchange market, either by *swaps* or outright purchases of currency forward, can be a powerful instrument of domestic and external monetary policy. It is particularly appropriate when there is a conflict between the internal and external interest-rate target. However, the central bank incurs foreign-exchange risks, though any losses need to be set against the broader benefits of the policy which includes the freeing of interest-rate policy for domestic targets. In fact, since the adoption of floating spot rates in the early 1970s the volume of forward intervention has been modest. There is also a potential balance-of-payments saving to the extent that not all external holders of domestic currency cover their spot purchases forward, but do benefit from high interest rates. Thus while the foreign currency cost of a *marginal* inflow is the same whether the covered interest-rate advantage derives from a high interest-rate or forward premium, the higher interest rate is paid on *existing* external holders of sterling whereas the advantageous forward rate is not. Overall, the evidence indicates that, as the speculators' schedule for forward exchange is inelastic, forward intervention can have a potentially powerful effect upon the capital account.

Bank of England Intervention in the Forward Market

In the United Kingdom forward intervention has not been used extensively as an instrument of domestic monetary policy. But since 1964 there have been two phases of Bank of England (BE) intervention in the forward market for sterling: (i) the period 1964 to 1967, and (ii) post-1973. The object of this section is to analyse the basic mechanics and rationale of such intervention. Rather anomalously, while the objective has been generally to indirectly support the spot rate, in the first period the BE was *buying* forward sterling, while in the post-1973 period it has frequently *sold* the currency forward.

(1) *1964–1967*

In the earlier period intervention was continuous, and took the form of BE purchases of forward sterling to limit the size of the forward discount. As noted in Chapter 10 the broad objective was to encourage covered arbitrage capital inflows which supported sterling in the spot market and the official reserves. Forward intervention was therefore designed to support the spot rate. The rationale was that, by itself purchasing the sterling being sold forward by arbitrageurs, the BE removed the necessity of the banks' selling spot sterling for dollars which would have occurred had the banks been forced to cover their open forward positions as a result of their counterpart forward purchases of sterling from their customers. In this way BE intervention meant that there was no spot covering (sales of sterling) by the banks in response to forward sales of sterling by speculators. Similarly, the effect on official reserves of covered capital inflows was not offset by the banks' spot covering of arbitrageurs' forward sales of sterling.

    The mechanics of the operation are described in Table 10.A.1 below. The key to the procedure is the effect of intervention on the banks' spot covering of their forward transactions with customers (both speculators and arbitrageurs, though only the latter are considered in the table).

(2) POST-1973: *BEAR-SQUEEZE*

In contrast the BE has on occasion in the post-1973 period, and before exchange controls were dismantled, intervened in a different way. It has intermittently attempted to *widen* the forward discount by *swap* transactions by simultaneously buying spot and selling forward sterling. This normally has the effect of raising euro-sterling interest rates and the spot rate, and making

TABLE 10.A.1

(1) *1963–7 situation*

Assume a covered spot capital inflow of 100:

(A) WITHOUT BE INTERVENTION IN FORWARD MARKET

Arbitrageur

(i) purchases spot sterling + 100
(ii) sells forward sterling − 100

His bank

(v) receives forward £ + 100
(vi) sells spot £ − 100

Bank of England

(iii) BE provides spot £
(iv) no transaction

Net spot sterling transactions + 100 at (i)
− 100 at (vi)

Net   0

(B) WITH BE FORWARD PURCHASE OF STERLING

Arbitrageur

(i) purchases spot sterling + 100
(ii) sells forward sterling − 100

His bank

Intermediation only

Bank of England

(iii) BE provides spot £
(iv) BE sells forward £ − 100

Net spot sterling transactions + 100 at (i)

Net   + 100

The difference, therefore, is that without forward intervention there are zero net purchases of spot sterling but with forward intervention there are 100 net purchases of spot sterling.

'short positions' in sterling more expensive. The BE in so doing hopes to discourage private spot sales by itself forcing down the forward rate (raising euro-sterling rates) to near to the future spot rate expected by speculators. The 'bear-squeeze' operation has been described succinctly by the BE (page 145 above).

Given the interest-parity condition in the euro markets, movements in the forward discount on sterling will, with a given euro-dollar rate, be mirrored by movements in the euro-sterling interest rate. Prior to the abolition of U.K. exchange control, and as the euro-sterling market is comparatively small and was previously isolated from the domestic sterling market by exchange control, a relatively small volume of such forward intervention could have a significant effect on the euro-sterling interest rate.

The BE could have three objectives in a 'bear-squeeze': (i) to minimise current pressure (downward) on the spot rate; (ii) to minimise pressure on the spot rate in the future; and/or (iii) 'punish' speculators who have sold sterling short in either the spot or the forward market.

The ultimate rationale is related to the spot market, and hence such intervention must in some way be rationalised and understood in terms of its direct or indirect effect upon the spot exchange rate.

To appreciate the mechanisms involved consideration has to be given to the *modus operandi* of forward speculation. Apart from straight spot sales of sterling, leads and lags, etc., speculators may either (i) sell sterling forward, or (ii) borrow (euro) sterling and sell the proceeds in the spot market for, say, dollars. The ultimate *net* effect upon the spot rate of these alternatives depends upon how banks (counterpart to their speculator customers) cover their forward position.

(i) *Speculators sell sterling forward*

Speculators sell sterling forward to their banks. The banks in turn, having purchased forward sterling, cover their open forward positions by selling sterling spot for dollars. This in itself will depress the spot rate. However, consideration must be given to how the banks 'finance' the spot sale of sterling. If they sell from an existing 'stock' of sterling balances the spot rate depreciates. If, on the other hand, they *borrow* euro sterling (exchange control previously prevented foreign banks borrowing sterling in the domestic market) there is likely to be no *net* effect upon the spot rate. This is because, the counterpart bank which is lending the sterling will, in all probability, itself acquire sterling funds by purchasing them spot for dollars (see Brown, 1978, p. 115).[1] This bank will likely purchase sterling spot and simultaneously sell it forward in a *swap* transaction. In the final analysis the spot *sale* of sterling by the bank which is acting as the counterpart to the speculators' forward sale of sterling is exactly offset by the spot *purchases* of sterling by the bank lending euro sterling.

Net pressure on the spot rate only results, therefore, if an existing 'stock' of sterling is being sold spot. In this case BE forward intervention offsets the *net* spot sale as in its *swap* operation it purchases sterling spot.

(ii) *Speculators borrow euro sterling*

The second method of speculation is where the speculator himself borrows euro sterling to sell spot for dollars. Similar considerations apply as in the previous case. If the sterling borrowed is from a given 'stock' there will be a *net* depreciation of the spot rate. On the other hand, if the bank which receives the demand for a euro sterling loan itself has to purchase spot sterling the two spot transactions again cancel.

It appears, therefore, that speculation by either method *may* depress the spot rate, though this is certainly not invariably the case.

The question to be considered is what *net* effect the BE's 'bear-squeeze' has on the spot rate. On the face of it, it might seem that there is no difference between the situation where the BE is selling sterling forward, and when such sales are made by private speculators. However, when the BE is intervening it is engaging in a *swap* transaction. Unlike the private speculator, when the BE sells sterling forward it simultaneously purchases sterling spot. Thus in those cases were private forward sales of sterling do induce *net* spot covering sales by the banks these spot sales are exactly offset by the BE's spot purchases. In those cases where forward sales by speculators do not induce *net* spot covering by banks the BE's intervention has a *net* positive effect upon the spot rate.

The operation with and without BE intervention is described in Table 10.A.2. In the latter case, it is assumed that the banks covering operations induce net spot sales of sterling.

EXCHANGE CONTROL

The situation has been transformed by the abolition of exchange control. First, speculators in the spot market are now not forced to finance their sales by borrowing in the euro-sterling market which previously had a substantial and immediate effect upon euro-sterling interest rates. With no exchange control domestic sterling funds and sterling borrowed in London may be used to sell sterling spot. The potential for speculation has been raised substantially.

Second, the leverage of forward intervention has been reduced markedly. As the euro- and domestic sterling markets are now fully integrated a much larger volume of forward intervention is needed to have the same impact upon the forward rate. This is because the effect upon the euro-sterling rate is now mitigated by arbitrage flows from the U.K. domestic money market. In effect, the BE is operating against a much larger volume of potential speculative funds. Nevertheless, in either direction, official intervention in the forward

TABLE 10.A.2.

(2) *Post-1973 situation*

Assume speculative forward sales of 100 by either speculators or Bank of England:

(A) WITHOUT BE INTERVENTION IN FORWARD MARKET

Speculator	*His bank*	*Bank of England*
(i) sells forward sterling −100	(ii) receives forward £ +100	(iii) no transaction
	(iv) sells spot £ −100	

Net spot sterling transactions −100 at (iv)

Net −100

(B) BE SELLS FORWARD STERLING TO REMOVE INCENTIVE FOR SPECULATOR TO DO SO

Speculator	*Bank*	*Bank of England*
(i) no transaction	(iv) receives forward £ +100	(ii) sells forward sterling −100
	(v) sells spot sterling £ −100	(iii) buys spot sterling +100

Net spot sterling transactions −100 at (v)
+100 at (iii)

Net 0

The difference, therefore, is that if the speculator sells forward sterling there is a net sale of 100 sterling spot. If the BE sells forward sterling with a simultaneous spot purchase the net effect on spot sterling is zero.

market remains a potentially powerful instrument of monetary policy, though it is now more feasible in the direction of supporting rather than depressing the forward rate. It remains an important and viable means of insulating domestic interest rates from interest-rate trends in other countries if they conflict with internal requirements in the United Kingdom.

SELECTED BIBLIOGRAPHY

Aliber, R. Z. (1962) 'Counter-Speculation and the Forward Exchange Market: A Comment', *Journal of Political Economy*, Dec 1962.

Auten, J. (1961) 'Counterspeculation and the Forward Exchange Market', *Journal of Political Economy*, Feb 1961.

Beenstock, M. (1978) *The Foreign Exchanges* (London: Macmillan) chap. 6.

Bloomfield, A. (1964) 'Official Intervention in Forward Exchange Market', *Banca Nazionale del Lavoro Quarterly Review*, Mar 1964.

Brown, B. (1978) *Money, Hard and Soft* (London: Macmillan).

Chalmers, E. (ed.) (1971) *Forward Exchange Intervention: U.K. Experience, 1964–67* (London: Hutchinson).

Day, W. H. L. (1976) 'Advantages of Exclusive Forward Exchange Rate Support', *IMF Staff Papers*, Mar 1976.

Einzig, P. (1961) *Dynamics of Forward Exchange* (London: Macmillan) chaps 31–50.

Fleming, J. M., and Mundell, R. (1964) 'Official Intervention in the Forward Exchange Market', *IMF Staff Papers*, Nov 1964.

Jasay, A. E. (1958a) 'Bank Rate or Forward Policy', *Banca Nazionale del Lavoro Quarterly Review*, Mar 1953.

Jasay, A. E. (1958b) 'Forward Exchange: Case for Intervention', *Lloyds Bank Review*, Oct 1958.

Tew, J. H. B. (1977) *Evolution of the International Monetary System, 1975–77* (London: Hutchinson).

11

Capital Account Policies and Financial Institutions

The broad options were outlined in Chapter 8, together with a summary of the main policy instruments applied by European Governments in the 1960s and 1970s to inhibit undesired capital inflows. Most of the specific measures noted in Table 8.1 (p. 108) are self-explanatory. In this chapter more detailed analysis is given of two measures: (i) the use of reserve requirements on bank and non-bank external borrowing; and (ii) the two-tier or dual exchange market. A review is also made of the limited empirical evidence about their effectiveness.

The particular choice of measures is determined in part by the institutional arrangements of the country, by the immediate monetary policy objectives of the authorities and by the general disposition towards either *market* or *control* mechanisms. The experience strongly suggests that when measures are adopted a comprehensive package is required. For instance, in June 1972 the Swiss authorities produced a package of measures to limit capital inflows which included: (i) a ban on foreign acquisition of Swiss financial assets; (ii) a ban on interest payments on non-resident bank deposits in Switzerland; (iii) a penalty rate on any increase in non-resident deposits; (iv) restrictions on non-bank borrowing abroad; (v) requests to banks to balance their foreign-currency positions daily; and (vi) mandatory reserve requirements on Swiss banks foreign liabilities. The experience also suggests that, at times of generalised exchange market pressure (as in the early 1970s), monetary authorities are forced to act simultaneously as action by one country diverts pressure to others. Thus in June 1972, the German authorities also imposed a series of defensive measures including: (i) an increase from 40 per cent to 50 per cent in the reserve ratio on non-bank external liabilities; (ii) a tightening of the coverage of the *Bardepot*; (iii) restrictions on the sale of domestic bonds to foreigners; and (iv) a further rise in reserve requirements on banks external liabilities.

As already noted, some of these external measures might normally be a regular and integral part of domestic monetary policy. This would apply, for instance, to currency swaps between the Swiss National Bank and the commercial banks in Switzerland. But more commonly they have been a response to substantial and volatile capital inflows associated either with a significant divergence of monetary policy between countries, or with exchange market speculation. Either way the objective of the measures is to alleviate pressure on the exchange rate and domestic monetary conditions induced by international capital movements.

I RESERVE REQUIREMENTS

BANKS' EXTERNAL LIABILITIES

Banking measures are the most common means of influencing capital flows, partly because banks are the most obvious channel for funds. Banks make the euro-currency markets and central banks are also familiar with banking policy techniques, many of which can be simply modified to deal with external operations. Most of the measures noted in the previous chapter are of a direct control nature; the major exception is reserve requirements on external liabilities to the extent that these are fixed at less than 100 per cent.

The most common policy instrument directed specifically at moderating capital inflows is the imposition of reserve requirements on bank's external liabilities. These require banks to maintain a proportion of the funds received from non-residents in an interest-free account at the central bank which thereby reduces the proportion of external funds the banks may use to acquire earning assets. The general effect is to lower the rate of interest banks can profitably pay on external deposits. At 100 per cent this reserve requirement mechanism becomes equivalent to a ban on interest payments on external liabilities though, with the prospect of a capital gain through an exchange-rate rise, there may still be an incentive for non-residents to acquire bank deposits.

Reserve requirements on external liabilities work in two ways; (i) they discourage the acceptance of external deposits (or their switching into domestic currency if the requirement is on *net* liabilities), and (ii) they neutralise part of any net inflow that does take place to the extent that the reserve part is not available for domestic credit creation. Germany has made extensive use of differential reserve requirements on external as opposed to domestic bank liabilities, and sometimes the difference has been substantial. They influence capital flows by determining the profitability of accepting external deposits at each internal/external interest-rate differential. The higher are reserve requirements on external liabilities the greater is the required differential between the domestic and the external borrowing rate to make it profitable for the banks to accept external liabilities for switching into domestic currency.

As noted in Table 8.1 (p. 108) reserve requirements on external liabilities may be imposed upon: (i) *gross* or *net*[1] external liabilities; (ii) foreign currency, domestic currency or total external liabilities; and (iii) either levels or changes in banks external liabilities. If the reserve requirement is placed upon *gross* external liabilities the incentive for banks to bid for funds is reduced, and the rate of interest offered on deposits will tend to fall. Reserve requirements placed upon *net* external liabilities create no disincentive for banks bidding for external funds providing they are not switched into domestic currency but are on-loaned in foreign currency. If the object is to minimise the domestic monetary or exchange-rate effect of a capital inflow, reserve requirements need to be imposed upon gross *domestic* currency external liabilities but need be applied only to *net* foreign-currency liabilities. Reserve requirements on *net* external liabilities create a clear incentive for banks: (i) to on-lend foreign currency deposits in the euro market, (ii) not to repatriate existing external assets and, (iii) to switch from domestic to foreign currency assets so as to increase external assets relative to external liabilities and thereby reduce *net* external liabilities. Imposition of reserve requirements on *gross foreign currency* external liabilities simply makes domestic banks uncompetitive in euro-currency market business (see Chapter 10).

The effect of reserve requirements levied against *gross* and *net* external liabilities may be considered for three different examples[2] of a capital inflow through the banks where: (1) domestic banks actively bid for external funds with a view to converting the proceeds into domestic currency to meet an existing domestic demand for bank credit; (2) non-residents take the initiative by depositing funds at the banks; and (3) non-residents deposit funds at a non-bank financial intermediary or commercial company. In the calculations to follow, the following symbols are used: R_d is the domestic interest rate on bank credit: R_b is the banks external borrowing rate; R_f is the banks external lending rate $(R_f > R_b)$; X is the volume of the capital inflow; r_f is the reserve requirement (per cent) on *gross* or *net* external liabilities; and r_d is the reserve requirement on domestic liabilities.

Example (1)   In order to lend domestically in domestic currency banks may actively bid for foreign-currency funds in the international markets with a view to selling the proceeds spot for domestic currency. The interest payments on borrowed foreign currency funds is given by $X R_b$. The interest earned on domestic lending is $X(1 - r_f) R_d$, i.e. the domestic rate of interest received on that proportion of borrowed funds available for domestic lending after r_f per cent is used to meet required reserves. Thus while interest is paid on the total of borrowed funds the bank acquires earning assets on the basis of an amount equal to only $X(1 - r_f)$. In equilibrium, at the margin, $\left(\dfrac{R_b}{R_d}\right) = (1 - r_f)$. It follows that: (i) the policy variable r_f can be set at a level which discourages external funding and a rise in the external component of high-powered money (with a fixed exchange rate), or a rise in the spot rate in the absence of official intervention; and (ii) the higher r_f is set by the central bank the wider has to be the difference between the bank's external borrowing rate and its domestic lending rate to make external funding profitable. There is therefore a symmetrical relationship between the differential $(R_d - R_b)$ and r_f. It also follows that the wider is the interest-rate differential the higher has to be the reserve requirement to discourage external funding of domestic lending.

Example 2   In the second example the initiative for the inflow is taken by non-residents and the banks are assumed to accept the external deposits offered. However, the banks are free to choose between on-lending the funds received to other non-residents or to switch the foreign-currency funds into domestic currency to lend domestically. In this example the imposition of reserve requirements on *gross* external liabilities lowers the return to the bank on any use of external funds but is neutral as between domestic and external lending. The reserves are required irrespective of the use made of the funds by the banks. In this case the profitability of accepting the funds depends upon the differential between the external borrowing rate on the one hand, and the domestic or external lending interest rate on the other.

Alternatively, if reserve requirements are imposed upon *net* external liabilities there is a clear incentive for the banks not to switch into domestic currency (which would represent an effective capital inflow into the country) but to lend externally. This is because the external liability is matched by an external asset and there is therefore no change in the banks' *net* external liability position, and hence no reserve requirement liability is incurred. If the banks switch into domestic currency the effective rate of return to the banks is: $X(1 - r_f) \cdot R_d$, while the return on external lending is XR_f. Providing $R_f > R_b$, and assuming $R_f < R_d$, the equilibrium condition is given by: $\left(\dfrac{R_f}{R_d}\right) = (1 - r_f)$. External lending is always profitable if $R_f > R_b$. The decision about external v. domestic lending is determined by the relationship between the differential between R_d and R_f on the one hand, and r_f (on *net* external liabilities) on the other hand. The higher is r_f and the lower is $(R_d - R_f)$ the greater is the incentive not to switch into domestic currency to finance domestic lending. Given that r_f is a policy variable it can, in principle, be set at a level to achieve a desired capital inflow. Thus, as noted earlier, if the objective of policy is to discourage capital inflows, reserve requirements on external foreign currency liabilities need be imposed only upon the *net* position.

Example 3   The inflow in this case is into non-banks (perhaps non-bank financial intermediaries), while reserve requirements are assumed to be imposed only upon banks' *gross* or *net* external liabilities. The banks' domestic liabilities rise (against the domestic recipient of the inflow), but external liabilities remain unchanged. Reserve requirements imposed on banks' *gross* external liabilities are therefore irrelevant. But banks still have the option of lending, either domestically or externally. If they lend externally, *net* external liabilities are reduced (as external assets rise while external liabilities remain unchanged). Therefore if reserve requirements are imposed upon *net* external liabilities the rate of return on domestic lending is given by: $X(1 - r_d) \cdot R_d$ while the return on external lending is given by: $X(1 - r_d) \cdot (1 + r_f) \cdot R_f$. When banks lend externally, the reduction in *net* external liabilities reduces the interest-free reserves required at the central bank. The volume of funds that can be loaned externally is therefore greater than the volume of funds that can be loaned domestically by an amount equal to the freed reserves. This creates an incentive to invest overseas unless R_d exceeds R_f by more than r_f (on *net* external liabilities). If this condition is not fulfilled the banks are induced to lend overseas so as to reduce their *net* external liabilities, and the domestic effect of the initial capital inflow to non-banks is neutralised. It also follows that, when reserve requirements are placed upon *net* external liabilities, there may be an incentive for banks to rearrange their portfolio and switch from domestic to external lending and induce a net capital outflow. The key determinant is again $(R_d - R_f)$ relative to r_f.

The analysis has more general application too. In a situation where a bank finds it profitable to increase its loan portfolio but is hampered by a shortage of reserves, in the absence of official control it has a choice between domestic and external business on both sides of the balance-sheet. Other things being equal the domestic and external interest rates, together with any difference between reserve requirements on domestic and external liabilities, will determine the banks' portfolio decisions. In this situation banks can choose between internal and external funding and lending, and the choice will be made on the basis of relative interest rates and reserve requirements.

RESERVE REQUIREMENTS ON NON-BANKS

One of the possible effects of constraints imposed upon banks (e.g. through reserve requirements) is a process of *disintermediation* whereby borrowers bypass the banking system. For instance, limitations on external bank borrowing may be circumvented by non-banks funding their requirements directly in external money markets. If the policy measures are designed to limit *net* capital inflows, such non-bank borrowing therefore offsets the desired effect. It was for this reason that in 1972 the German monetary authorities imposed a cash deposit scheme (*Bardepot*) on external borrowing by non-banks. Under this regulation non-bank borrowers funding externally were required to deposit 40 per cent of the proceeds (50 per cent in June 1973, and 20 per cent in February 1974 until it was lowered to zero in September 1974) in an interest-free account at the Bundesbank. In effect reserve requirements were imposed upon non-bank borrowers, which effectively raised the cost of external funding. But the borrower would also need to consider any potential change in the domestic currency cost of the borrowing due to exchange-rate changes. Clearly, an appreciation of the domestic currency against the currency borrowed lowers the effective cost of the loan. If the *Bardepot* were 50 per cent the company would need to borrow the equivalent of DM 200 to invest DM 100 and the interest cost would double. But the effective cost is also determined by the movement of the exchange rate against the borrowed currency.

EFFECTIVENESS OF MEASURES

There is little systematic empirical evidence about the effectiveness of measures to limit capital inflows. One investigation[3] of policy in Germany concluded that, while measures to limit capital inflows (e.g. reserve requirements on banks' external liabilities and the *Bardepot*) had substantial effects within the relevant sector, they were almost totally offset by increased flows through other channels. This induced the authorities to extend the coverage of the measures, but their effect upon the overall capital account was still limited. Thus initially the imposition of reserve requirements on banks' external liabilities had a substantial direct impact on external bank liabilities (a reduction of DM 4.5 billion). But this was offset by a DM 3.9 billion rise in non-bank external liabilities, and it was for this reason that the *Bardepot* was introduced. This was effective in terms of non-banks, whose external liabilities declined by close on DM 6 billion. But in turn the capital inflow was diverted to other channels, e.g. the long-term capital account.

Offsets to capital controls in Germany occurred in five main ways: (1) the forward premium of the Deutsche Mark, and expectation of a rising spot rate, meant that non-residents were prepared to hold DM deposits even at a zero rate of interest;[4] (2) German banks and companies sold DM bonds to non-residents in order to circumvent the *Bardepot* requirement on external borrowing; (3) non-residents purchased bonds and other long-term assets that were not subject to the limitation on non-resident holding of DM assets; (4) capital flows occurred on a substantial basis through leads and lags in commercial payments and; (5) German banks were able to circumvent liabilities on external liabilities by transferring loan business against domestic residents to their branches in Luxembourg. In this way the domestic borrower incurred a liability to a foreign branch of a German bank which was not subject to the reserve requirements imposed by the Bundesbank. Overall, the evidence suggests that control measures have only a limited effect and have to be extended to encompass an increasingly large number of alternative channels. Eventually these measures tend to introduce their own distortions, and it was largely for this reason that the resolution of the supposed incompatibility of fixed exchange rates, domestic monetary control and freedom of international capital movements was eventually made by abandoning fixed exchange rates after capital controls had been attempted on a large scale in the late 1960s and early 1970s.

EURO AND DOMESTIC MARKET

As noted in Chapter 7 (p. 78), bank deposits may be held in domestic money markets or in euro markets, but controls and reserve requirements may be imposed by a central bank only upon banks located in its own country. One effect of controls and differential reserve requirements against domestic v. non-resident liabilities is to induce non-residents to switch their deposits to the euro market in the same currency, perhaps at foreign subsidiaries of domestic banks. For instance, as noted in Chapter 7 (p. 94), in 1973 official reserve requirements on banks in Germany discriminated heavily against external liabilities with a 35 per cent reserve requirement on non-resident liabilities compared with 13–14 per cent on domestic liabilities. This had the effect of inducing non-residents to hold euro-DM deposits rather than deposits at banks in Germany and, as a result, the euro-DM interest rate moved substantially below domestic interest rates in Germany (see Chart 7.5 (p. 92)).

However, given the mechanics of the euro market analysed in Chapter 9, the effect upon high-powered money in Germany is the same irrespective of where the non-resident DM deposit is held. Suppose an American holder of dollars converts into Deutsche Marks and the Bundesbank supports the dollar in the exchange market. Irrespective of whether the U.S. resident holds the Deutsche Marks in Germany or at a euro bank, high-powered money is created within the German banking system.

The legal cash ratio is assumed to be 10 per cent and the initial balance-sheet of the German bank is:

Liabilities		Assets	
German deposits	1000	Cash	100
Foreign deposits	0	Loans	900
Foreign banks	0		
TOTAL	1000	TOTAL	1000

A capital inflow of 50 with Bundesbank intervention produces:

Liabilities		Assets	
German deposits	1000	Cash	150
Foreign deposits	50	Loans	900
Foreign banks	0		
TOTAL	1050	TOTAL	1050

Two portfolio adjustments are now made: (i) the U.S. resident switches his DM holdings to a euro bank in Luxembourg, and (ii) the German bank increases its earning assets to maintain the cash ratio at 10 per cent. Therefore:

Liabilities		Assets	
German deposits	1450	Cash	150
Foreign deposits	0	Loans	1350
Foreign banks	50		
TOTAL	1500	TOTAL	1500

The transfer of the funds by the non-resident to the euro bank has no effect on the total of bank deposits in Germany, which may increase by some multiple of the original inflow into Deutsche Marks. The monetary effect derives from the Bundesbank's foreign-exchange market intervention and not from the location of the deposit.

In circumstances where capital control measures still make it worth while to hold Deutsche Marks in the euro market, the rationale of measures to limit capital inflows into Germany is indirect. They may nevertheless have some effect:

(1) The lower interest rate on euro DM assets (which may be the only asset available to non-residents) may limit the demand for Deutsche Marks.
(2) The constraint imposed on DM portfolios may limit demand; the volume of assets held when only euro deposits are available could be less than when the investor has a choice across the whole spectrum of euro and domestic DM assets.
(3) The lower euro-DM interest rate may induce borrowers to borrow in the euro DM to convert into other currencies, thereby inducing an offsetting capital outflow from Deutsche Marks.

The important analytical and practical point is simply that, following upon the analysis of Chapter 7, whether non-resident holdings of a currency are held in the euro or domestic market makes little difference to the domestic monetary effect of capital movements. Changes in the external component of high-powered money occur at the point when the central bank intervenes in the exchange market, and are not affected by non-residents' decisions as to whether to hold the currency in the euro or domestic money market. Insulation requires measures to inhibit spot purchases of the domestic *currency*.

II DUAL EXCHANGE MARKET

A rather complex mechanism for insulating the domestic money supply and spot exchange rate from capital flows is to operate a *dual* exchange-rate system. Two broad approaches have been adopted by different countries. With the partial segregation practised by the United Kingdom (until 1979) and the Netherlands, some capital account transactions must be conducted through a separate market where no official intervention takes place. Thus, until exchange controls were abolished in 1979, if a U.K. resident wished to purchase foreign securities the foreign currency had to be purchased in a separate investment currency market where the exchange rate simply reflected the balance of supply and demand between those U.K. residents selling foreign securities and those buying them.

The broader segregation, which is the focus of attention in this chapter, makes a more fundamental distinction. The essence of this approach is that current account transactions are conducted through an *official* market at a fixed exchange rate, while capital account transactions are channelled through a *financial* market at a different exchange rate. There may or may not be official intervention in the *financial* market.

The *dual* exchange market may be operated in two ways with respect to the monetary effects of external transactions. If the object is to create a fixed exchange rate for current account transactions and yet insulate the domestic money supply only from external capital movements, this can be achieved simply by the central bank intervening in the *official* market while refraining from intervention in the *financial* market. The external component of high-powered money changes in line with the current account surplus or deficit, but the *financial* rate adjusts to clear any excess demand for foreign or domestic currency due to capital account transactions. On the other hand, complete insulation from all external transactions can in principle be achieved with the benefit of a fixed rate for current account transactions if the central bank sells/buys in the *financial* market the foreign currency bought/sold in the *official* market.[5] A current account surplus forces the central bank to buy foreign currency in the *official* market to prevent the exchange rate rising. The domestic monetary counterpart is offset by equivalent sales against domestic currency in the *financial* market. The net result is a stable exchange rate for trade and no change in the external component of high-powered money.

Thus the basic rationale of the *dual* exchange market is to insulate the domestic economy from the monetary effects of capital movements, while enabling trade to be conducted at a fixed exchange rate. Dependent upon the intervention strategy, it also enables the money supply to be insulated from all external transactions even with a fixed exchange rate.

CAPITAL MOVEMENTS

The effect of a *dual* exchange market on capital movements is complex. Capital movements may respond to changes in the *financial* rate relative to the *official* rate for two reasons: (1) such differential movements alter the effective rate of return to non-residents at each domestic interest-rate level; and (2) they may induce expectations of speculative profits if the movement of the *financial* rate relative to the *official* rate induces expectations of further movements. The normal procedure of *dual* markets is for capital transactions to be conducted in the *financial* market while the earnings on investment are transferred through the *official* market. It is likely that capital inflows will be moderated at each interest-rate level as the *financial* rate of the domestic currency moves to a *premium*[6] over the official rate. If the domestic interest rate is 10 per cent while the *financial* rate is at a 4 per cent premium, the effective rate of return on non-residents' investment in the country is 9.6 per cent. This is because the capital inflow occurs at a less advantageous exchange rate for the investor than that at which the interest payments are repatriated.

It follows therefore that the *neutral* intervention strategy outlined above has an equilibrating effect on the balance of payments if the current account is in deficit and the central bank's purchases of domestic currency in the *official* market are offset by equal sales in the *financial* market. In this case the *financial* premium narrows and, at constant interest rates, this induces a larger capital inflow as the effective rate of return rises as noted above.

BASIC MECHANISMS

To be effective the two markets must be kept separate in that all current account transactions (and only current account transactions) must pass through the *official* market which ensures the same for capital transactions in the *financial* market. There should be no transfers between the two markets which requires various forms of control to ensure that transactions are conducted through the appropriate market.

In practice separation can never be complete, and if there are arbitrage links between the two markets the basic mechanisms are undermined. Thus, if some capital flows through the *official* (fixed-exchange-rate) market then: (i) the sustainable differential between the two exchange rates is reduced and this may reduce the volume of equilibrating capital movements, and (ii) the official rate and domestic monetary conditions are not immune from the effect of capital movements. However, in the neutral intervention case the effect of such arbitrage on the *financial* premium could be offset by official intervention in the *financial* market. For instance, if a capital inflow takes place through the *official* market the effect upon the premium of the financial rate could be offset by corresponding purchases of domestic currency in the *financial* market. But in practice central banks have been reluctant to intervene in *financial* markets, particularly on the large scale that would be necessary if there were substantial evasion of the regulations stipulating the market through which different transactions are to take place.

The anomaly is that the larger the differential between the two exchange rates the greater is the incentive for evasion and arbitrage between the markets. In practice the practical degree of exchange control cannot sustain a total separation and it may be for this reason that in the three major countries (Belgium, France and Italy) that have adopted the *dual* market the differential never exceeded 5 per cent. The evidence suggests that there are leakages and, in the absence of a completely neutral intervention policy, speculative and other capital flows do exert pressure on the *official* exchange rate and domestic monetary conditions. As with many measures to influence capital flows, in the final analysis a major potential leakage is through leads and lags in trade payments.

CONCLUSIONS

In principle a *dual* exchange market offers a convenient means of reconciling a fixed exchange rate for current account transactions while maintaining domestic monetary control. However, to work effectively, and to keep the two exchange rates apart, a policy of neutral and symmetrical official intervention in the two markets is normally required. In practice the system has not worked particularly well, partly because the two markets cannot be kept entirely separate, but also because of a clear reluctance by central banks to intervene in the *financial* market. For these reasons the evidence indicates only limited success in insulating the *official* rate and monetary conditions from the effect of capital inflows and outflows.

SELECTED BIBLIOGRAPHY

Argy, V. (1971) 'Monetary Policy and Internal and External Balance', *IMF Staff Papers*, Nov 1971.
Barattieri, V. (1971) 'Analysis of the Two Tier Exchange Market,' *Banca Nazionale del Lavoro Quarterly Review*, Dec 1971.
Fleming, J. (1974) 'Dual Markets and Other Remedies for Disruptive Capital Flows', *IMF Staff Papers*, Mar 1974.
Hewson, J., and Sakakibara, E. (1977) 'Effectiveness of German Controls on Capital Inflow', *Weltwirtschaftliches Archiv*, pp. 645–64.
Lanyi, A. (1975) 'Separate Exchange Markets for Capital and Current Transactions', *IMF Staff Papers*, Nov 1975.
Mills, R. H. (1972) 'Regulations on Short Term Capital Movements; Recent Techniques in Selected Countries', *Federal Reserve Board Discussion Paper* (Washington, D.C.: Federal Reserve Systems).

12

The Independence of Monetary Policy

One of the major analytical and practical issues in the analysis of the open economy is the extent to which governments are able to pursue independent monetary policies. As noted in earlier chapters, one strand of the theoretical literature establishes that a key difference between fixed and floating exchange-rate systems is the degree of monetary independence afforded to governments. The broad conclusions of this theoretical analysis are that when the exchange rate is fixed the domestic monetary counterpart of foreign-exchange market intervention effectively means that the monetary authorities lose control over the domestic money supply. On the other hand, the domestic money supply is largely insulated from external developments with a floating exchange rate.

With a fixed exchange rate the monetary effects of the balance of payments occur irrespective of whether the surplus/deficit is on current or capital account.[1] However, in practice the monetary links between countries, and in particular the difficulty of pursuing an independent monetary policy, derive predominantly from international capital movements. Thus with a fixed exchange rate a domestically induced rise in high-powered money (e.g. through open-market purchases of bonds by the central bank) tends to induce a fall in domestic interest rates, a capital outflow and hence an offsetting reduction in high-powered money. The initial increase in the domestic component of high-powered money is at least partly offset by a lower external component and, in the process, the central bank has exchanged foreign for domestic assets. While the relationship is complex there is for most countries a strong negative correlation between movements in the domestic and external components of high-powered money. Also, the effects of monetary policy in one country may in this way be transmitted internationally. Thus, with a high degree of interdependence (particularly associated with the capital account), a fixed-exchange-rate regime limits the possible degree of divergence of both national inflation rates and domestic money supplies and interest rates.

However, monetary independence is a question of degree. It was noted in an earlier chapter that if domestic and foreign securities are perfect substitutes (i.e. the F schedule is perfectly elastic) monetary interdependence is complete. In this case no independent monetary policy is possible, interest rates are determined at the world level and the monetary authorities are unable to *sterilise* the domestic monetary effects of capital movements. It is this model that dominates much of the theoretical literature. In this chapter consideration is given to the precise institutional mechanisms linking the balance of payments and the domestic money supply and in particular the extent to which, in practice, offsetting capital flows limit the pursuit of independent monetary policy. It is established that, with fixed exchange rates, the linkage between the balance of payments and the domestic money supply is critically dependent upon the precise institutional structure in individual countries. For instance, in Germany virtually all balance-of-payments transactions affect the domestic money supply while, because of the reserve currency role of the dollar, the U.S. money supply is largely immune from external influences. The United Kingdom lies somewhere between with current account and private sector capital flows having standard domestic monetary effects, while the money supply is unaffected by capital flows into and out of public sector debt.

The broad conclusion is that, while *offsetting capital flows* are frequently substantial, governments do in practice have a degree of monetary independence even with fixed exchange rates. This is because of several important *insulation* mechanisms and the ability of governments to *sterilise* externally induced changes in the money supply. In the analysis to follow, *insulation* mechanisms refer to certain features of the system (such as movements in the forward exchange rate in response to changes in interest rates), which automatically insulate either domestic interest rates or money supplies from monetary developments in other countries. *Sterilisation*, on the other hand, refers to deliberate policy measures to counteract externally induced changes in the money supply. An important distinction is therefore made between the three related concepts of *offsetting capital flows*, *insulation mechanisms* and *sterilisation*. However, it also appears that while *sterilisation* for most countries is feasible when practised in isolation, it works by passing on monetary problems to other countries. This means that it is effective only to the extent that at least some countries remain passive in the face of externally induced changes in domestic monetary conditions.

THE BASIC MECHANISMS

Emphasis is given in the analysis to high-powered money rather than the money supply more broadly as it is, in principle, the monetary component more directly under the influence of the monetary authorities. High-powered money (or the monetary base of the banking system) may for simplicity of exposition be defined as the reserves of the banking system at the central bank[2] and, in a fractional reserve banking system, changes in the supply of this component may induce a multiple change in the total volume of bank deposits. The monetary base has a domestic component (roughly corresponding to central bank credit to the domestic economy) and an external component equal to the central bank's external reserves. High-powered money therefore corresponds to the sum of domestic and foreign assets of the central bank, with a counterpart in the form of commercial banks reserves (deposits) at the central bank.

The determination of high-powered money (HPM) is summarised in the following identity:

$$\Delta HPM \equiv (GD + F) - (MD + NMD) - B + \Delta R + \Delta CB_b,$$

where GD is the Government's financial deficit, F the volume of maturing public sector debt, MD and NMD official sales of marketable and non-marketable debt to non-banks, B sales of public sector debt to banks[3], R external reserves of the central bank, and CB_b commercial bank borrowing from the central bank. Other things being equal, a budget deficit or maturing public sector debt increases the domestic money supply and HPM as bank deposits are created when payment is made by the Government and the banks reserves at the central bank are correspondingly increased. On the other hand, non-bank purchases of new public sector debt extinguish bank deposits and reserves of the banking system as, in the final analysis, most transactions between the public and private sectors which are conducted through the banking system involve changes in commercial banks' deposits at the central bank.

The major sources of changes in HPM are therefore: (i) the Government's net budget position (public sector borrowing requirement in the United Kingdom); (ii) central bank transactions in public sector debt; (iii) the balance-of-payments surplus; and (iv) direct borrowing by commercial banks from the central bank. For instance, an open-market purchase (of $£X$) of bonds by the central bank changes the balance-sheet positions of the banks and central bank as follows:

Central bank				Commercial bank			
Assets		*Liabilities*		*Assets*		*Liabilities*	
Domestic assets	+X	Commercial banks'		Reserves at central		Deposit of seller of	
Foreign assets	—	reserves	+X	bank	+X	debt	+X
	+X		+X	TOTAL	+X		+X

The external component of high-powered money changes as the counterpart to foreign-exchange market intervention by the central bank. A German exporter paid in dollars sells dollars for Deutsche Marks so as to increase his DM bank deposit. If, to prevent the Deutsche Mark rising on the exchange market, the Bundesbank buys the dollars it creates a DM deposit in favour of the exporter. But in the process the exporter's bank also acquires reserves at the Bundesbank as in practice the central bank buys the dollars with Deutsche Mark from the exporter's bank. In this way high-powered money has been created and, in principle, and unless it is offset by other measures by the central bank to neutralise it, a multiple expansion of the money supply is made possible. This is true irrespective of whether the balance-of-payments surplus is on current or capital account. Thus, with a fixed exchange rate, intervention in the foreign-exchange market has the same effect upon HPM as do open-market operations in public sector debt. The balance-sheet effects of intervention where the central bank purchases X of foreign currency are summarised below:

Central bank				Commercial bank			
Assets		Liabilities		Assets		Liabilities	
Domestic assets	−	Commercial banks'		Reserves at		Exporters	
Foreign assets	+X	reserves	+X	central bank	+X	deposit	+X
	+X		+X		+X		+X

On the other hand, if the Bundesbank refrains from intervention the German exporter sells the dollars for Deutsche Marks to an existing holder of Deutsche Marks. There is a change in the ownership of bank deposits, but the total German money supply remains unchanged. The result is that the exchange rate rises. In the face of a balance-of-payments surplus the German monetary authorities are faced with the choice of allowing either the supply of high-powered money to rise or its currency to appreciate.

More formally the following identities and equations are established:

(1) $HPM \equiv H_T + R_T$ {(where $H_T \equiv (H_p + H_e)$ and $R_T \equiv (R_p + R_e)$)}
(2) $\Delta R_T \equiv C + K$
(3) $K \equiv \Delta D_f - \Delta F_d$
(4) $C = a + b(y)$
(5) $K = g + e(i_f - i_d - f) + S,$

where H_T and R_T are the total domestic and external components of HPM, and each has a policy and endogenous element.[4] C and K are the current and capital account balances, D_f represents foreign purchases of domestic bonds and F_d the purchase of foreign securities by domestic residents; y is real income, i_f and i_d the foreign and domestic interest rates; f the forward premium and S the volume of speculative capital inflows. When considering the independence of monetary policy a key element is the two-way causal relationship between H and R via K and sterilisation measures. Offsetting capital inflows imply that $\uparrow H_p \rightarrow \downarrow \Delta R_e$, while effective sterilisation policies mean that $\uparrow \Delta R_e \rightarrow \downarrow H_p$. Both imply a negative correlation between H_T and R_T.

INSULATION AND STERILISATION

Some degree of monetary independence is possible when the interest-rate sensitivity of international capital movements is less than perfect. In this case the domestic interest rate is not uniquely determined at the world level, though the more sensitive are international capital movements to interest-rate differentials the greater the external reserve flows implied by an attempt to maintain an independent monetary policy. Monetary independence secured through an active *sterilisation* policy may therefore be possible only at the cost of substantial external reserve accumulations or losses. Monetary independence is also secured through a series of *insulation* mechanisms. In some countries automatic mechanisms exist which, even though capital mobility may be very high, prevent domestic monetary conditions being totally dominated by international capital movements. In these ways a degree of monetary independence is secured without the necessity of deliberate *sterilisation* measures.

This may usefully be considered in terms of a mechanical representation of the causal links between an initial policy induced change in the domestic component of HPM in country A ($H_{p(A)}$) and the ultimate induced change in HPM in country B (HPM_B):

$$\Delta H_{p(A)} \rightarrow \Delta H_{T(A)} \rightarrow \Delta HPM_{(A)} \rightarrow \Delta i_A \rightarrow \Delta(i_A - i_B - f) \rightarrow \Delta K$$
$$\rightarrow \Delta R_{e(B)} \rightarrow \Delta HPM_B,$$

where the symbols are as previously defined. There are several links in the process whereby monetary policy in country A is ultimately transmitted to country B, and at various stages automatic adjustments may occur which limit the degree of transfer of monetary changes. Specifically, when considering whether, with fixed exchange rates, capital movements transmit monetary policy internationally seven main links are identified between:

(1) the policy induced change in the domestic component of HPM in country A and the total domestic component and total volume of HPM in that country;

(2) the resultant net change in HPM in country A and interest rates in that country;

(3) the change in interest rates in country A and the interest-rate *differential* relevant for international capital movements;

(4) changes in interest-rate differentials and international capital movements;

(5) capital movements and the endogenous external component of HPM in country B;

(6) changes in the external component of HPM in country B and the total HPM in that country and

(7) an initial change in aggregate HPM in country B and the ultimate change.

In each of these links a series of *insulation* mechanisms may limit the transfer of the initial monetary policy impulse. Some of these mechanisms may also limit the domestic effectiveness of monetary policy measures. For instance, in the first link banks may respond to a change in the policy element of the domestic component of HPM by reducing their net indebtedness to the central bank, i.e. if the domestic component of HPM is demand rather than supply determined changes in Hp may be partly offset by changes in H_e in identity (1) on page 172. Through this mechanism the change in the total domestic component of HPM in country A may be less than the initial policy induced change; only if HPM is entirely supply-determined and the banks passively accept any change in net free reserves at the central bank will the two be equal. In the second channel, interest rates will tend to fall in response to the rise in HPM only providing the demand function is stable and does not shift in line with changes in HPM. The relationship between changes in the money supply and interest rates is certainly not as clear cut as in the standard Keynesian model.

In the third channel an important *insulating* mechanism is an equilibrating movement in the forward exchange rate. In Chapter 6 it was noted that such movements in the forward exchange rate may be substantial and may occur quickly, with the result that the change in the covered interest-rate differential is less than the initial change in interest rates. Herring and Marston (1977) calculate that, over their estimating period, a 1 per cent change in the euro-dollar rate induced a 0.73 percentage point equilibrating change in the forward premium of the Deutsche Mark if the German interest rate is held constant, and 0.52 p.p. movement if the latter is also allowed to adjust. In simulation exercises they concluded that the induced change in Germany's external reserves was reduced from DM 13.2 billion to DM 6.3 billion when the forward rate is allowed to respond to changes in uncovered interest-rate differentials. Thus, changes in forward exchange rates are a powerful *insulating* mechanism at least with respect to covered capital movements. Even allowing for such changes there are other factors (exchange control, sovereign risk, threat of exchange control, desire for diversified portfolios, etc.), which in practice may limit the response of wealth-holders to changes in appropriate interest-rate differentials (channel (4)).

With respect to channel (5) capital movements, even in the fixed exchange-rate case, need not invariably induce changes in the external component of HPM. This is particularly important in the case of the United States and the United Kingdom. As noted in the next section the money supply in the United States (being a reserve currency centre) is almost entirely insulated from external monetary influences. The United Kingdom is discussed in the following section, where it is established that the portfolio preferences of the overseas sector may automatically insulate the domestic money supply from the effect of international capital movements.

As with channel (1) there may also be offsetting movements between the external and domestic components of HPM if banks respond to externally induced changes in net free reserves by changing their borrowing from the central bank. Thus in channel (6) there may be *insulation* mechanisms through the portfolio behaviour of the banks. Finally, *sterilisation* measures may neutralise any initial externally induced change in high-powered money.

The analysis may also be widened from focusing upon high-powered money to the money supply more generally. The basic identity becomes $\Delta M \equiv \Delta D - \Delta R$, where M is the domestic money supply, D is total domestic credit creation, and R is the central banks' external reserves. The concept of offsetting capital flows implies that exogenous changes in D induce offsetting changes in reserves so that the change in the money supply is less than the initial change in domestic credit. But, quite apart from sterilisation policy, causality may also run from changes in reserves to domestic credit. Thus, an exogenous capital inflow may not induce a corresponding rise in the domestic money supply if it induces an offsetting reduction in D. This may arise, for instance, if the inflow is into the domestic corporate sector, and the implied rise in corporate liquidity induces less borrowing from the domestic banking system. Similarly, to the extent that exogenous inflows have a favourable impact on confidence and/or expectations that domestic interest rates will fall, the non-bank demand for public sector debt may rise. This means that the effect of a given public sector borrowing requirement on domestic credit creation is reduced.

All these considerations are consolidated into the following equations and identity:[5]

(1) $\quad \Delta HPM \equiv \Delta H_T + \Delta R_T$

(2) $\quad \Delta R_e = x + a(\Delta H_T)$

(3) $\quad \Delta H_p = y + b(\Delta R_e),$

where a (the *offset coefficient*) and b (the *sterilisation* coefficient or policy reaction function) both have values between 0 and -1. Thus in equation (2) a change in external reserves and the external component of high-powered money is inversely related to changes in the domestic component of high-powered money. The value of a is determined by: (i) the extent to which interest rates respond to changes in high-powered money (i.e. the elasticity and stability of the demand function for high-powered money); (ii) the interest-rate sensitivity of international capital movements; (iii) the response of the forward exchange rate; (iv) the degree of exchange control; (v) the response of spot speculative capital flows to changes in interest rates; and (vi) in the U.K. case, the portfolio preferences of wealth-holders regarding the type of assets acquired. The value of b indicates the extent to which policy-makers respond to externally induced changes in high-powered money by attempting to change the domestic component (e.g. by open-market operations, currency swaps with the commercial banks, changes in reserve requirements, etc.).

The ultimate power of monetary policy is determined by the values of a and b; for a given value of b, the nearer to -1 is a the less powerful is monetary policy, and for given values of a the closer to -1 is b the more powerful is monetary policy. However, the closer are the coefficients a and b to -1, the greater will be the change in external reserves and policy-induced change in the domestic component of high-powered money. For instance, if $a = -0.5$ and $b = -1$, and the policy target is for a net rise in HPM of 100, the increase in the domestic component of HPM must ultimately be 200 and there will be a net fall in external reserves of 100. The higher are a and b the more the quest for monetary independence implies substantial changes in external reserves.

THE UNITED STATES CASE

The United States, being large and a reserve currency centre, is largely immune from external-induced changes in the money supply through foreign-exchange market intervention. The mechanics of the relationship between central bank intervention and the U.S. money supply is complex and outlined in detail in the *Federal Reserve Bank of St. Louis Review*.[6]

When intervention is designed to support the dollar the general monetary effects may be summarised as: (i) a rise in *high-powered money* in the surplus countries; (ii) no effect on the U.S. money supply; (iii) some initial easing of U.S. interest rates; and (iv) some initial easing of interest rates in the surplus country following the rise in the money supply. For the sake of brevity we consider the case where intervention is undertaken by the central bank in the surplus country (e.g. the Bundesbank). The following stages are identified:

(1) A U.S. resident (importer of German goods) buys Deutsche Marks from his New York bank which in turn buys Deutsche Marks from a bank in Germany. At the U.S. bank the importer's dollar deposit is reduced, while that of the German bank is increased. A change in the ownership of U.S. bank deposits has occurred but at this stage no change in total,
(2) The German bank sells dollars for Deutsche Marks
(3) The Deutsche Bundesbank buys the dollars being sold by the German bank (and credits the bank's reserves at the Bundesbank) to prevent an appreciation of the Deutsche Mark. The dollar proceeds thereby acquired by the Bundesbank are deposited at the FED (a Federal Reserve Bank), and there is a consequential equal loss of reserves by the U.S. commercial bank. On the basis of $\$Y$ imports the cumulative changes in the U.S. bank balance-sheet at this stage are:

Liabilities			Assets	
U.S. importer		$-Y$	Reserves	$-Y$
Foreign bank	$+Y$	$-Y$	Treasury bills	—
			Loans	—
TOTAL		$-Y$	TOTAL	$-Y$

At this point: (i) German bank reserves in Deutsche Marks at the Bundesbank have risen (increase in *high-powered money*); (ii) the German money supply has risen (German exporter's DM deposit is higher); (iii) U.S.bank reserves have been reduced (the counterpart to the Bundesbank's deposit at the FED); and (iv) the U.S. money supply is lower due to the lower deposit of the U.S. importer which at this stage is not counterbalanced by any equivalent increase.

(4) Portfolio adjustments by the U.S. Treasury and the Bundesbank are now likely. As the Bundesbank earns no interest on FED deposits it buys, say, U.S. Treasury bills from the U.S. Treasury. The Bundesbank's holding of bills rises and its FED deposit is reduced, while the Treasury's deposit at the FED is increased following the sale of bills to the Bundesbank.

(5) If the Treasury does not desire an increased level of deposits at the FED, the deposit acquired is used to buy bills or Treasury securities from U.S. banks or non-banks.[7] When the bills are purchased from the U.S. commercial bank, the bank regains its lost reserves at the FED and, as it holds fewer Treasury bills, can increase its domestic loans. At this stage the cumulative balance-sheet of the U.S. commercial bank is as follows:

Liabilities			Assets		
US Importer		$-Y$	Reserves	$-Y$	$+Y$
Foreign bank	$+Y$	$-Y$	Treasury bills		$-Y$
Domestic depositor		$+Y$	Loans	$+Y$	
TOTAL		--	TOTAL		—

(6) The U.S. money supply has been restored though there is now a higher volume of bank loans, which is likely to involve some rise in the velocity of circulation of money and interest rates. If, alternatively, the Treasury buys bills from the non-bank public, the cumulative balance-sheet positions becomes:

Liabilities			Assets		
US importer		$-Y$	Reserves	$-Y$	$+Y$
Foreign bank	$+Y$	$-Y$	Treasury bills		—
Domestic investor		$+Y$	Loans		—
TOTAL		—	TOTAL		—

(7) The important point is that as the Bundesbank holds more Treasury bills, fewer are issued and held within the United States and hence the initial loss

of bank reserves (U.S. *high-powered money*) is restored by virtue of the U.S. treasury issuing fewer securities.

The net result is that: (i) German bank reserves have risen; (ii) U.S. bank reserves and money supply are unchanged; and (iii) the U.S. Treasury bill rate is lower by virtue of the increased total demand for bills at initial interest-rate levels (from the Bundesbank). There is therefore an asymmetrical effect on the German and U.S. money supplies. The U.S. money supply is immune from the balance of payments while changes in Germany reflect a balance-of-payments surplus (or deficit). It should be noted that the insulation of the U.S. money supply derives from decisions of: (i) the foreign central bank to hold Treasury bills rather than deposits at the FED; and (ii) the Treasury in responding to higher deposits at the FED by actions which reduce bill-holdings of U.S. residents. Neither are inevitable.

Thus, with fixed exchange rates, the United States may have a dominant position in determining monetary conditions in the world economy. A more expansionary policy in the United States than in Europe may pose difficulties for monetary control in Europe. This was viewed by some analysts as a major and inherent defect of the Bretton Woods system, as it was unrealistic to expect the conduct of U.S. monetary policy to be based on the requirements of world monetary stability.

THE UNITED KINGDOM CASE

The relationship between the balance of payments and the U.K. money supply is also more complex than in Germany, as is the definition of *high-powered money*. In the U.K. case the effect of a balance-of-payments surplus on the money supply depends upon whether the surplus is on Current or Capital account, and in the latter case also upon the portfolio preferences of the overseas sector.[8] The intervention agency in the United Kingdom is the Exchange Equalisation Account (EEA) whose assets are held in foreign currency (e.g. U.S. Treasury bills) and sterling (U.K. Treasury bills). Any receipt of sterling (intervention to buy sterling on the exchange market) by the EEA is immediately invested in U.K. Treasury bills, and this reduces the Exchequer's residual financing through the banking system. That part of the Exchequer deficit which is not financed by sales of debt to the EEA, the overseas sector or domestic non-banks is financed through the banking system via the latter's purchase of Treasury bills. As these are reserve assets of the banks (analogous to *high-powered money*) this residual financing increases the money supply and facilitates a potential multiple rise in bank deposits.

A Current account deficit (with a balanced Capital account and official foreign-exchange market intervention) increases the sterling assets of the EEA which reduces the residual financing of a given Exchequer deficit through the banking system. The supply of reserve assets and the money supply are therefore less than would otherwise have been the case. The money supply is therefore reduced by a Current account deficit and increased with a surplus.

The monetary effect of capital flows is more complex. Suppose the Current account is balanced but there is a net capital inflow. The EEA purchases foreign currency (to stop an appreciation of sterling) with sterling acquired through liquidating Treasury bills. The Exchequer receives less financing from the EEA and must therefore sell more debt elsewhere. If the non-resident who has purchased sterling (the capital inflow) invests in Treasury bills the overseas sector in effect purchases the bills being liquidated by the EEA. There is therefore no change in the Exchequer's residual financing of its deficit, the supply of reserve assets or the U.K. money supply. *Sterilisation* of the monetary effect of the balance of payments is in this case automatic. On the other hand, if the non-resident acquires a private sector asset (e.g. a bank deposit) the increased supply of Treasury bills (from the EEA) must be absorbed by the banking system. The supply of reserve assets to the banking system is therefore increased, although as sterling liabilities of banks against non-residents are not included in measures of the U.K. money stock there is no immediate rise in the money supply. There may be a subsequent rise as, with higher reserves, the banks are able to increase their domestic lending. In the final analysis external flows induce an immediate rise in the money supply only to the extent that sterling is placed in the hands of non-bank U.K. residents.

It follows that the monetary effect of the balance of payments is not measured in the United Kingdom by the overall balance-of-payments deficit/surplus (change in external reserves). The *monetary account*, the significant part for monetary analysis, is the Current account plus the private sector Capital account. A Current account deficit matched by an equal capital inflow is not neutral on the domestic money supply when the overseas sector purchases public sector debt. It also means that *the domestic money supply is not immune from external developments with a floating sterling exchange rate.* Although in the floating-rate case bank reserves are not affected by the domestic counterpart of Bank of England intervention in the foreign-exchange market, a Current account deficit matched by a capital inflow may involve an initial transfer of bank deposits to foreigners, who in turn purchase public sector debt. In this case, there is a loss of reserve assets to the banking system.

STERILISATION V. OFFSETS: EMPIRICAL EVIDENCE

Before considering the empirical evidence of offsetting capital flows and *sterilisation* a methodological problem is noted. There is, for most countries, a clear negative correlation between changes in the domestic and external components of high-powered money. However, while a clear conceptual distinction can be made between offsetting capital flows and *sterilisation*, the empirical evidence is more difficult to interpret. This is because both give rise to a negative correlation between changes in external reserves and in the domestic component of high-powered money. Offsetting capital flows imply that a rise in the domestic component of high-powered money *causes* a fall in external reserves via a capital outflow. Conversely, a policy of *sterilising* capital inflows implies that a rise in external reserves induces the monetary authorities to reduce the domestic component of high-powered money.

While there is no dispute about the statistical correlation between changes in external reserves and the domestic component of high-powered money, the interpretation varies between analysts.[9] For instance, Willms (1971) concluded that the German monetary authorities were able to *sterilise* around 85 per cent of the monetary effects of capital flows. Porter (1972) concluded that around 80 per cent of changes in reserve requirements was offset by the effect of capital flows, and that the data observed by Willms were more consistent with the offsetting capital flows hypothesis than the alternative *sterilisation* mechanism. A simultaneous equations approach (attempting to test separately for both mechanisms) was applied by Argy and Kouri (1974), who found in favour of the offsetting capital-flows hypothesis. Kouri and Porter (1974) estimated offset coefficients for several countries which ranged between -0.42 and -0.77 with the highest being for Germany. The O.E.C.D. (1973) also indicates that as much as 85 per cent of restrictive monetary policy measures in Germany was offset by capital flows. Herring and Marston (1977) subsequently argued that Argy and Kouri had mis-specified the central banks' reaction function (in particular, it had not allowed for banks borrowing from the Bundesbank) and supported the interpretation of Willms. They attempted to overcome the problem of interpreting causality by investigating both offsetting capital flows and *sterilisation* through a complete model of the monetary sector in Germany.

Neumann (1977) also supports the power of the German monetary authorities to *sterilise* changes in the external component of *HPM* and concluded that overall, in the period 1959–72, the sterilisation coefficient was 86 per cent (i.e. for every change of 100 in external reserves the rise in *HPM* was only 14). Of this, two-thirds was due to sterilisation *policies*, while as much as one-third was due to the banks adjusting their borrowing from the central bank (this was defined above as an *insulating* rather than *sterilisation* measure). Neumann's evidence for the sterilisation coefficient is summarised below and indicates that *sterilisation* and insulation were feasible for both rising and falling reserves with the banks reacting by borrowing heavily from the Bundesbank when reserves were falling. It would appear therefore that commercial banks reacted to changes in their domestic reserves by adjusting their borrowing from the central bank and hence for this reason, as well as policy sterilisation, changes in external reserves and the external component of the monetary base were not fully reflected in changes in high-powered money.

TABLE 12.1   Sterilisation coefficients (per cent)

	Whole period	Period of rising reserves	Period of falling reserves
Policy-induced	0.557	0.597	0.249
Commercial bank borrowing	0.303	0.205	0.769
TOTAL	0.859	0.798	1.018

Herring and Marston (1977), in a detailed analysis of the German monetary sector, concluded that the Bundesbank was able to sterilise 90 per cent of the monetary effect of changes in external reserves even though, without sterilisation, capital flows would offset 78 per cent of the effect of policy-induced changes in the domestic component of *HPM*. As already noted, they also concluded that the forward exchange rate offered a significant element of insulation.

PROBLEMS OF STERILISATION

On the face of it, a policy of *sterilisation* would appear attractive most especially for governments faced with a conflict between the requirements of internal and external balance. However, there are serious problems in practice, and the conditions where it can be practised for lengthy periods are probably limited. First, it works against the requirements of balance-of-payments adjustment in that it prevents the automatic monetary elements in the balance-of-payments adjustment process. In this sense it delays what, in the long run, must be effective balance-of-payments adjustment and also implies that, in one sense, it is an option more available to surplus than deficit countries which are constrained by limited external reserves. A second problem is that continuous *sterilisation* necessarily implies volatile reserve movements, especially if several countries are simultaneously attempting to sterilise the monetary effects of external imbalances. It also implies, for surplus countries, a continuous build-up of external reserves which may both aggravate tensions in the international monetary system and increase the risk exposure of the central bank through a continuous accumulation of balances in potentially weak currencies. This was a real concern of central banks when they were accumulating substantial balances in U.S. dollars in the late 1960s and early 1970s, and was instrumental in forcing President Nixon to formally end the official convertibility of the dollar into gold.

But the most serious problem with *sterilisation* is that, if it is effective in one country, it works only by passing the monetary problem on to others. If other countries passively accept this, the burden of monetary adjustment is necessarily borne by them who, if in surplus, accept a rise in *HPM* and if in deficit a reduction. If partner countries simultaneously attempt full *sterilisation* (i.e. the burden cannot be shifted to non-sterilising countries) there develops instability in external reserve flows. This occurs as no country is prepared to accept the inevitable monetary adjustment and the system becomes inherently unstable unless monetary policies are co-ordinated. The more countries that attempt *sterilisation*, and the greater is the degree of such measures, the greater is the instability of reserve flows and the less effective is *sterilisation* in any one country.[10] Instability therefore derives from inconsistent monetary policies and was a particular problem under the Bretton Woods system where, as already noted, automatic sterilisation occurred in the United States though Europe was not prepared to passively accept the domestic monetary implications of the U.S. deficit.

CONCLUSIONS

The general conclusion is that while *offsetting capital flows* are frequently powerful, most European governments have some degree of independence of monetary policy with fixed exchange rates through certain *insulation* mechanisms, and their ability to *sterilise* at least part of the domestic monetary effects of capital flows. The empirical evidence suggests that while, in the short run, partial *sterilisation* is feasible, and has in fact been practised widely, it is at the cost of a higher volatility of external reserves. Problems also arise when several countries attempt inconsistent *sterilisation* based upon conflicting monetary policies. It follows that a stable fixed-exchange-rate system requires a higher degree of co-ordination of monetary policies than was practised in the 1960s. In particular, 'rules of the game' are needed with respect to *sterilisation* and the extent to which the balance-of-payments adjustment process is to be eased by automatic monetary adjustments. There remains, however, considerable doubt about the ability and wisdom of central bank *sterilisation* measures in the long run. Such measures, together with *insulation* mechanisms, may offset the monetary effects of short-run balance-of-payments disturbances. But there is no practical long-run alternative to framing monetary policy consistent with external equilibrium. A totally independent monetary policy, except for the United States, is not feasible with fixed exchange rates.

SELECTED BIBLIOGRAPHY

Argy, V., and Hodjera, Z. (1973) 'Financial Integration and Interest Rate Linkages in Industrial Countries', *IMF Staff Papers*, Mar 1973.
Argy, V., and Kouri, P. (1974) 'Sterilisation Policies and the Volatility in International Reserves', in *National Monetary Policies and the International Financial System*, ed. R. Z. Aliber (Chicago: University of Chicago Press).

Balbach, A. (1978) 'The Mechanisms of Intervention in the Exchange Market', *Federal Reserve Bank of St. Louis Review*, Feb 1978.

DeGrauwe, P. (1975) 'Interaction of Monetary Policies in a Group of European Countries', *Journal of International Economics*, Aug 1975.

DeGrauwe, P. (1976) *Monetary Interdependence and International Monetary Reform* (Westmead: Saxon House).

Herring, R., and Marston, R. (1977) *National Monetary Policies and International Financial Markets* (Amsterdam: North-Holland) chaps 5, 6 and 7.

Holbick, K. (ed.) (1973) *Monetary Policy in Twelve Industrial Countries* (Boston: Federal Reserve Bank of Boston).

Kouri, P. (1974) 'International Capital Flows and Portfolio Equilibrium', *Journal of Political Economy*, May/June 1974.

Kouri, P. (1975) 'The Hypothesis of Offsetting Capital Flows: A Case Study of Germany', *Journal of Monetary Economics*, 1975.

Kouri, P., and Porter, M. (1974) 'International Capital Flows and Portfolio Equilibrium', *Journal of Political Economy*, May/June 1974.

McKinnon, R. I. (1974) 'Sterilisation in Three Dimensions: Major Trading Countries, Eurocurrencies and the US', in *National Monetary Policies and the International Financial System*, ed. R. Z. Aliber (Chicago: University of Chicago Press).

Miles, C. N., and Bull, P. A. (1978) 'External and Foreign Currency Flows and the Money Supply', *Bank of England Quarterly Bulletin,* Dec 1978.

Neumann, M. (1977) 'A Theoretical and Empirical Analysis of the German Money Supply Process 1958–1972', in *Monetary Policy and Economic Activity in West Germany*, ed. S. Frowen *et al.* (Guildford: University of Surrey Press).

O.E.C.D. (1975) *Role of Monetary Policy in Demand Management: Experience of Six Countries* (Paris: OECD).

Porter, M. (1972) 'Capital Flows as an Offset to Monetary Policy: German Experience', *IMF Staff Papers*, July 1972.

Willms, M. (1971) 'Controlling Money in an Open Economy: The German Case', *Federal Reserve Bank of St. Louis Monthly Review,* Apr 1971.

13

The Structure of World Interest Rates

A central feature of the analysis of earlier chapters has been the complex linkage of monetary conditions between countries brought about by international capital movements. An important aspect of the international monetary system is therefore the extent to which, under various exchange-rate regimes, countries are able to pursue independent monetary policies. In particular, the extent to which interest rates in different financial centres move together is one measure of the degree of interdependence of national monetary systems.

In the simple model described in Chapter 2 the degree of international capital mobility and the exchange-rate regime were both factors influencing the extent to which national interest rates could diverge. With both fixed and floating exchange rates a monetary expansion in one country (inducing a decline in interest rates) would tend to induce a corresponding movement in interest rates in other countries, though the mechanism linking them is different in the two regimes. With a fixed exchange rate, and in the absence of sterilisation, the linkage derives from the domestic monetary counterpart of central bank intervention in the foreign-exchange market. In the floating exchange-rate case the linkage derives from the effect upon the demand for money of exchange rate induced changes in the level of income. In both regimes interest rates in different countries tend, in general, to move in parallel. In one polar case (where the external equilibrium schedule is infinitely elastic) there is no monetary independence with either a fixed or floating exchange rate and the interest rate is determined at the 'world level'.

This conclusion has dominated much of the theoretical literature. And yet the evidence of previous chapters (particularly Chapters 6, 7 and 12), and the conclusions of this chapter, do not conform to this extreme theoretical proposition. Contrary to the implication of much recent theoretical literature, while the evidence suggests a high degree of monetary interdependence, it is clear that the world monetary system is not totally integrated, and some degree of monetary independence is attainable under a fixed exchange-rate regime. The object of this chapter is to review the empirical evidence with respect to international interest-rate relationships.

Measurement of financial integration may be made in terms of four alternative approaches: (1) the interest-rate sensitivity of international capital movements; (2) the extent of divergence from interest-rate-parity conditions; (3) the links between changes in high-powered money in different countries; and (4) the extent to which the levels or movements in national interest rates are highly correlated. The first three have been discussed in detail in Chapters 6, 7 and 12. The fourth is the subject of this chapter but, as it is closely related to the interest-parity approach, the analysis of Chapter 6 is briefly summarised.

INTEREST PARITY

The parity condition requires the forward premium (per cent) between two currencies to be equal to the interest-rate differential between homogeneous financial assets. When this condition is met, any exogenous factor causing an initial *ex ante* divergence from the parity condition induces simultaneous equilibrating movements in some combination of four 'prices': the spot rate, the forward exchange rate and the two interest rates. Equilibrium may be restored by either arbitrage flows or, in the efficient markets' case, by automatic adjustment of prices or interest rates by market-makers. Within the euro-currency markets, where the parity condition is invariably met, a major equilibrating mechanism is provided by banks operating in highly competitive exchange and money markets. In this case immediate adjustments to prices ensure the parity condition without an actual flow of arbitrage funds. When the parity condition between two currencies is met only within the euro markets, the *partial* parity condition is met. *Global* parity requires not only parity within the euro markets, but also between the relevant national money markets. In this case the following conditions apply: (i) the covered differential between euro-currency interest rates approximates to zero; (ii) the covered differential between national interest rates approximates to zero; and, hence, (iii) the domestic and euro-market interest rates in the same currency are equal. The reasons why partial parity is invariably sustained while global parity is not are discussed in Chapter 7. The interest-parity analysis highlights two major reasons why interest rates in different countries, and on homogeneous financial assets in different currencies, may vary in both directions and magnitude: (1) movements in the forward exchange rate, and (2) actual or potential exchange control. The former may be due to either speculation or arbitrage reactions to changes in interest-rate differentials.

THE EURO-DOLLAR RATE[1]

Most empirical studies conclude that the euro-dollar rate plays a key role in international arbitrage and interest-rate linkages. The evidence also suggests that: (i) in normal times there is a close relationship between U.S. domestic and euro-dollar interest rates; (ii) this relationship was less pronounced during the period of U.S. capital controls and when Regulation Q was effective; (iii) both rates are simultaneously determined by the same factors (e.g. U.S. monetary policy) as the domestic and euro sectors are different and competing segments of the total dollar market; (iv) movements in the euro-dollar rate have had a significant impact on European interest rates; and (v) movements in European interest rates have in general had only a small[2] impact on dollar interest rates, though this impact was higher during the period of U.S. capital controls (1963–74) which prevented arbitrage flows from the U.S. money market when the euro-dollar rate moved above the U.S. domestic rate (see Chart 13.2). It has been largely via the euro-dollar market that U.S. monetary policy has, at various times, had a significant impact on interest rates and general monetary conditions in Europe. When arbitrage between the two competing components of the dollar money market is not constrained by capital controls interest rates in the two segments are determined simultaneously. Being subject to the same forces it is inappropriate to regard the euro-dollar rate as being *caused* by interest rates in the United States.

WORLD INTEREST RATES

The pattern of short-term interest rates in five countries is shown in Chart 13.2 for the period 1960–78. Comparing interest rates in Europe with those in the United States it is apparent that while trends in the United States have had an important effect on interest rates in Europe, the correlation is less than perfect. The correlation is more pronounced in terms of direction of change than levels, though interest rates in most European countries have shown some degree of independence from those in the United States for sometimes lengthy periods. This might be expected for countries such as France and the United Kingdom where arbitrage flows are limited to some extent by exchange control. But it is also true of Germany and Switzerland. In general, however (though with notable particular exceptions in some periods), the trend of European interest rates between 1960 and 1974/5 followed that of U.S. interest rates.

The most dramatic example was in the period 1968–71 when, under the influence of at first a tight U.S. monetary policy followed by a substantial easing of U.S. monetary conditions, European interest rates rose sharply to a peak around the end of 1969, followed by a sharp decline during 1970 and early part of 1971. As already noted, this was largely a product of the conjuncture of: (i) sharp swings in the stance of U.S. monetary policy (first restrictive, then expansionary); (ii) Regulation Q, which restricted bank deposit rates at a level below market interest rates in 1969; and (iii) U.S. capital controls. The net effect was a very sharp rise in the euro-dollar rate (from $6\frac{1}{4}$ per cent in the middle of 1968 to over 11 per cent in 1969 – Chart 13.1) which induced similar sharp rises in European interest rates under the influence of substantial arbitrage flows to the euro-dollar market. It is interesting to note from Chart 13.1 that, following the non-operation of Regulation Q after 1970 and the abolition of U.S. capital controls at the

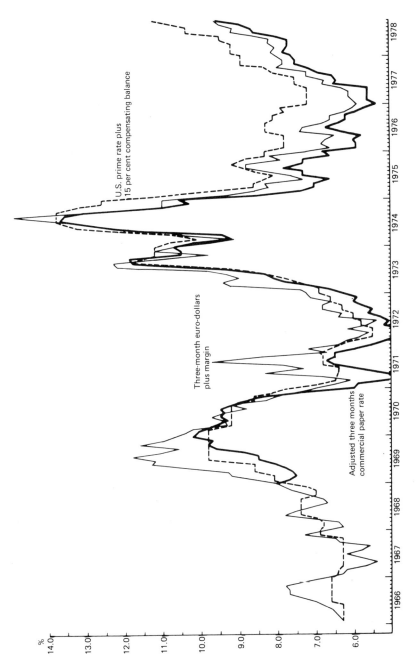

U.S. prime rate plus
15 per cent compensating balance

Three-month euro-dollars
plus margin

Adjusted three months
commercial paper rate

CHART 13.1   Borrowing arbitrage: New York and euro-dollar market[1]

CHART 13.2   Structure of world interest rates

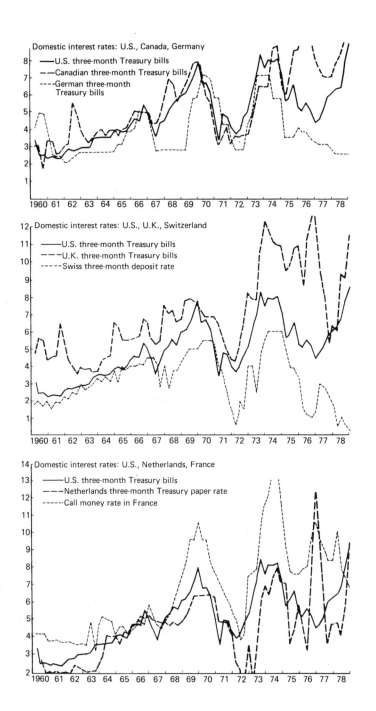

beginning of 1974, in subsequent periods of sharply rising U.S. interest rates (1974 and 1977/8) no wide differential between the euro-dollar rate and U.S. interest rates emerged. Indeed, domestic bank lending rates were high relative to euro-dollar rates in the period 1977–9, and the differential that previously emerged when interest rates were high was reversed.

Since 1974/5 the divergence of interest rates, in both level and direction, has increased and U.S. interest rates seem to have been less dominant. Particularly wide differentials have occurred in the post-1974/5 period. Even in the earlier period U.S. rates were not always dominant. For example, the German Treasury bill rate did not follow the dramatic rise in U.S. interest rates in 1967 and 1968, though by 1969 and the early part of 1970 the German interest rate rose sharply from 2.8 per cent to over 7 per cent and followed U.S. interest rates down during the second half of 1970.

With the exception of 1962 and the period 1975–7 interest rates in Canada followed U.S. rates fairly closely. In Switzerland interest rates paralleled those in the United States fairly closely between 1960 and 1970 though a substantial divergence developed during the 1970s. During 1971 Swiss interest rates declined sharply and while they followed the *trend* of U.S. interest rates in the period 1972–6, the absolute differential was sometimes substantial (e.g. $4\frac{1}{2}$ per cent in 1973 and 1976). In the U.K., which had substantial exchange control on resident capital outflows, interest rates have almost invariably been above corresponding rates in the United States. But with a few exceptions the trend followed that of U.S. rates fairly closely with a notable exception of 1977 when the U.K. Treasury bill rate declined from around 14 per cent to below $5\frac{1}{2}$ per cent at a time when U.S. rates were rising. Also, in the period 1974–6, U.K. rates were substantially higher than in the United States. A similar pattern is discerned for interest rates in France, though interest rates were also substantially higher than in the United States in 1969 and 1970, and the direction of change was poorly correlated in the period after the middle of 1975.

The most significant divergence in interest-rate trends occurred in 1977 and 1978 when the U.S. Treasury bill rate firmed sharply (from $4\frac{1}{2}$ per cent to over $8\frac{1}{2}$ per cent), while market rates in Switzerland and Germany declined markedly. By the end of 1978 the Swiss deposit rate was $\frac{1}{4}$ per cent while the U.S. Treasury bill rate had risen to $8\frac{1}{2}$ per cent producing an unprecedented interest-rate differential. Both Germany and Switzerland were free of exchange control and there was therefore a corresponding widening of the forward premium against the dollar. The divergent movements of dollar and European interest rates was associated predominantly with differences in general economic performance (with the U.S. economy distinctly more expansionary than most European economies), and associated differences in domestic liquidity conditions. Towards the end of 1977 interest-rate movements were also dominated by substantial speculative pressure against the dollar in the exchange market with interest rates in Europe responding to the domestic monetary effect of the resultant central bank intervention in the exchange markets. It was also in this period that the hitherto fairly close relationship between the U.S. dollar/DM exchange rate and the uncovered U.S./German interest-rate differential broke down.[3] In these two years the Deutsche Mark steadily appreciated against the U.S. dollar while the differential in favour of U.S. interest rates widened steadily to an unprecedented 6.3 percentage points. This divergence was associated in large part with a major portfolio diversification as private wealth-holders and some central banks (including some in OPEC) attempted to reduce the proportion of their portfolios and external reserve held in U.S. dollars. These two years afford a good example of how the trend of interest rates may diverge due to speculative and portfolio diversification transactions, and when perceived risk is increased.

ECONOMETRIC EVIDENCE

The impressionistic evidence from Chart 13.2 suggests that while interest rates moved quite markedly in parallel over the 1960s and early 1970s, interest rates in Europe were not totally dominated by the United States. Similar conclusions are reached through econometric analyses of similar data. Two alternative forms of econometric tests are reported below: (i) models of interest-rate determination in individual countries which incorporate external influences; and (ii) correlation of interest-rate trends in selected countries. Examples of the former are given by Herring and Marston (1977) and of the latter by Logue *et al.* (1976).

(i) *Herring and Marston (1977)*

Interest-rate equations are tested for five countries using two-stage least squares as the euro-dollar rate (the foreign rate of interest) is itself partly influenced by national interest rates in Europe. The equations tested for domestic and external determinants of short-term market interest rates. The main results for the period 1960 to 1971 are summarised in Table 13.1, though in each case some variables have been excluded (e.g. dummy variables for speculative factors, seasonal variables and factors specific only to individual countries). The main conclusions of the analysis may be summarised: (i) in all cases the foreign rate of interest was a significant determinant though the coefficient was significantly less than unity; (ii) domestic factors such as increases in the demand for money induced by movements in domestic incomes and prices were also significant; (iii) noninterest external factors (such as exogenous changes in external reserves) entered the equations with the right sign indicating that changes in the external component of high-powered money had some influence on domestic interest rates; and (iv) measures to restrict capital flows tended to increase the degree of monetary independence in the short run.

The external interest-rate coefficient for France understates the true influence of external interest-rate factors as the discount rate is also adjusted partly in response to changes in external interest rates. When allowance is made for this, the external interest-rate coefficient rises to 79 per cent. The apparently low coefficient for Switzerland does not indicate the absence of powerful arbitrage capital flows, but rather the strong convention of the central bank exercising moral suasion over domestic banks' interest-rate policy.

TABLE 13.1 Herring and Marston interest-rate equations

	$i_\$$	RFX	G	N	DR
Netherlands	+0.871	−1.196	+10.569	+0.164	
Italy	+0.345	−0.305	+0.047	−0.36	
Switzerland	+0.345	−0.199	+0.031	+0.156	
United Kingdom[1]	+0.187	−2.584	+2.899	−0.328	+0.571[2]
France	+0.577	−0.021			+0.618

$i_\$$ = euro-dollar rate; RFX = exogenous component of external reserves except for U.K. where it represents the current account; G = index of change in prices or output variable; N = employment (+) or unemployment (−) variable; DR = discount rate.
[1] Discount rate.
[2] Lagged one period

The equation for the United Kingdom (based on a period prior to the abolition of exchange control) also needs careful interpretation as, unlike the other cases, the U.K. interest-rate is the administered discount rate rather than a freely adjusting market rate. An equation linking the U.K. discount rate and the Treasury bill rate indicates that the latter is almost totally dominated by bank rate. In turn the key market interest rate (three-month local-authority deposit-rate) is determined powerfully by the Treasury bill rate through arbitrage in the London money market. The evidence suggests that the major causal link between external and U.K. rates is through a policy reaction to changes in the euro-dollar rate, with bank-rate adjustments made to prevent undesired interest-rate differentials emerging. Overall, Herring and Marston estimate that in the period investigated, a 1 percentage point change in the euro-dollar rate induced a 0.44 percentage point change in bank rate.

In general the analysis confirmed that, notwithstanding a high degree of capital mobility, European monetary authorities retained a significant degree of control over domestic rates both because of exchange control and also because they were able to sterilise a proportion of the domestic monetary effects of capital flows. Also equilibrating movements in forward exchange rates offered a significant degree of insulation from the effect of movements in dollar interest rates. On the basis of simulation exercises their analysis indicated that a 1 percentage point rise in the euro-dollar rate induced the following rises in European interest rates: Netherlands 0.91 per cent; Italy 0.32 per cent; Germany 0.30 per cent; Switzerland 0.35 per cent; United Kingdom 0.45 per cent; and France 0.58 per cent. In the U.K. case Herring and Marston conclude that the authorities were capable of sterilising virtually all of the domestic monetary impact of foreign-exchange flows and the interest-rate response noted above is more a reflection of a deliberate policy decision to keep interest rates in line with those in the euro-dollar market so as to limit the incentive for capital outflows.

(ii) *Logue, Salant and Sweeney (1976)*[4]

An alternative statistical technique of factor analysis was applied to levels and changes in uncovered interest rates in seven countries over the period 1958–74. This measures the extent of covariability of interest rates and isolates the extent to which common factors underly interest-rate movements. The evidence suggested that most of the variation in national interest rates over the estimating period could be related to a single factor and hence financial integration was high. This single common factor accounted for 85 per cent of the variance in interest-rate levels and 41 per cent of changes. While factor analysis does not identify the nature of the common factor the results confirm the existence of an 'international factor' in interest-rate determination.

CONCLUSIONS

The empirical evidence indicates a high, though less than perfect, correlation between interest-rate trends in different countries. But this in itself does not imply any particular model of causation and need not imply a high degree of capital mobility or movement of funds between countries. Four general factors may account for a high correspondence of interest-rate trends. First, interest rates may be linked through international arbitrage and capital movements. With a fixed exchange rate this would also imply sympathetic movements in high-powered moneys. Second, interest-rate trends in different countries may reflect common causes such as synchronisation of the business cycle or common inflationary expectations. Third, a high correlation could be achieved without actual capital movements if interest-rate policy is adjusted to external considerations. Fourth, the efficient-market hypothesis suggests that prices may simultaneously adjust to new information and before arbitrage flows occur. In the fourth case, for instance, a change in high-powered money in country A may induce an adjustment to interest rates in country B without inducing a significant transfer of funds between the two countries, and hence also without causing changes in either high-powered money in country B or in the exchange rate between the two currencies.

On the other hand, interest rates may not move precisely in parallel, especially in the short run, because of: (i) the insulating mechanism of the forward exchange rate;[5] (ii) the practice of sterilising the monetary effect of balance-of-payments transactions; (iii) exchange control on either capital inflows or outflows; (iv) transactions costs; and (v) changes in perceived risk in line with interest-rate changes and sometimes because of them. Also portfolio balance theory would not predict that interest rates move precisely in parallel, as investors increase the proportion of portfolios invested in any particular country, so the compensation required for further adjustment tends to increase.

The overall conclusion with respect to interest-rate linkages is that, until 1975, the general *trend* of European interest rates tended to follow that of the United States fairly closely, though in the short run significant variation in both direction and magnitude could occur. Interest rates in Europe appear not to have been totally dominated by U.S. monetary policy with the forward exchange rate, sterilisation measures and exchange control offering some degree of monetary independence. There is some evidence that in the period of floating exchange rates interest rates in Europe have been less dominated by monetary developments in the United States and particularly in 1977 and 1978. Floating exchange rates do seem to offer a higher degree of insulation from monetary developments overseas: it is inconceivable that with rigidly fixed exchange rates European and U.S. interest rates could have diverged as much as in 1977 and 1978 (Chart 13.1, p. 187).

SELECTED BIBLIOGRAPHY

Aliber, R. Z. (1978) 'The Integration of National Financial Markets', *Weltwistschaftliches Archiv* (1978) pp. 448–77.
Argy, V., and, Hodjera, Z. (1973) 'Financial Integration and Interest Rate Linkages in Industrial Countries', *IMF Staff Papers*, Mar 1973.
Corden, W. M. (1972) *Monetary Integration*, Essays in International Finance, No. 93 (Princeton University Press).
Fase, M. (1974) 'The Interdependence of Short-Term Interest Rates in the Major Financial Centres of the World: Evidence 1961-72', *Kyklos* (1974) pp. 93–6.
Herring, R. H., and Marston, R. M. (1977) *National Monetary Policies and International Financial Markets* (Amsterdam: North-Holland).
Kenen, P. B. (1976) *Capital Mobility and Financial Integration: A Survey*, Studies in International Finance, No. 39 (Princeton University Press).
Kouri, P. J. K. (1977) 'International Investment and Interest Rate Linkages under Flexible Exchange Rates', in *The Political Economy of Monetary Reform*, ed. R. Z. Aliber (New York: Allan Held, Osman).
Kwach, S. Y. (1971) 'Structure of International Interest Rates', *Journal of Finance*, Sept. 1971.
Logue, D. E., Salant, M. A., and Sweeney, R. J. (1976) 'International Integration of Financial Markets: Survey, Synthesis and Results', in C. H. Stem *et al.*, *Eurocurrencies and the International Monetary System* (Washington: American Enterprise Institute for Public Policy Research).
Marston, R. (1974) 'American Monetary Policy and the Structure of the Euro-Dollar Market', *Princeton Studies in International Finance*, No. 34 (Princeton, N.J.: Princeton University Press).

14

The Issue of Monetary Independence

One of the central issues under review has been the degree of monetary independence available to individual countries in a world of efficient international money markets. In fact there are two related issues to be considered: (1) the actual degree of monetary independence; and (2) whether monetary independence is in the final analysis a significant policy issue. If monetary independence does not confer on policy-makers an effective means of securing their policy objectives, the lack of independence is of only second-order importance.

The context established at the outset was the possibility of two 'incompatible trinities' (domestic and external). The latter implies that in a world of substantial capital movements, domestic monetary control is potentially undermined when the exchange rate is fixed. The policy-maker is, in these circumstances, constrained to choose any two of: (1) a fixed exchange rate; (2) control over the domestic money supply; and (3) freedom of international capital movements. This has become particularly significant during the 1970s with a higher priority being given in many countries to fairly precise control over domestic monetary aggregates. Several monetary authorities have sought to conduct policy on the basis of publicly announced monetary targets. In this context, and faced with the external 'incompatible trinity', several European governments at first moved to control international capital movements, and later abandoned the regime of fixed exchange rates that had previously prevailed (with the exception of Canada) for thirty years.

The domestic 'incompatible trinity' (particularly relevant for the United Kingdom) relates the Government's fiscal policy to the level of interest rates and the rate of growth of the money supply. In the United Kingdom, for instance, the monetary authorities are constrained to choose between: (i) the level of the public sector borrowing requirement (PSBR); (ii) the level of domestic interest rates; and (iii) the growth of the domestic money supply. For a given PSBR and monetary target interest rates adjust to whatever level is necessary for the Bank of England to sell the required volume of public sector debt to non-banks. Alternatively, if policy is directed at the level of interest rates, with a given PSBR the money supply becomes the residual and determined by the non-bank demand for public sector debt at the prevailing level of interest rates.

Either form of incompatibility taken alone poses potentially serious policy dilemmas. These have frequently been experienced, for instance, by the U.K. monetary authorities in their domestic monetary policy when, for a decade, the PSBR has been substantial. Even more so is this the case when the two are combined. It is in these circumstances that policy is most severely constrained. Thus, in a situation where the PSBR is given, a precise money supply target may be undermined by capital inflows in response to the level of interest rates that is required to sell the required volume of public sector debt. While this combined dilemma exists in a powerful way in the United Kingdom, it was to some extent alleviated by exchange control and the automatic sterilisation that occurs if the capital inflow represents non-resident purchases of public sector debt (see Chapter 12).

The two key issues therefore in the question of monetary independence are: (i) the interest-rate sensitivity of international capital flows (which determines the offset-coefficient); and (ii) the power of sterilisation mechanisms. Although some capital flows are uncovered the former in turn is dependent predominantly upon the extent to which the forward exchange rate adjusts to interest rates, and the sensitivity of capital movements to changes in covered interest-rate differentials. Sterilisation, as noted in Chapter 12, may be: (i) automatic (the reserve currency case and partly so in the United Kingdom); (ii) induced by portfolio adjustment by banks and others (e.g. repayment of debt to the central bank if bank reserves rise due to a capital inflow); or by (iii) deliberate policy response. The particular importance of the automatic sterilisation in the U.S. case is that monetary trends in Europe may, when exchange rates are fixed, be powerfully influenced by the monetary policy being conducted in the United States. Indeed, one of the factors contributing to the eventful breakdown of the Bretton Woods regime was the resistance to U.S. monetary dominance in a situation where, not unexpectedly, U.S. monetary policy was not conducted in the interests of European countries. Major monetary conflicts arose between the United States and Europe and these were particularly powerful when Regulation Q and U.S. capital controls were operative.

FINANCIAL INTEGRATION

Financial integration is the extent to which financial markets are connected. It relates to: (i) the degree to which transactors in any one market seek to maximise their portfolio objectives through diversification; (ii) the extent to which they are free to do so; and (iii) the efficiency of information transfers. An early view of financial integration focused upon the volume of arbitrage flows between markets. But more recent analysis concentrates as much upon the flow of information. As noted in earlier chapters, the concept of efficient markets implies that the movement of interest rates in different countries may be highly correlated even though the volume of funds flowing between them may be small. Ironically, on this basis the more efficient and integrated are financial markets in different centres the smaller is likely to be the volume of arbitrage funds passing between them.

This form of integration becomes particularly powerful through the simultaneous operations of banks in euro-currency and domestic money markets, and in forward exchange markets. The mechanisms through which this is secured are: (i) profitable arbitrage opportunities can never be sustained between different euro-currency markets as all the requirements for total integration are satisfied; and (ii) except for exchange control, and changes in risk as between domestic and euro markets, domestic and euro-currency rates in the same currency move very closely in parallel. In the former the only reason why euro-currency interest rates diverge (in either level or direction) is through movements in the forward exchange rate. It follows therefore that a major factor limiting the size of the offset coefficient, and the extent to which interest rates in different countries move in parallel, is equilibrating movements in the forward exchange rate.

Two alternative measures of the degree of interdependence between countries are given by the correspondence of interest-rate movements and parallel changes in the monetary base. The more significant of the two is the measure in terms of high-powered money because interest rates may also be linked through common causes (e.g. inflation expectations in the early 1970s, international convergence of business cycle trends, or a deliberate *policy* response to movements in external interest rates). The last, however, would be necessary only to the extent that, in the absence of such a response, capital flows would be induced by interest-rate differentials. Interest rates might also be closely related without a close correspondence of monetary base movements in the efficient markets case. Sympathetic movements in the monetary base between countries due to international financial integration requires an actual movement of funds between countries. This is the significant issue when monetary policy focuses upon control of monetary aggregates. It is also in this sense, and not in terms of interest rates, that floating exchange rates increase the degree of monetary independence.

THE EVIDENCE

The evidence indicates that, with fixed exchange rates, over the 1960s the offset coefficient was significantly less than unity and the sterilisation coefficient was greater than zero. Combined they suggest that, while capital did respond to interest rates and a strong negative correlation between the domestic and external components of high-powered money existed for many countries, a degree of monetary policy independence was possible at least in the short run. Similarly, while national interest rates clearly moved sympathetically, they were not totally dominated by any single factor, though trends in the United States did have a powerful influence on world interest rates. In the period since generalised floating spot rates, the divergence of interest-rate trends has increased somewhat (particularly in 1977 and 1978), though substantial common elements remain. An important caveat to any conclusions on the experience of floating rates is that intervention has at times been substantial, and some European currencies have operated a rigid fixed-rate system between themselves.

The evidence also indicates that the major factors insulating national money markets, even with a fixed exchange rate, are: (i) equilibrating movements in forward exchange rates; (ii) exchange control; (iii) domestic sterilisation measures; and (iv) portfolio balance considerations. In the last-mentioned respect, except in the euro-currency markets, the arbitrage schedule is clearly less than infinitely elastic. This implies that financial assets between countries are not perfect substitutes and that differential risk factors limit the extent of international capital movements. The forward exchange rate has been a particularly powerful insulating mechanism (in terms of both interest rates and the monetary base), and official intervention in the forward exchange market is a potentially powerful monetary policy technique under varying spot exchange-rate systems. The increased independence of interest rates observed in the period of floating spot rates is due in part to larger movements in forward rates than in general occurred in the period of fixed spot rates.

Overall, the evidence is firmly against either of the two polar cases outlined in Chapter 2. While capital clearly does respond to interest rates the external equilibrium schedule has an elasticity which is most certainly less than infinity at least in the short run. Indeed, the experience of floating spot rates has not produced an unambiguous relationship between movements in interest rates and exchange rates.

MONETARY CO-ORDINATION

The neo-Keynesian model outlined in Chapter 2 indicates that when the exchange rate is fixed monetary policy has no permanent effect upon domestic income and employment; changes in the domestic component of the monetary base are offset by induced changes in the external component. But the empirical evidence suggests that, except in the very long run: (i) the offset is not total, and (ii) sterilisation measures are feasible. If the offset coefficient is greater than zero but less than unity, a desired monetary target can be attained providing allowance is made for the offset which implies a larger *ex ante* increases in the domestic component than the desired *ex post* rise. But this strategy, together with *ex post* sterilisation measures, inevitably increases the volatility of external reserves and the potential for monetary policy conflicts between countries.

The evidence outlined in Chapter 12 indicates that if one country attempts to sterilise the monetary effect of its balance of payments, this can be successful providing partner countries are prepared to accept the monetary consequences of their corresponding balance-of-payments position. As sterilisation delays balance-of-payments adjustment, the compatibility of monetary targets between countries is an important determinant of the stability of a fixed-exchange-rate system. If targets are not consistent, and several countries simultaneously seek to sterilise the monetary effects of their inconsistent balance-of-payments targets, the volume of capital flows increases, reserve flows become explosive and no country achieves its desired monetary target. However, partial sterilisation (implying partial success in independent monetary policies) may be stable though the potential for conflict and instability increases as the number of countries seeking to sterilise external monetary effects rises, and the degree of sterilisation increases. In the final analysis, the breakdown of the Bretton Woods fixed-exchange-rate system can be attributed in part to the incompatibility of balance-of-payments targets, and the conflict of monetary policy between the U.S. and major surplus countries.

The theoretical and empirical results indicate that a fixed-rate system is viable in the long run only providing: (i) monetary and balance-of-payments targets are consistent, or (ii) a sufficient number of countries are prepared not to attempt total sterilisation. Either way, potential conflict can be avoided by some mechanism for co-ordinating monetary policy.

POLICY IMPLICATIONS

The overall conclusion of the empirical evidence, subject to its limitations, is that the degree of monetary integration in the world economy is high but, at least in the short run, less than complete. The evidence suggests that within the world system there are important insulating mechanisms which limit the transfer of monetary conditions between countries and, again in the short run, partial sterilisation of the monetary effects of capital movements, and the balance of payments generally, is feasible. Thus some monetary independence is possible even with fixed echange rates. But the long-run degree of monetary independence is less certain and the empirical evidence is not clear, partly because the long run is not easily susceptible to econometric testing.

An important distinction is made between what might be termed *constitutional* and *effective* sovereignty. The former defines a national government's ability to use instruments of policy at its own discretion and independently of other countries. But *effective* sovereignty relates to the power of governments to independently determine the value of significant target variables in the economy, such as the level of employment, real income and the balance of payments. Thus there may be scope for a government to decide upon the rate of growth of monetary aggregates with floating rates, and in this case *constitutional* sovereignty is unimpaired. But whether such an independently determined policy can influence the target variables in the desired way is open to question. If the instruments of policy are not effective, perhaps because of the constraints imposed by an open economy, the government has little *effective* sovereignty even though its *constitutional* sovereignty is unquestioned.

The power of monetary policy and the exchange rate to influence real magnitudes in the economy in the long run has been brought into question by recent *monetarist* analysis. This analysis questions whether the apparent monetary independence gained by floating exchange rates is of long-run value if monetary policy is unable to affect the long-run values of real income and employment. Similarly, if the exchange rate is not a powerful balance-of-payments adjustment mechanism in the long run the case for floating rates is weakened. While a floating exchange rate may enable a government to decide upon its own monetary policy this is viewed as conferring only the ability to choose the domestic inflation rate. While this might be of value in the short run, its longer-run significance is questionable.

The complex theoretical background to this may be briefly summarised in terms of three basic *monetarist* propositions:

(1) In the long run, monetary policy has no influence on the level of real income as the policy-maker is not able to choose a desired position on a short-run Phillips Curve. This is based on the well-known notion of a vertical long-run Phillips Curve at the natural level of unemployment.

(2) In the long run, for a small open economy, a balance-of-payments deficit with a fixed rate or a depreciating floating rate are symptoms of an excess supply of money.

(3) Exchange-rate adjustments have no long-run effect upon the balance of payments or level of real income.

The first proposition is well known though not universally accepted. It implies that, with a floating exchange rate, monetary policy determines only the long-run rate of inflation. The monetary independence gained by floating rates is, therefore, of only limited value.

The second proposition has been termed 'the monetary theory of the balance of payments'. In its most extreme form the balance of payments and movements in the exchange rate are the mechanisms through which an excess supply or demand for money is adjusted. Thus with a fixed exchange rate in a small economy the creation of money balances in excess of the long-run growth of real income (determined independently of monetary policy) is reflected in a balance-of-payments deficit which eliminates the excess supply of money.

The third proposition doubts the equilibrating power of floating rates on two grounds: (i) in the short run, the implied change in domestic real wages has little effect upon trade flows as the time lag is quite long; and (ii) in the long run, the initial effect upon real wages is offset by a higher price level due to resistance to the cut in real wages. This view argues that the exchange rate is not an effective adjustment mechanism. As economies become more open the benefits of devaluation in enhancing the competitive position of exports are quickly lost by the upward impetus given to import prices which eventually filters through to the prices of all goods. The gains to trade are temporary and soon overtaken by the effect of the exchange-rate change on the domestic rate of inflation. This is the 'vicious circle' of exchange-rate movements. As *money-illusion* is eroded, wage-earners are likely to resist the cut in the real wage resulting from an exchange-rate depreciation. New wage demands are therefore made and the vicious circle continues. The adjustment power of an appreciating currency in surplus countries is similarly limited. It follows that if exchange rates are only a weak adjustment mechanism, and effective only in the short run, little effective *real* sovereignty is surrendered by fixing exchange rates. Floating rates since 1973 have clearly not permitted governments to pursue domestic objectives without regard to the balance of payments, and the independence conferred through the release from obligations to support the exchange rate at particular levels has proved to be very limited. There is little that exchange-rate adjustments can secure that cannot equally be achieved by an appropriate monetary policy, and the exchange rate is not an efficient policy instrument in the face of an inappropriate monetary policy.

However, none of these propositions are universally accepted particularly by policy-makers whose time horizons are seldom in terms of the monetarists' 'long run'. The debate is also complicated by different views about the efficacy of exchange-rate changes as a means of adjusting real wage differentials and the balance of payments between countries. As already noted, if exchange-rate changes have little long-run impact on the balance of payments the case for fixed exchange rates is strong. If, on the other hand, the exchange rate is a powerful policy instrument, a real degree of sovereignty is surrendered by forgoing the use of this particular instrument of policy. The debate is complicated even further by differences of view as to: (i) the time period over which any effectiveness of the exchange-rate mechanism operates; and (ii) the time period over which monetary policy has real effects on the economy as opposed to purely price effects. The evidence seems to suggest that both have effects in the short run but little impact in the long run; and that the short run has become shorter over the 1970s. Indeed, the recently developed *rational expectations hypothesis* questions the plausibility of the assumption that the analytical long run may stretch into several years. If economic agents correctly appreciate the ultimate consequences of policy measures and their own actions they rationally act immediately to anticipate these consequences and this accelerates the convergence on the ultimate equilibrium position which, through a gradual learning process, might otherwise take several years.

The central issue, therefore, is the length of the short run in relation to the policy-makers' time horizon. But the monetarist analysis summarised above implies that, if monetary policy has no long-run effect on real income, and a floating rate in response to monetary policy determines only the rate of inflation, no *effective* economic sovereignty is lost by fixed exchange rates with monetary policy conducted to secure balance-of-payments equilibrium.

The appropriate long-run strategy of policy implicit in these arguments may be summarised:

(i) fixed exchange rates;

(ii) monetary policy directed towards maintaining balance-of-payments equilibrium in the long run;

(iii) co-ordinated monetary policy at the international level; and

(iv) policy measures to reduce the short-run costs of pursuing a long-run monetary policy and to shorten the time period of the long run.

Such a strategy would imply a marked change in the conduct of monetary policy, and would require the policy-maker to focus more on long-run considerations than has been the practice for decades. This requires not only changed attitudes of policy-makers, but also of the electorate. Such a strategy is advocated for consideration not so much because of abstract notions related to the virtues of long-term policy horizons, but through increasing doubts about the efficacy and wisdom of constantly adjusting to short-run situations. The benefits of short-term measures are frequently transitory and, even when valuable at the time, distract attention from longer-term requirements.

The experience of decades also indicates that, while the practical problems are great, there is a strong presumption in favour of devising institutional mechanisms for increased co-ordination of policies at the international level. Many of the problems in the international monetary system have their origin in incompatible monetary policies. On the face of it there is an implied loss of sovereignty through fixed exchange rates on two counts: (i) the surrender of the use of the exchange rate as an instrument of policy; and (ii) the inability to choose the stance of domestic monetary policy. However, both elements may be challenged as, in the long run, the loss of *effective* economic sovereignty is not as great as might appear because the present degree of *effective* sovereignty is limited. The same argument applies in the issue of policy co-ordination. If incompatible policies are in any case adjusted *ex post*, the concomitant costs of instability could be avoided by *ex ante* co-ordination. Little *effective* sovereignty is thereby surrendered by *ex ante* co-ordination. Overall, therefore, monetary policy of any one country has to be compatible both with its own exchange-rate policy but also with monetary policy of other countries. This is the implication of international financial integration.

Notes and References

CHAPTER 2

1. Monetary policy is defined in terms of policy changes in the domestic component of high-powered money.

2. Y = real national income (output); C = domestic consumption expenditure; I = domestic investment; i = domestic interest rate; G = government expenditure on goods and services; X = exports of goods and services: r = spot exchange rate; M_p = imports; M = supply of high-powered money; L = demand for high-powered money; H = central banks' holdings of domestic assets; R = external reserves: K_1 = capital flows related to interest-rate differentials; K_2 = speculative capital flows; r_e = expected future spot exchange rate; T = current account balance $(X - M_p)$; B = overall balance-of-payments surplus/deficit.

3. An exchange-rate depreciation causes the F schedule to move to the right as, at a more depreciated exchange rate, external equilibrium is consistent with a higher level of income and/or lower interest rate. Similarly, the IS curve moves to the right as the higher volume of exports implies a higher equilibrium income at each rate of interest.

4. We abstract from the effect that a change in the exchange rate may have on the real value of money balances.

5. See A. K. Swoboda (1972).

6. R. N. Cooper (1976).

7. For an analysis of the difference made to the analysis by alternative budget financing methods see D. T. Llewellyn (1974).

8. It is assumed that an increased money supply induces a fall in interest rates which assumes an essentially Keynesian short-run liquidity preference theory. In particular it assumes that the demand for money function is independent of the money supply and that a rise in the money supply does not induce expectations of faster inflation causing the demand for money to rise at given interest-rate levels.

9. This assumes that the elasticities of demand for imports and exports sum to greater than unity in which case the rise in overseas prices induces an *ex ante* balance-of-payments surplus and hence appreciation of the exchange rate. This would not be the case, for instance, following the rise in oil prices in 1973 as the elasticity of demand for oil is low and the import capacity of oil-exporting countries is limited. The domestic economy would not be insulated

from external inflation in this case; indeed domestic inflation may be generated through the depreciation of the exchange rate.

10. The negative effect on income must be greater in case 2.8c than in 2.8b (ie greater when the elasticity of LM exceeds that of F) as the exchange-rate appreciation is greater; i.e. F_2 is equivalent to a more appreciated exchange rate than F_0 in Figure 2.8c but depreciated against F_0 in Figure 2.8b. This can be reasoned in terms of the required change in the interest rate for external equilibrium. If the elasticities of the IS and F schedules were the same in Figures 2.8b and 2.8c, any difference in the two cases derives from the elasticity of the LM curve. In case 2.8c the demand for money with respect to the rate of interest is greater than in 2.8b. Thus a given fall in income induces a smaller fall in the rate of interest in case 2.8c than in 2.8b. It follows that in case 2.8c, as the same reduction in income ($y_0 y_1$) as in case 2.8b would induce a smaller reduction in the interest rate, there would be a smaller interest-rate-induced capital outflow. This would be insufficient to restore external equilibrium in case 2.8c.

11. See D. J. Ott, and A. F. Ott, (1965), and D. J. Ott, A. F. Ott, and J. H. Yoo (1979), *Macro Economic Theory* (Tokyo: McGraw-Hill) chap. 11.

12. See Oates, W. E. (1966).

CHAPTER 3

1. See, for instance, S. Black (1976) and P. Kouri (1976).

2. See M. V. Whitman (1975).

CHAPTER 4

1. The latter is done in Beenstock (1978) chaps 2–4.

2. This is not strictly true, as the bank with which he opens a forward position may require the deposit of a proportion of the funds committed by the speculator. Nevertheless, to the extent that this margin is less than 100 %, the speculator gains leverage by speculating in the forward rather than the spot market.

3. This is the way most countries quote spot and forward exchange rates. The U.K. tradition, however, quotes exchange rates in terms of foreign currency per pound sterling. In February 1977 the spot exchange rate against the dollar was £1 = \$1.7128. In the formula and in the diagrams below, this is reversed and would become $1/1.7128 = 0.5838$, i.e. \$1 is equivalent to £0.5838.

4. Analogously to the Keynesian liquidity preference function, the representation of expectations by a stable schedule assumes that the structure of expectations is itself independent of movements in the forward exchange rate. In other words, it is assumed that movements along the schedule do not induce shifts in the schedule. This makes implicit assumptions about the way

expectations are formed, and is an important qualification to be noted when the dynamics of the model are investigated.

5. See, for instance, M. Beenstock (1977) chap. 6.

APPENDIX

1. This is a wider range than appears in much of the theoretical literature which defines inelastic expectations as when a movement in the spot rate induces expectations of a return to its initial level and elastic expectations as when a movement in the spot rate creates expectations of a further move in the same direction.

2. Clearly, this may be an unstable system dependent upon how elastic expectations are. See V. Argy and M. Porter (1972).

CHAPTER 5

1. Indeed, within the same dealing-room, dealers quote a forward rate by comparing two euro-currency interest rates, while they quote a non-dollar euro-currency rate on the basis of the euro-dollar rate and the relevant forward exchange rate!

2. This is because banks have borrowed euro-DM, sold spot for dollars and invested the proceeds in the euro-dollar market.

CHAPTER 6

1. I.e. interest arbitrageurs expose themselves to exchange-rate risks by not covering their spot transactions in the forward market (see Chapter 4).

2. K^f is holdings of external assets; W is wealth; i_d is the domestic interest rate; i_f is the foreign interest rate; R is a measure of risk; and Z represents all other determinants.

3. See R. M. Stern and E. E. Leamer (1970).

4. C^s is short-term claims on foreigners, W is a U.S. wealth measure; RT^{UK} is the U.K. domestic interest rate; RT^{US} is the U.S. three-month bill rate; $DF1$ is proxy for the VCFR programme, IET is proxy for the interest-equalisation tax; RED is the euro-dollar interest rate; $M1$ is the Jaffee–Modigliani credit-rationing index; V is the U.S. income velocity of money; and X is exports.

5. L = external liabilities; C = external claims; i_g = German inter-bank rate; $i_\$$: euro-dollar rate; W_f: stock of wealth held by non-residents; $NO1$ = dummy variable for periods when a ban on interest payments on deposit liabilities to non-residents was applied; $SPEC$ = dummy variable for periods of speculative disturbances; fp = forward premium; S = seasonal variables; fpa = forward premium adjusted for the official swap rate for periods when the Bundesbank increased its swap (forward) commitments and W_g = stock of wealth held by German residents, (*) denotes endogenous variables.

CHAPTER 7

1. For a more detailed discussion of the analytical framework and empirical results see R. B. Johnston (1979).

2. R. B. Johnson (1979).

3. The sustained wide differential between the euro-sterling and domestic inter-bank rates in 1974 (at times as wide as 5 percentage points) was not eliminated by external holders also because the British Government were offering an exchange guarantee to official non-resident holders of sterling balances but only on sterling held in the London money market.

4. In 1973 official reserve requirements on German banks discriminated heavily against external liabilities with a 35 % reserve requirement on external liabilities against 13–14 % on domestic liabilities. In addition, a 60 % reserve requirement was imposed upon the growth of German banks' time liabilities against non-residents.

5. Measurement error can arise because published data may not relate to quotations made in the different markets at precisely the same point in time, and because data frequently relate to 'middle rates' at which few transactions actually take place. This is a particularly important qualification when the difference between 'bid' and 'ask' rates are wide.

APPENDIX

1. For a detailed discussion of some of the domestic monetary effects see D. T. Llewellyn, 'End of Exchange Control: Monetary Implications', *The Banker*, Dec 1979.

CHAPTER 8

1. For a review of policies see O.E.C.D. (1972); *The Economist* (Survey), 27 Jan 1973; *Annual Reports on Exchange Restrictions* (IMF); R. H. Mills (1972), and S. I. Katz (1969).

CHAPTER 9

1. It has been noted that net liquidity creation by U.K. euro banks via maturity transformation increased markedly after September 1973 (see M. Villani, 'Concept of Net Liquidity Applied to the Euro Dollar Market', *Economic Notes*, vol. 7, no. 1).

2. The reader is referred to many excellent descriptions and analyses of the detailed aspects of the markets, e.g. G. W. McKenzie (1976); G. L. Bell (1973); E. Clendenning (1970); R. I. McKinnon (1977); and F. Klopstock (1968).

3. For most purposes this definition will suffice though, more technically,

the major issue is the form of regulation rather than location. Thus, a euro-dollar market could in principle exist in New York if non-resident deposits at banks in New York were to be exempt from the regulations (e.g. over reserve requirements) that apply to deposits by domestic residents.

4. 'Margins' include compensating balances borrowers may be required to maintain at lending banks.

5. Regulation Q enables the Federal Reserve to place an upper limit on the interest rates banks pay on deposits.

6. A. K. Swoboda (1968).

7. This would not apply if the transfer was from the domestic market of one currency to the euro segment of another as, dependent upon how the transfer is financed, there may be a reduction in the credit capacity of the banking system subject to the loss of deposits. Thus an outflow from Germany to the euro-dollar market may reduce the monetary base in Germany while not increasing that of the United States. This is discussed in detail later in this chapter.

8. There may, however, be an indirect effect due to the difference in reserve · requirements on *time* and *demand* deposits, and between domestic and external liabilities. There may also be a counterpart Federal Funds market transaction if the euro bank keeps its U.S. bank deposit at a different bank than Corporation *A*.

9. Other than indirectly through any net freeing of bank reserves in the United States due to the lower (zero in 1978) reserve requirements against external liabilities which includes deposits of euro banks.

10. Assuming that the French corporation would not otherwise have borrowed elsewhere or that the alternative bank and credit now released is absorbed by another borrower. This, as argued below, presupposes either an initial world excess demand for credit or demand being sensitive to the lower interest rates charged by euro banks.

11. See J. Hewson and E. Sakakibara (1974).

12. For a review of other estimates see G. W. McKenzie (1976) chap. 6 and G. Dufey and I. Giddy (1978) chap. 3. See also D. Logue *et al.*, pp. 279–304, for a discussion of alternative multiplier concepts, and M. Willms (1978). As already noted, Group of Ten central banks have agreed not to hold their dollar reserves in the euro-dollar market. But other central banks are not subject to this constraint, and many central banks of developing countries do maintain a high proportion of their external reserves in the euro markets.

13. In cases (6), (7) and (8) there may be slight credit effects within the United States by virtue of differences in reserve requirements as between different types of bank deposit. If, in the process of the financial flows noted, there are changes in the structure of U.S. bank deposits between *time* and *demand* deposits, there may be slight credit effects deriving from changes in the banks' excess reserves. This is because reserve requirements are in general higher on *demand* than on *time* deposits. As the initial flow to the euro-dollar

market from U.S. residents is likely to involve the liquidation of *time* deposits, while the total volume of U.S. bank deposits is unchanged, *time* deposits have been transformed into *demand* deposits. As higher reserves are therefore needed, there might be a slight negative effect upon U.S. bank lending if the banks initially had no excess reserves.

14. The ratio between equity capital and deposits is around 1:18 in the United States and for euro banks is typically around 1:40.

15. Whereby reserve requirements are placed on euro-currency loans made by foreign branches of U.S. banks to U.S. residents. In fact this was abolished in August 1978.

16. See G. W. McKenzie (1976) chap. 8.

CHAPTER 10

1. See W. Day (1976).
2. *Bank of England Quarterly Bulletin* (Dec 1976) p. 430.

APPENDIX

1. B. Brown, *Money, Hard and Soft* (London: Macmillan, 1978).

CHAPTER 11

1. *Net* external liabilities are equal to the banks total (*gross*) external liabilities less external assets. Thus *net* external liabilities are unchanged if banks lend externally the proceeds of external borrowing or the deposits by non-residents.

2. The following paragraphs draw heavily upon V. Argy (1971).
3. J. Hewson and E. Sakakibara (1977).
4. Ibid.
5. This inevitably exposes the central bank to arbitrage gains or losses.
6. The *financial* rate will be at a premium when the country would have been a net importer of capital had all transactions taken place at the fixed *official* rate.

CHAPTER 12

1. An important qualification is entered in the case of the United Kingdom (see p. 178).
2. The U.K. banking system is more complex than this though, in principle, the broad analytical conclusions apply.
3. If, in the United Kingdom, the concept of *HPM* relates to reserve assets, this must exclude those sales of public sector debt to the banking system which are reserve assets, e.g. Treasury bills.

4. The policy element of H would include the effect of central banks' open-market operations in government debt, while the endogenous element includes commercial bank borrowing from the central bank. The policy element of R includes, for instance, currency swaps between the central bank and commercial banks, and the endogenous element relates to offsetting capital flows. Therefore, HPM has a domestic and external component and each has policy and endogenous components.

5. HPM is total high-powered money; H_T is the domestic component; H_p is the policy component of H_T; R_T is the central banks' external reserves and external component of high-powered money; and R_e is the endogenous element of R_T.

6. A. B. Balbach (1978).

7. In practice it may simply issue correspondingly fewer bills in the following week.

8. For a fuller discussion see C. M. Miles and P. A. Bull (1978).

9. The major studies are: V. Argy and Z. Hodjera (1973); V. Argy and P. Kouri (1974); P. De Grauwe (1975); P. De Grauwe (1976); R. Herring and R. Marston (1977); P. Kouri (1974); P. Kouri (1975); P. Kouri and M. Porter (1974); M. Michaely (1971); M. Neumann (1977); O.E.C.D. (1975), M. Porter (1972); M. Willms (1971).

10. See, in particular, DeGrauwe (1975) and DeGrauwe (1976).

CHAPTER 13

1. For a detailed analysis of the determination of the euro-dollar interest rate see V. Argy and Z. Hodjera (1973); R. Marston and R. Herring (1977); and R. Marston (1974).

2. This is largely because the euro-dollar rate is at least partially insulated from movements in European interest rates through offsetting movements in forward exchange rates. It follows that the influence of European interest rates would likely increase if forward rates were pegged by official intervention.

3. See O.E.C.D., *Economic Outlook* (Dec 1978) p. 38.

4. D. Logue, M. A. Salant, and R. J. Sweeney (1976).

5. Even in the *global parity* condition interest rates more precisely in parallel only if the forward premium is determined unambiguously by speculators or by central bank intervention.

Index